The Tarot Key

UNLOCK THE SECRETS OF YOUR SOUL

ALIYAH MARR

www.parallelmindzz.com
tools & toys for creative people

Library of Congress Cataloging-in-Publication Data

Marr, Aliyah

The Tarot Key, Unlock the Secrets of Your Soul/Aliyah Marr—1st ed.

ISBN-13:978-1517529437
ISBN-10: 1517529433

1. Tarot 2. Divination 3. Personal Growth 4. Motivational
5. Transpersonal 6. Self-help 7. Self-Realization

think
əpᴉsdn
down™

DEDICATION

This book is dedicated to those who protected and preserved all forms of ancient wisdom despite all odds and opposition.

The eyes only see what the mind is prepared to comprehend.

~ Henri Bergson

CONTENTS

GRATITUDE

I wish to express my appreciation for the help from my friends and family who were very patient with me during the nine-month creation of this book. But the real thanks go to Robyn Swick for editing the manuscript. Truly, she is my Queen of Swords; the Tarot's archetype for a good editor. With a great eye for the misplaced comma and the run-on sentence, she successfully sliced through the confusion and helped me produce a book that I hope honors the mystery and timeless beauty of the Tarot.

PREFACE

My romance with the Tarot started out as a blind date.

In 2004, I created a conceptual art project that explored the nature of proximity and meaning; I wanted to design a computer game that would randomize the titles to paintings that I had already created. I decided to model my game on the Tarot since it contains cards with pictures on the faces. I designed *The Transformational Tarot* as a virtual deck of 116 cards; some of the cards contain an untitled image while others display only a single word. When you "shuffle" the deck, the program creates a spread of randomly chosen image and words.

My experiment was very successful, but not in the way I intended. About halfway through the project, after I had programmed the game and created the cards, I realized that I had somehow made the transition from creating a conceptual art project to creating an actual tarot deck. I tested it on myself, and found it was eerily accurate. Then I ran it online and asked for feedback. The results were surprising: my game was reviewed in a magazine and endorsed by the editor. People loved it; many readers said it was the best reading they had ever had.

At the time when I created this computer game, I thought the images and symbolism of what I called the "traditional" tarot were uselessly archaic; I did not resonate with the images I saw in the Rider Waite Smith deck or other traditional decks. Years later, when a traditional tarot deck came into my hands, I found myself studying it in earnest.

Learning the Tarot by studying what others think the cards mean was very dry and difficult for me. The meanings traditionally assigned to some of the cards didn't jibe with my interests or intuition. I had just written my first book on creativity, and I intuitively saw that the Tarot, like art, is a tool for personal evolution; a way to access your intuition and higher guidance.

Over the years that I worked with the cards, I developed a blended reading technique called the SEER System™ which makes it easy to interpret the cards at a glance. My passion for the cards is the same thread that connects and informs all my work; a seeker's quest for the answers to the questions that haunt all of us: what is the hidden reality that lies behind all things?

INTRODUCTION

The Tarot is an ancient tool for self-actualization that gives you to access a vast library of intuitive, innate knowledge that may be otherwise inaccessible to you. From the view of the scientist, you are using the visual side of your brain—the right hemisphere—when you look at the images on the cards. An anthropologist or art historian may see that you are digging into a long-buried treasure house of cultural clues. A psychologist would immediately see the archetypes in the images of the Major Arcana.

The study of the Tarot is a deep probing into the nature of the deeper reality that underlies all things; an attempt to understand that which can never be completely understood by the rational brain. The depth and breadth of that knowledge is simply much vaster than the human mind can comprehend. It is our nature to seek a single all-inclusive answer for all the questions that constantly elude us, but failing to find it doesn't stop us from seeking it. The Tarot is the search for the Holy Grail—the well of creativity, wisdom, and personal power that lies within us.

The Tarot is a magical work of art that changes with each viewer, and with each reading. It is a map of human consciousness that is responsive to the degree you are open to what it has to say to you; it teaches you more about you every time you read the cards, even if you read for someone else. Collectively, the cards are an interactive spiritual book of ancient wisdom. Each card is a door to a wealth of information that slowly reveals itself to you over time.

Why this book?
There are a lot of books out there on the Tarot; what makes this book different? As the creator of two tarot decks, and the author of several books on creative empowerment, I have a unique view of the Tarot. Portions of my view are echoed in other books, but I have brought elements from diverse fields of study and mastery in a new synthesis that I believe can help anyone who is interested in the Tarot.

My purpose with this book is to provide a guide to the Tarot to help tarot novices learn this amazing tool quickly. It is also a reference book for experienced tarot readers. My experience as an artist and teacher taught me to value individual expression and intuition above all else. So rather than tell you how to interpret each card, I give you clues about the mythic archetypes and symbols in the cards and let your imagination take you on your own personal journey.

It takes the same qualities to be an artist that it takes to read tarot: openness, intuition, an understanding of symbols, and general visual literacy. The images on the cards show a fluid landscape of symbols and universal archetypes that are surprisingly modern and timeless in their import. The Tarot is us: it is the seeker and the sage, the answer and the question, the quest and the Grail, all at the same time.

The Tarot asks the same existential and universal questions that mankind has asked since the beginning of time: What is out there beyond our senses? How can we access our true creative power? And how can we understand, align, and create with the forces in our lives?

ONE BOOK FITS ALL

In this book, I show you how to work with two decks: the *Rider Waite Smith Tarot* and with my own deck, *The Tarot of Creativity*. These decks are complimentary; the meaning of each card from one deck adds to the depth of the meaning of the equivalent card in the other deck; however each card system is complete in itself and can be read alone as well.

The Rider Waite Smith deck tends to be very blunt, worldly, and includes some negative interpretations, while *The Tarot of Creativity* is more positive and modern in its titles and interpretations; *The Tarot of Creativity* is designed to provide you with advice even in a negative situation or consequence.

This book was designed to work with any deck. If you are a beginner, you will find it easy to learn to read the cards and develop your own intuition. My revolutionary blended system for reading the cards allows you to pick up any deck and interpret the images instantly. If you are an experienced tarot reader, this book can enhance and deepen your knowledge of the cards.

Introducing the SEER SYSTEM™
In this book, I introduce my system for reading the cards which I call The SEER System;™ it blends four ways of seeing the cards, and rewards the user with instant ways of interpreting the images, numbers, and symbols in each card.[1] It presents a very intuitive way to learn and read the cards.

Dealing From Two Decks
Reading more than one deck at once is called doing a "comparative tarot reading." This technique gives more depth to a reading than possibly can be obtained from one deck. Pioneered by Valerie Sim, the process involves comparing the same card from two or more decks in order to gain additional insight into the card or the spread.

It works best with decks that use the same numbering system, and that are compatible in tone. A comparative tarot reading can be easily done by shuffling and reading from one deck while keeping the other deck in order, so you can pull the corresponding cards from it to enhance your reading.

---

1 The Glossary of Symbols at the back of this book contains a complete list of symbols and their meanings.

I like to keep a tarot app on my phone for card readings, and then pull the corresponding card from *The Tarot of Creativity*. The app ensures true randomization, while responding very effectively to my intent and reading expertise. The depth provided by *The Tarot of Creativity* reading is very enlightening, as it tends to provide more positive information for me than any other deck.

In contrast, the Rider Waite Smith deck bluntly "tells it like it is." Its message can sometimes seem like a dire prediction that I can't do much about, but when I consult the alternative meanings of the cards in *The Tarot of Creativity*, the reading takes me in a positive direction, and provides advice on what I can do.

Even if you don't want to do comparative tarot readings, or if you only own one deck, the additional information in this book can increase the depth of your readings. If you have only one deck, such as the *Rider Waite Smith Tarot*, you will still benefit from the information provided in this book for the corresponding *Tarot of Creativity* card. You can even use this book to help you do readings in the absence of any deck, as I will show you later. Alternatively, *The Tarot Key* can be used to learn the Tarot or add depth to your knowledge without even having a deck.

Twice the Meaning

The Tarot Key can work with any tarot, but it is designed to work specifically with the imagery and meanings of *The Rider Waite Smith Tarot* and with *The Tarot of Creativity*. In this book I use the following two acronyms:

RWS = *Rider Waite Smith Tarot*
TOC = *The Tarot of Creativity*

The Rider Waite Smith deck dates from the beginning of the 20th century. It is arguably the most popular tarot deck of all time. Illustrator Pamela Colman Smith was commissioned by academic and mystic A.E. Waite to draw the cards, and the Rider Company published the deck in 1910. It is said that Waite specified the imagery of the Major Arcana cards, and left Pamela Smith to design all the remaining lower cards. I suspect that Pamela Smith had much more to do with the design and symbology of the deck than anyone knew.

While the images are simple, the details and backgrounds hold a wealth of symbolism. Some imagery remains close to that found in earlier decks, but overall the Waite Smith designs represent a substantial departure from their predecessors. The RWS deck demonstrates a considerable knowledge of numerology and the esoteric ideas of The Golden Dawn. The cards were numbered using the Roman numeral system.

The Tarot of Creativity was designed to trace the natural creative process through the cards. It encourages the individual to learn how to work with the laws of nature both within us and outside of us. The suits in the TOC each outline a particular path that the Querent can follow: these are named as classical elements but they symbolize the unique gifts of man. The cards of the TOC use the same numerological and titling system of the *Rider Waite Smith Tarot*, but add a contemporary title in a modern font on each card. The deck uses modern Arabic numbers to make them more accessible. This familiar numbering system makes it easier for most people to read the number for each card. It also facilitates a reading technique in which you sum up the cards in a spread, which I will show you how to do. This sum gives you the "meta message" of the reading.

A Note on the Pronouns Used in this Book
English tends to be a male-biased language. In other books I have tried to mix up the gender references to provide a more balanced model. Most of the figures represented in the Tarot are already mixed, however, whenever I refer to the Querent or the seeker, it may be overwhelmingly male. I have chosen to do this simply to make it easier to read. The *Rider Waite Smith Tarot* imagery, which follows alchemical traditions, often represents the subconscious as a female figure, while the self-conscious is symbolized as male. I discuss this more completely in the sections related to these concepts.

THE TAROT OF CREATIVITY

The Major Arcana

All true modern tarot decks consist of at least twenty-two cards: the Major Arcana, which represent the fifth path to enlightenment, higher than the other four paths represented by the suits.

> Arcana: noun: arcanum; plural noun: arcana
> 1. secrets or mysteries.
> 2. the twenty-two trump cards (the major arcana) or the fifty-six suit   cards (the minor arcana)[1]

In traditional tarot decks, the Major Arcana represent the laws of the universe and the principles of consciousness; it is here where most of the archetypes and the majority of the symbols in the Tarot are to be found. It is said that the Fool wanders through the other cards of the Major Arcana on his journey through life, learning from the archetypical figures that he encounters on his path.

The number of each card in the Major Arcana is very important, and this is retained in *The Tarot of Creativity*. Tarot scholars sometimes refer to the Major Arcana cards as "keys" that help the seeker "open the lock" on the treasure chest of arcane knowledge and access the secrets locked inside. In *The Tarot of Creativity* the Major Arcana are identified by the Ouroborus symbol that surrounds the numbers at the top of the card; this helps distinguish them easily from similarly numbered cards in the lower suits. The twenty-two Major Arcana cards represent universal archetypes: in the Rider Waite Smith deck the images often express these archetypes in the form of mythological figures. Each archetype in a traditional tarot carries a message or a teaching: in *The Tarot of Creativity*, the contemporary meaning is directly inscribed in the title of the cards. The traditional titles of the Major Arcana cards can be misleading, especially for the modern reader.

---

1   www.merriam-webster.com/dictionary/arcana

For instance, if you get The Hierophant in a reading from a traditional deck, how would you know what this card means? You look at the image, and you see an ecclesiastical figure in the robes that resemble that of the Pope. If you don't respond to religious imagery, this might put you off so that you aren't able to see the meaning of the card, which has to do with listening to your higher guidance. This is why the Major Arcana cards in *The Tarot of Creativity* have been titled with the attributes of the archetype— as a kind of keyword for the card. The cards retain the traditional title below the new title in shadow text, so that the experienced tarot reader can identify the card according to the traditional system. The two titles—a modern interpretation of the card followed by the traditional title—allow for instant comprehension and individual interpretation at the same time.

For example: Key #20, Judgment, is not about judgment at all, in fact, the card meaning is the *inverse* of the contemporary interpretation of the word: the Judgment card isn't about judging anything, but about getting *past* judgment, into a place of clarity, balance, tolerance, and understanding.

The traditional way of titling the cards may have been an intentional *blind* to conceal the real meaning of the cards. The title on the equivalent card in *The Tarot of Creativity* is THE EPIPHANY, which is meant to convey the transformational meaning of the card: an epiphany is a sudden breakthrough in understanding.

Epiphany (1) a usually sudden manifestation or perception of or insight into the reality or essence of something, usually initiated by some simple, homely, or commonplace occurrence or experience (2) an intuitive grasp of reality through something (as an event) usually simple and striking (3) an illuminating discovery, realization, or disclosure

The Suits

Tarot scholars often assign an order to the suits. The ordering of the suits is done differently by various tarot practitioners, for instance, one technique arranges the suits according to the seasons. This may be because the Tarot was often used as a divinatory tool, and the suit of a card could be used to determine when something might happen.

The suits in *The Tarot of Creativity* represent the four classical elements, which correlate with the suits of traditional tarot decks. Each element is also a path on the journey of the earthbound Soul. *Parallel Mind, The Art of Creativity* introduced a diagram for visualizing the four bodies of man.

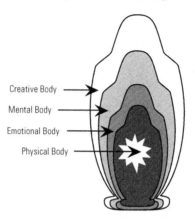

A human being can be visualized as several bodies in one: a physical body, an emotional body, a mental body, and a creative body. They are like shells enclosing one another; like Russian dolls, one enclosed inside the other. The body in the center is the physical body, the emotional body encloses it, next is the mental body; the top layer is the creative body. Each body is progressively more ethereal, with the dense physical body at the center and the outermost shell representing the pure energy of creative inspiration. This model is key to understanding how our thoughts can manifest in our physical body and in our material reality.

Another useful metaphor is to visualize each of these as a musical note: when the total person is healthy, the combination of notes from each body produces a harmonic chord. Disease produces a discordant sound. When the physical, mental, emotional, and creative bodies are producing notes of harmony then the whole person is healthy.[1]

The suits in both traditional decks and in *The Tarot of Creativity* represent the same four parts that combine to make the totality of ourselves; each "body" is a tool we can use to consciously create anything. Used together, these tools can transform the whole self, and help us create our life path. I arranged the suits in *The Tarot of Creativity* to reflect the process of

1 *Parallel Mind, The Art of Creativity*, Aliyah Marr

creative manifestation, but this same arrangement works with any deck and gives you inside information on how to create the life of your dreams. The suits in this order show us the path of creative manifestation.

1. Fire—> 2. Air—> 3. Water—> 4. Earth

The elements/suits proceed from the most etheric (Fire/Wands—energy/intent/spiritual plane) to the densest (Earth/Pentacles—matter/physical plane). We have been taught to create backwards, from matter to energy, we have been taught to focus exclusively on the material results: "When my business is successful, then I will be happy." We must learn to first create the *feeling* of what we want first—happiness—and then allow the physical expression of that feeling to appear.

The Pip Cards
Cards Ace-10 are sometimes called the "pip" cards. In the TOC cards 2-10 contain the image of the element of the suit and are labeled with two words, one "upright" and one "reversed"—you can choose to read the meaning of just one word, or read them together as a phrase. Often, the reversed meaning of the card is the energy of the upright word taken a little further, as in the Ten in which the upright word is GENEROSITY and the reversed word is ABUNDANCE, which reveals that the secret source of abundance is in the cultivation of generosity.

The meaning of the card when seen this way is: *a generous Spirit experiences abundance.* The implication is that in order to experience abundance, you have to first generate the feeling of a generous nature. In other words, if you feel that you are in survival mode, you are only open to experiences that reflect thoughts that support survival: that of barely having your needs met. To experience abundance, you have to *choose to see* abundance.

The Court Cards—In the TOC, the royal cards represent creative mastery of each suit or path of mastery. In a departure from traditional tarot decks, the court cards in the TOC deck are labeled with a numerical value, which aids in interpreting the card's numerological meaning.

The Tarot of Creativity is available directly from the artist:
www.parallelmindzz.com

THE ROOTS OF THE TAROT

No one really knows where the Tarot came from, but there are definite clues in the cards themselves. The Tarot (first known as trionfi and later as *tarocchi, tarock*, and others) is a pack of playing cards (most commonly numbering 78), used from the mid-15th century in various parts of Europe to play a group of card games such as Italian *tarocchini* and French tarot.

From the late 18th century until the present time the Tarot has also found use by mystics and occultists for divination as well as a map of mental and spiritual pathways. The English and French word "tarot" derives from the Italian *tarocchi*, which has no known origin or etymology. When it spread, the word was changed to *tarot* in French and *tarock* in German.

Playing cards first entered Europe in the late 14th century, probably from Mamluk Egypt, with suits of Swords, Batons or Polo sticks (commonly known as Wands by those practicing occult or divinatory tarot), Cups, and Coins (commonly known as disks or pentacles by practitioners of the occult or divinatory tarot) These suits were very similar to modern tarot divination decks and are still used in traditional Italian, Spanish and Portuguese playing card decks.

The first known documented tarot cards were created between 1430 and 1450 in Milan, Ferrara and Bologna in northern Italy when additional trump cards with allegorical illustrations were added to the common four-suit pack. These new decks were originally called carte da trionfi, triumph cards, and the additional cards known simply as trionfi, which became 'trumps' in English.

The first literary evidence of the existence of carte da trionfi is a written statement in the court records in Florence, in 1440. The oldest surviving tarot cards are from fifteen fragmented decks painted in the mid 15th century for the Visconti-Sforza family, the rulers of Milan. Picture-card packs are first mentioned by Martiano da Tortona probably between 1418 and 1425, since the painter he mentions,

Michelino da Besozzo, returned to Milan in 1418, while Martiano himself died in 1425. He describes a deck with 16 picture cards with images of the Greek gods and suits depicting four kinds of birds, not the common suits. However the 16 cards were obviously regarded as 'trumps' as, about 25 years later, Jacopo Antonio Marcello called them a ludus triumphorum, or 'game of trumps.' [1]

The Rider-Waite-Smith Tarot

For the purposes of this book, I am going to trace the roots of the Rider Waite Smith deck, which dates from 1909. The influences on the imagery and concepts of this deck are well documented and rather easy to trace.

The Egyptian/Hermetic Connection

Regardless of the fact that paper was not invented until the 13th century, many people still believe that the Tarot has origins in ancient Egypt. The breadcrumb trail that seems to point to Egyptian ideas goes way back to the Egyptian god Thoth and the Greek god Hermes. The medium of the cards may not have existed, but the ideas in the Tarot are ancient philosophical ideas; the Major Arcana represent universal archetypes found worldwide.

> During the Middle Ages and the Renaissance, the writings attributed to Hermes Trismegistus, known as Hermetica, enjoyed great prestige and were popular among alchemists. The "hermetic tradition" consequently refers to alchemy, magic, astrology and related subjects.
>
> Hermes Trismegistus may be a representation of the syncretic combination of the Greek god Hermes and the Egyptian god Thoth. Both Thoth and Hermes were gods of writing and of magic in their respective cultures. Thus, the Greek god of interpretive communication was combined with the Egyptian god of wisdom as a patron of astrology and alchemy. In addition, both gods were psychopomps, guiding souls to the afterlife. [2]

The Rider-Waite-Smith tarot deck (originally published 1910) is arguably one of the most popular tarot decks in the English-speaking world. The cards, drawn by illustrator Pamela Colman Smith, were commissioned by academic and mystic A. E. Waite and published by the Rider Company.

---

1   en.wikipedia.org/wiki/Tarot
2   en.wikipedia.org/wiki/Hermes_Trismegistus

Both Smith and Waite were high-standing members of The Hermetic Order of the Golden Dawn, which was a society established for "the continued preservation of that body of knowledge known as Hermeticism or the Western Esoteric Tradition," so we can assume that they would base the tarot deck they created upon Hermetic concepts.

Western Esotericism
The Western Esoteric movement comprises mystical and magical ideas and movements focused on the pursuit of gnosis, a term which has been defined as 'direct spiritual insight into cosmology or metaphysics.'

> The origins of Western esotericism are in the Hellenistic Eastern Mediterranean, then part of the Roman Empire, during Late Antiquity, a period encompassing the first centuries of the Common Era. This was a milieu in which there was a mix of religious and intellectual traditions from Greece, Egypt, the Levant, Babylon, and Persia, and in which globalization, urbanization, and multiculturalism were bringing about socio-cultural change. One component of this was Hermetism, an Egyptian Hellenistic school of thought that takes its name from the legendary Egyptian wise man, Hermes Trismegistus.[1]

The Six Characteristics of Esotericism

1. Correspondence
Everything in Nature is a sign that can be read. The microcosm and macrocosm interplay. Synchronicity is a sign from Nature and the divine.

2. Nature is Alive
Nature is not just pieces of matter, it is a living entity that evolves and expands.

3. Imagination and Mediation
Imagination is a power that provides access to innumerable worlds and levels of reality; it is the intermediary between the material world and the divine.

---

1   en.wikipedia.org/wiki/Western_esotericism

4. Experience of Transmutation

Transmutation is Gnosis and the Illumination of the Self and Mind. Transmutation marks the birth of a new awareness: enlightenment.

5. Practice of Concordance

There is one common root from which all esoteric knowledge grows.

6. Transmission

Master-Disciple initiation into arcane knowledge.

These are the general principles that run like a thread, or more like a river, through the Tarot. One of the strongest concepts is the Hermetic idea of correspondence expressed in the common phrase: "as above, so below."

As above, so below

These words circulate throughout occult and magical circles. They are recorded in Hermetic texts, although they originated in the Vedas. The actual text of that maxim, as translated by Dennis W. Hauck from The Emerald Tablet of Hermes Trismegistus, is:

> That which is Below corresponds to that which is Above, and that which is Above corresponds to that which is Below, to accomplish the miracle of the One Thing. Thus, whatever happens on any level of reality (physical, emotional, or mental) also happens on every other level. This principle, however, is more often used in the sense of the microcosm and the macrocosm. The microcosm is oneself, and the macrocosm is the universe. The macrocosm is as the microcosm and vice versa; within each lies the other, and through understanding one (usually the microcosm) a man may understand the other. [1]

Tarot and the Tree of Life

Tarot is often used in conjunction with the study of the Hermetic Kabbalah. In these decks all the cards are illustrated in accordance with Kabbalistic principles. The most influential tarot deck exemplifying Hermetic and Kabbalistic ideas is the Rider-Waite-Smith deck, which bears illustrated scenes on all the suit cards.

1 en.wikipedia.org/wiki/Hermeticism

Hermetic Kabbalists see the cards of the Tarot as keys to the Tree of Life. The twenty-two cards including the twenty-one Trumps plus the Fool or Zero card, are often called the "Major Arcana" or "Greater Mysteries" and are seen as corresponding to the twenty-two Hebrew letters and the twenty-two paths of the Tree; the ace to ten in each suit correspond to the ten Sephiroth in the four Kabbalistic worlds; and the sixteen court cards relate to the classical elements in the four worlds. While the Sephiroth describe the nature of divinity, the paths between them describe ways of knowing God.[1]

The Tree of Life is represented throughout the Tarot, especially the Major Arcana: it is the tree that frames The Magician card, it is shown behind the man in The Lovers card, and it is the tree from which The Hanged Man is suspended.

Tarot and the Zodiac

It is reasonable to conjecture that if the Tarot is a repository for arcane knowledge and if the Tarot originated before or during the Renaissance then it very probably would incorporate one of the most important ancient systems of knowledge in the cards—astrology. Obvious references to astrology are seen in the imagery: Justice is often shown holding scales—the sign of Libra—while the lion in the Strength card is a clear reference to Leo. Many of the symbols and archetypes in tarot imagery are clearly referring to astrological correspondences. Animals are often used to portray human qualities. Human figures often represent psychological archetypes which in turn are pictorial metaphors for universal principles or laws of nature.

The Lost Art of Alchemy

The titles of the cards, especially the Major Arcana, reveal alchemical and hermetic ideas. Alchemy, as opposed to modern day science, attempts to work with nature instead of exploiting it; the goal of the alchemists was to achieve personal evolution by aligning themselves with the forces of the universe and nature.

Alchemists claimed that they were trying to make base metals into gold, and they were on a search for something they called "the philosopher's

---

1   en.wikipedia.org/wiki/Hermetic_Qabalah

stone." They hid their real goal of personal transformation under terms that the materialists of the ruling class could understand.

The philosopher's stone that the alchemists desired was not outside them, nor was it something that allowed them to gain any worldly power, instead, it was nothing less than the transformation of their pineal gland. The alchemist's goal of personal transformation is the same as that of all mystical practices: the opening of the "seed" of their personal consciousness—as the transformed pineal gland—to the wheeling stars of the firmament. When transformed, the pineal gland becomes the "third eye" that allows "spiritual vision;" it allows the inevitable recognition of our innate and inseparable connection with all that is. Religious iconography records the shape of this tiny gland in the symbol of a pine cone. The hat on the head of The Hierophant could be interpreted as a stylized representation of this symbol.

Tarot practitioners might have had the same goals as the alchemists, but they hid their interests under the guise of "fortune telling," and so the cards were able to survive to today, relatively unscathed. It is conjectured by tarot scholars that they used something called a "blind" to help hide the original meanings of the cards from unfriendly eyes.

> The word alchemy was borrowed from Old French alquemie, alkimie, taken from Medieval Latin alchymia, and which is in turn borrowed from an Arabic "al-kīmiyā" which meant the 'philosopher's stone.' The Arabic word is borrowed from Late Greek chēmeía.
>
> This ancient Greek word was derived from the early Greek name for Egypt, Chēmia, based on the Egyptian name for Egypt, "kēme:" 'black earth' (as opposed to red desert sand). [Black earth was known to be fertile, and it is a good description for the feeling of gratitude and reverence that the ancient Egyptians felt for the Earth.] [1]

One obvious blind was to title the Major Arcana with obscure, alchemical, and astrological titles. It seems pretty obvious that the Tarot was designed as an alchemical map. Its origins cloaked by the mists of time, it has been used for divinatory purposes by people who either had no idea of its real purpose, or chose to hide their knowledge in the pictures on the

1   en.wikipedia.org/wiki/Alchemy

cards; images that Carl Jung, many centuries later, would define as universal archetypes.

Alchemical symbolism has been used by psychologists such as Carl Jung who reexamined alchemical symbolism and theory and presented the inner meaning of alchemical work as a spiritual path. Jung began writing his views on alchemy from the 1920s and continued until the end of his life. His interpretation of Chinese alchemical texts in terms of his analytical psychology also served the function of comparing Eastern and Western alchemical imagery and core concepts and hence its possible inner sources (archetypes).

Jung saw alchemy as a Western proto-psychology dedicated to the achievement of individuation. In his interpretation, alchemy was the vessel by which Gnosticism survived its various purges into the Renaissance. Jung viewed alchemy as comparable to a Yoga of the East, and more adequate to the Western mind than Eastern religions and philosophies.

The practice of Alchemy seemed to change the mind and spirit of the Alchemist; spontaneous changes in the minds of Western people undergoing any important stage in individuation seems to produce, on occasion, imagery known to Alchemy and relevant to the person's situation. Jung [wrote] that the transmutation was performed in the mind of the alchemist. He claimed that material substances and procedures were only a projection of the alchemists' internal state, while the real substance to be transformed was the mind itself.[1]

Many people believe even today that the goal of the alchemist was to turn base metal into gold. This was a ruse to throw profane opportunists off the trail. The alchemists sought to transform themselves: they sought to turn the "base metal" of lower consciousness into the "gold" of higher consciousness. They used obscure terms to define and mask their process. These terms are preserved in the traditional keywords of each card in the Tarot. These keywords are known only to those who seriously study the Tarot; they are not to be confused with the titles on the cards.

---

1   en.wikipedia.org/wiki/Alchemy

The mythological and archetypical figures on the cards demonstrate what is needed at each stage in the personal alchemical process in order to progress to the next card—which symbolizes the next stage of consciousness. When seen this way, through the psychological and archetypical concepts embedded in the images and in the titles of the cards, the Tarot is obviously an alchemist's manual for turning the base metal of an unconscious individual into the gold of a self-realized man.

A clue to the cards' alchemical roots can be found in the suits of the deck. The lower cards, called the Pips, are like a regular playing card deck, with four suits. Each suit represents an element: Wands are Fire, Swords are Air, Cups are Water, and Pentacles are Earth. The "lower" suits represent four ordinary paths of mastery, and the trials that those paths will undoubtedly subject the seeker to.

All the paths lead to wisdom, but each presents its own particular set of challenges, as well as its own way to dissolve obstacles and come to a state of enlightenment. The Tarot mirrors the path of the ancient alchemist or mystic. The alchemist wants to discover the laws of the universe, and he wants to learn how to use the laws of nature to manifest his desires. Like a shaman or wise man of ancient times, he doesn't attempt to control or dominate the forces that surround him so much as learn how to work with them.

Ultimately, the alchemist finds that the map to the universe is inside his own soul; and the philosopher's stone, that he thought was his goal at the outset of his journey, has been within him all along. The Tarot is the map for the self-realized individual, the journey that never ends; the discovery that the entire universe is ultimately centered in you.

The Divine Feminine: The Hidden Side of Yourself

All of these secret esoteric practices had to uncover the "dirty secret" of the patriarchal paradigm, the willful attempt to kill off of the Feminine Side of Divinity, the Goddess inside ourselves. The archetype of the Goddess is the same as the "anima" of Jungian psychology; it resides as the natural counterpart of every man, it is the unexpressed feminine side in the man, as the animus is the unexpressed male side in the woman.

> [Femininity is] the left, the side of the heart, the shield side has been symbolic, traditionally and everywhere of the feminine virtues and dangers: mothering and seduction, the

tidal powers of the moon and substances of the body, the rhythms of the seasons: gestation, birth, nourishment, and fosterage; yet equally malice, and revenge, irrationality, dark and terrible wrath, black magic, poisons, sorcery, and delusion; but also fair enchantment, beauty, rapture, and bliss.

And the right, thereby, is of the male: action, Weapons, hero-deeds, protection, brute force, and both cruel and benevolent justice; the masculine virtues and dangers: egoism and aggression, lucid luminous reason, sunlike creative power but also cold unfeeling malice, abstract spirituality, blind courage, theoretical dedication, sober, unplayful moral force. [1]

The "incarnational wound" of the lion in the Strength card is the trauma that the ego has suffered as a result of the unnatural inequality of the patriarchal system. The Devil card shows clearly what happens when instead of honoring and respecting the Divine Feminine, you choose to dominate, exploit and rape the Earth or her representatives, women.

Christ said, "Whatsoever you do to the least of my people, that you do unto me.." Christ is saying that any injury inflicted upon another is reflected as an inner wound in the self of the persona inflicting the harm; when a man harms a woman or the Earth, his inner self—the Divine Feminine, or "anima"—is wounded in the same degree. The holistic view of the "oneness of all things" is what is called "Christ consciousness"—it is essential for the goals of any kind of spiritual enlightenment.

I looked at myself, I mated with myself, I gestated myself, I gave birth to myself, I am myself. [2]

A recognition of the equality of the Divine Feminine Goddess and her reunion with the Divine God is at the heart of any holistic philosophy or esoteric practice. The "marriage" of the God and Goddess is an internal matter, a way of "wholing" the self; it represents the healing of the incarnational wound, the primal wound of separation. No healing can be accomplished without recognizing the parts that make up the whole that have to be reunited within the self.

---

1   Joseph Campbell, Creative Mythology (New York: Viking, 1968), pp 288-89
2   An alchemical proverb

The Quintessence

The Tarot was built upon the fifth suit, the Major Arcana. Many early decks have only this suit. These cards are considered more important than any other card. In the game of tarot—as in life—these cards "trump" all others; within this "higher" suit, the cards show an obvious progression, with the cards of the higher number trumping the lower number cards. This progression begins with The Fool (Key #0)—Spirit descending into physical existence—and ends with The World (Key #20). The attainment of The World is the ultimate goal of The Fool, and the end of his journey through the cycle of earthly existence.

While the suits of the lower cards represent the four elements that make up life on Earth, the trump suit is the classic "Fifth Element." Alchemists call the fifth element, the "Quintessence," which means "ether," or the air of the gods; the fifth element corresponds to fifth suit of the Tarot, the Major Arcana. Quintessence is the fifth and highest element in ancient and medieval philosophy that permeates all nature. The cards in this suit contain pictures that communicate directly with the image-based right brain through the use of symbols and archetypes.

By bypassing words, the images on the cards were very effective at imparting certain concepts that would have been trivialized by putting them in words. Images made it possible for the tarot to communicate with people who spoke a different language or who couldn't read. There are many cards in the Major Arcana that express alchemical ideas and processes: The Sun, The Moon, Temperance, The Lovers, The Magician, The Chariot, Strength—each card in the Major Arcana demonstrates a singular alchemical principle; the procession and order of the Major Arcana represent the process of transmutation, or personal evolution.

Numerology and the Tarot

Numerology is one of the cornerstones of the Tarot. Pythagoras, the Greek philosopher and mathematician (569-470 B.C.), is said to be the father of modern numerology, but it is speculated that he got his information from the "Mother" numerology system, called "Chaldean numerology" which originated in the part of the world that anthropologists have identified as "the cradle of civilization," Mesopotamia.

The Chaldean and the later system developed by Pythagoras were both alphanumeric systems that assigned meanings to numbers and numbers to letters. Pythagoras believed that there is a direct esoteric relationship between numbers and the creative nature of the universe. Each number in both systems is believed to possess a unique signature vibration; the system includes the base numbers one through nine, with two Master numbers, 11 and 22, which are never reduced.

In the art of numerology, each letter of the alphabet is assigned a number, which allows the adept to arrive at the hidden meanings behind names and words. The system is simple: a handy chart of the letter-number equivalents is included in the Numerology section at the back of this book for your convenience. It is easy to memorize the meanings of the numbers and letters, and use this knowledge to enhance your readings.

Letters to Numbers

In the art of numerology, each letter of the alphabet is assigned a number, which allows the adept to arrive at the hidden meanings behind names and words. The system is simple: a handy chart of the letter-number equivalents is included in the Numerology section at the back of this book for your convenience. It is easy to memorize the meanings of the numbers and letters, and use this knowledge to enhance your readings.

The Strength Versus Justice Argument

There is a long-standing argument about the numbering of tarot cards. Early tarot decks did not have numbers on any of the Arcana cards, while later decks placed the Justice card after The Chariot as the eighth card of the Major Arcana. In the *Tarot of Marseilles*, Justice was the eighth card and Strength was the eleventh card, but the influential Rider-Waite-Smith deck switched the position of these cards in order to make them better fit astrological correspondences, or so some people believe.

Waite is said to have had a vision that these two cards should be switched though he apparently never said why. If you are new to tarot, you may be surprised at the vehemence of the various factions that support each numbering system. Those who argue for the "traditional numbering system of the Tarot" are referring to the practice started by the *Tarot of Marseilles* which is not the earliest version of the Tarot. The earliest decks were unnumbered; when the decks started to acquire numbers there were many transposed cards, not just the eight and the eleven.

Many people who believe that the Tarot outlines very esoteric knowledge conjecture that these two cards were deliberately transposed in order to confuse non-practitioners and protect secret knowledge that was hidden inside the cards. This was called a "blind" and if true, it means that the readers of tarot with the knowledge of numerology had to get used to transposing the numbers of the cards in their heads in order to render an accurate reading.

In my own exploration of the Tarot. I have found that the RWS numbering system seems to follow the rules of numerology[1] that I use. Numerology within the Tarot reveals the path of creative manifestation and what I see as the esoteric path of personal development, and this is why my deck, *The Tarot of Creativity*, follows this system. Justice as Key #11 has always made sense to me, because I see the pillars on the card as a gateway and the figure of the Goddess Justice as the gatekeeper to knowledge reserved for the initiate.

Justice is a natural correspondence with the sign of Libra. Eleven is also the first Master number, meaning "illumination" and this corresponds with the meaning of Justice as an initiation and gateway to higher consciousness. The Strength card feels right as Key #8 for the astrological correspondence of Leo, as well as for the meaning of the number eight. There are many other reasons for this preference, which will become apparent as each of these cards is outlined in this book.

Ultimately, most people use the system that they first learned. In the end, a deck that makes sense to you personally is the one to use. If you happen to have a deck that reverses the RWS order, then I recommend that you use the corresponding card meaning rather than the number to help you understand the card. For instance, if you have a number eight Major Arcana card in your deck and it is titled, "Justice," then you might want to go to the corresponding section for number eleven in this book for the interpretation of the card's meaning. Fortunately, these two numbers (#8 and #11) are the only ones that are commonly transposed.

---

1   The Numerology section at the back of the book supplies meanings for each number.

ARCHETYPES, QUANTUM MECHANICS, & SYNCHRONICITY

How does the Tarot work? I have to admit to being a skeptic in the beginning. I even created my first deck without any belief in it or any real experience with the cards. I thought the Tarot was for credulous fools. But after I created the *Transformational Tarot* computer game, I tested the programming by running a few readings of my own: the results were eerily accurate. When I posted my game online, people wrote me that their readings were the best they ever had.

But my rational mind balked at the evidence. I had to explore the ideas of consciousness and quantum physics to arrive at an answer.[1] Obviously, the random program I had designed was influenced by the people running it, or perhaps the subconscious of the player was choosing to translate the reading in a more meaningful way than was possible in a completely random environment. So, that meant that the random program was not truly random, or that meaning was being seen where there was none—or a third option: something else was at work.

Archetypes

Jungian psychology contains a few key concepts that can be used to show how the Tarot might work. Carl Jung coined the term "archetype;" he believed that there was a collective conscious shared by all peoples, no matter their native beliefs or culture; archetypes are the universal fruits of that consciousness.

Archetypes are very powerful symbols that directly communicate with a part of our brain that deals primarily in images—the right brain. Each image holds a great deal of non-verbal information which is much more accessible and direct than verbal or written language. The Tarot contains many archetypes, especially in the Major Arcana. You could say that the lower cards are related to folklore and fairy tales, populated with common folk, animals, and royal courts; these cards represent the common, lower paths of personal development. The archetypical images in the Major Arcana are related to the esoteric mysteries of consciousness and the structure of the universe. The lower cards delineate a practical path through one of the suits, but each suit is a path of realization in itself. The trumps represent the path

---

1 To explore the relationship between mind and matter read *The Holographic Universe* by Michael Talbot.

of the esoteric student. The lower cards show the minutia of daily life—the trials and tribulations of ordinary consciousness—while the higher "trump" cards represent universal concepts related to self-realization.

To anyone with the slightest interest in mythology, the archetypes in the Tarot are clear to see. For example, a goddess or god represents a guiding principle for humanity: the universal concept *behind* the figure is what makes it an archetype. An archetype is a symbol that conveys a universal concept, usually in the form of an image, that is instantly understood no matter its geographic origin; archetypes transcend cultural boundaries and temporal beliefs.

Christ, for instance, represents a universal archetype of the principle of Love. The Christ Child, in his innocence (lack of beliefs) and purity, sends a powerful message about how to achieve enlightenment by returning to the original state of innocence and purity of purpose that we had in the Garden of Eden. His message is to become "like a child"—in becoming like him, you are able to "ascend" in frequency through the power of unconditional Love. It doesn't matter whether you believe that Christ is God, or whether you think he was an ascended master, a prophet, or simply a good man. His example communicates an archetype that embodies the principles of wholeness, unconditional love, and unity that speak to all of us.

Someone once defined God as a principle of wholeness, and this is the best definition that I can find; it supports the ideas in many ancient philosophies and esoteric knowledge worldwide, and in the images of the Tarot itself (see the definition for the symbol CIRCLE). Since the Tarot shows us archetypical images of goddesses, angels, and devils that might seem to support certain beliefs, I think it is necessary to address what I see as the higher purpose of the Tarot. To do that, I will try to define as best as I can the underlying concepts and terms that are in this book.

The Tarot is meant to be taken symbolically, not literally. For instance, the Devil represents an archetype of the misuse of power: in the Tarot, the image of the Devil is the reverse of The Lovers card. The principle of Love shown in The Lovers/LOVE card, indicates a holistic awareness, inclusion, unity consciousness, acceptance, equality and abundance; the Devil is the opposite side of the coin, indicating a focus on a materialistic view to the exclusion of everything else. Believing in the Devil lends power to this concept of separation, thereby increasing the archetype's influence. You give this concept life by believing in it and contributing your emotional power to it. This is why the Devil card in *The Tarot of Creativity* is titled "The

Shadow." To Carl Jung, the archetype of the Shadow defines everything in yourself that you cannot see, or don't want to see. It is an archetype that is understood the world over. Why? Because the creative system of duality requires shadow to balance the light. Or rather, the shadow defines the light as the light defines the shadow. A dualistic system creates out of the polarity of opposites; it can be no other way. Without the negative side, the system of duality would be like a teeter-totter that has only one side, or like a person trying to walk with only one leg.

Synchronicity is an ever present reality for those who have eyes to see. ~ Carl Jung

Synchronicity

"Synchronicity" is another unique term that was coined by Carl Jung. Synchronicity is the occurrence of two or more events that appear to be meaningfully related but not causally related. Synchronicity holds that such events are "meaningful coincidences;" it implies that, just as events may be connected by causality, they may also be connected by meaning. Man is compelled by his nature to search for meaning—he is compelled to make order out of apparent chaos. This organizing principle of the mind may be what creates reality itself. Carl Jung defines synchronicity:

> Meaningful coincidences can be thought of as pure chance; but as they accumulate, as the correspondence becomes more exact and elaborate, their probability decreases and they become un-thinkable, thus becoming impossible to be thought of as mere randomness, and lacking all possible causal explanation, one must see in said events a manifestation of order.[1]

According to mystics, reality was created by the cosmic mind as a mirror for the consciousness of Itself. The phenomenon of synchronicity that Jung defined is one of the ways for the connected nature of the under-lying reality of consciousness to reveal itself.

In a game such as the Tarot, the natural process of synchronicity is given free play. The randomizing of the cards initiates the process, as you clear your mind of all preconceptions or wishes. Then as you deal the cards, you find that the cards seem to reflect an inner voice. The relationship of the

1   Carl Jung

cards to each other and their positions in the spread are all meaningful, and are interpreted according to knowledge and beliefs that you already have.

When you put this together with the question you asked, the information becomes even more personalized, and intimately meaningful. Perhaps the Tarot should be called the "synchronicity game," a device that allows the Higher Self to use the magic of synchronicity to speak to you in a language of images and words.One of Jung's favorite quotes on synchronicity was from *Through the Looking-Glass* by Lewis Carroll.

"Living backwards!" Alice repeated in great astonishment. "I never heard of such a thing!"

"But there's one great advantage in it, that one's memory works both ways."

"I'm sure MINE only works one way," Alice remarked. "I can't remember things before they happen."

"It's a poor sort of memory that only works backwards," the Queen remarked.

The Queen is implying that memory can work backwards as well as forwards because memory is a form of consciousness. This is another way to say that consciousness transcends time and space, or rather, that consciousness is not subject to the rules of matter, or general physics.[1]

The Quantum Explanation
The running of a random computer program, or a good card shuffle, allows synchronicity free play. And it allows the mind to peer behind the curtain of the holographic universe to see how consciousness creates reality, as in the famous "double-slit" quantum experiment, where the expectations of the viewer influenced the (apparent) outcome of the experiment.

Quantum mechanics is a form of physics that is subject to the rules of consciousness, rather than to the rules of density or physical matter. Consciousness rules the world of the subatomic; it is the energy *behind* the world of appearances.

---

1   The movie, *Interstellar*, explores this concept

The creator can never stand outside his creation.
This is an immutable law of consciousness.[1]

The quantum nature of consciousness and the way the mind is geared engenders the eventual realization that there is no such thing as empirical reality; because without the existence of an objective observer who can stand *outside the experiment,* there is no chance that an objective reality exists. It would mean that there is no tree that can fall in the forest without someone to hear it fall, or more precisely, without someone to *expect* it to make a sound when it falls.

The implicate or sea of awareness was known to ancient mystics, and alchemists; it is what the mystics might refer to as the cosmic mind stuff; it is a sea of consciousness that underlies everything else. In the Tarot the quantum implicate is represented in the card The High Priestess, while the "explicate," or *unfolded order* is the world of appearances, represented in the next card in the Major Arcana, The Empress.

The Empress card represents the natural world of matter—Newtonian physics. The world of the senses is the result of the energy, or rather the potential, underlying the form, the quantum implicate represented by The High Priestess. The Tarot teaches the principles of the universe and what happens with the application of directed consciousness in the first seven cards of the Tarot. The tarot allows us to tap into this awareness through our intuitive interpretation of the images.

---

1 *Unplug From the Matrix: Truth is Sometimes Stranger Than Fiction*, Aliyah Marr

THE PURPOSE OF THE TAROT

Not everyone sees the Tarot as I do, as a tool for personal empowerment and evolution. Chances are if you are attracted to this book, you resonate with this philosophy, and are intrigued by the subliminal, universal messages that seem to underlie the card images and titles. To me, the deck shows a system for understanding the underpinnings of duality, while it hints at the larger reality that lies underneath.

What I call the *Higher Self* or *Spirit* is not God, it is the larger part of you, the part that could not come wholly into this level of density, this material existence. The self-conscious is the ego/mental body that thinks (erroneously) that it has to be in charge. The subconscious is the emotional/physical body. These three parts together form what I call "the divine triad" of the enlightened individual.

Most of us are not able to overcome the ego; however we try, we always fail because the ego cannot be fought or overcome. If the ego dies, so does the whole person. The only way forward is to demote the ego from its position of control, which it assumed upon entry to *The Matrix*, which features power over others as a theme and fear-separation as its core programming. You have to make friends with all parts of yourself in order to achieve harmony, cooperation, and wholeness. The enlightened individual goes from a being at war with himself to a being at peace in whatever world he finds himself.

The whole point of esoteric practices like the Tarot is to reestablish the natural system of the divine triad with the Higher Self or Super Conscious as the director, the ego as the personal assistant or executor of the will of the Higher Self, and with the subconscious/physical body as the energy source, and place for manifestation on the material plane. In order to experience the harmony of the divine triad, the Tarot teaches us to purify ourselves of all unconscious thoughts and emotions. Higher awareness is always a conscious choice, not a default condition.

The purpose of tools like the Tarot is to put you in contact with your Higher Self by accessing your natural intuition. In order to do that, you must learn how to choose your vibrational signature. As long as you consistently resonate with the frequencies of the lower emotions and dense, disempowering belief systems you cannot "hear" the messages of Spirit, or your Higher Self. If you cannot hear the voice of your Higher Self, you are like a boat without a rudder on the sea of life.

The Language of the Higher Self

As an artist, it is obvious to me that the Tarot is a visual language of archetypes and symbols, but it is more than that: it is a map masked as a game that outlines a path for the seeker of personal empowerment. The Tarot is meant to address the way our greater psychic awareness, aka the Higher Self, communicates through symbols. A deck of cards with images is a perfect language for the symbol-based reality of the right brain.

The right brain gathers information from disparate sources and synthesizes the bits and pieces in order to derive a meaning or construct something new. The left brain catalogues information and data like the hard drive of a computer. In the enlightened, whole individual, the right brain is the creative brain, while the left brain is in charge of executing the directives of the Soul that are coming in from the right brain in practical, physical ways. Thus, in the enlightened individual, the left brain becomes the "personal assistant" of the Higher Self; its job is to bring the rarefied intent of the Higher Self into physical form. The left brain is a crucial component in creative manifestation: it has very practical physical skills.

In the unenlightened individual, the system of creative manifestation takes an unconscious turn, still manifesting, but in a way that doesn't serve the greater evolvement of the individual. The monsters of undigested fears and overwhelming negative emotions populate the dreams and the reality of the person's field, eventually spilling out like a sickness into the collective conscious.

Only when we are open enough to see that consciousness may be greater than that which can be contained in the physical brain, can we understand that reality may be much more than we can currently comprehend. To understand the way reality works at the quantum level, the individual has to first realize that thoughts and emotions influence perceptions, if not reality itself.

> *I am the Smoky Mirror, because I am looking at myself in all of you, but we don't recognize each other because of the smoke in-between us. That smoke is the Dream, and the mirror is you, the dreamer.* [1]

Once that first step has been taken away from literal, materialistic, so-called "rational" explanations, it is possible to open up to a psychic reality

1   Ruiz, Don Miguel, *The Four Agreements*

that runs parallel to material existence, a veritable river of consciousness and information that is infinitely vast, broad, and deep. All the most ancient systems of knowledge assert that physical existence is created by the mind, which projects the reality the individual then experiences. Perception is a "smoky mirror"—smoky to the degree of the individual's realization of their role in creating what appears in the mirror, and possibly even the mirror itself.

The analogy of tarot to language is obvious: each card in a reading can be seen as a word in a sentence. In a language, a word is made up of characters that are each symbols that stand in for a packet of information. As the symbol-characters are strung together to create a sentence, so the symbols and archetypes in a card can be assembled by the brain into a cohesive unit of meaning. And in the same way that words are strung together to create a meaningful sentence, so images on the cards in a reading can be assembled in a coherent and meaningful sentence.

The Major Arcana cards are referred to as "keys;" they are indeed keys to the mystery of the universe, the YOU-and-I-verse that exists within our psyches. The Tarot opens the door to understanding the mysteries that have haunted man for thousands upon thousands of years, ever since the first being thought to look at the skies, and see a meaning enclosed inside a mystery.

And so, we come full circle, to the alchemist's concept of the Quintessence: what they termed, "the realm of the gods," as a reality, unseen, but able to be reached. This psychic, psychological realm is where the archetypes, once revered as the gods, overseers, protectors, and idealized prototypes of man, still exist as images, deeply engrained into the collective conscious.

This is the rich cultural treasure that is our heritage as human beings. Eventually the seeker comes to understand that the ultimate mystery he sought to understand was never "out there" at all; it is a mystery of the mirror, the mirror that is the mind, which is ultimately an explanation wrapped in an enigma.

ANATOMY OF THE TAROT

A reading consists of two major players: the person doing the reading, called the Reader, and the person requesting the reading, called the Querent (based upon the root, "question"), or Seeker in this book. Of course, if you are doing the reading for yourself, you are both parties. The two decks referenced in this book are referred to by the following acronyms:

RWS = Rider Waite Smith tarot
TOC = The Tarot of Creativity

The Major Arcana

The Major Arcana are the heart of the Tarot. These cards are the highest cards in the deck. Also called the "Trumps" because they trumped all the lower cards in the deck, if you are playing it as a game. This term also refers to the ancient Roman triumphal march, when returning victorious from a campaign. The Major Arcana represent the progress of the Soul in its journey through life. In the TOC, the Major Arcana cards are indicated by the Ouroborus symbol that surrounds the numbers.

> The Ouroborus is the symbolic rendition of the eternal principles presented in the Emerald Tablet. The great serpent devouring itself represents the idea that "All Is One," even though the universe undergoes periodic cycles of destruction and creation (or resurrection).
>
> In Orphic and Mithraic symbology, the Ouroborus was called the Agathos Daimon or "Good Spirit" and was a symbol for the "Operation of the Sun." In Greek terminology, the Ouroborus was the Aion, which Herakleitos likened to a child at play. To the Greeks, the Aion (from which our word "eon" is derived) defined the cosmic period between the creation and destruction of the universe. [1]

The Suits

The suits represent the four worldly paths to personal mastery through natural human qualities; these can be either weaknesses or strengths, depending on the card, the orientation of the card, and the other cards in a

---

1 en.wikipedia.org/wiki/Ouroboros

reading. The suits in the Tarot are analogous to the four suits in a playing card deck, but they contain one more card in the court cards, for a total of fourteen cards in each suit.

The suits each demonstrate one of the paths of the seeker, and shows a progression of understanding as the numbers increase, with lessons at each stage or number. Each suit represents a path or tool on the journey of personal evolution, and are seen as representative of the four elements of the Earth. The final fifth suit is the Major Arcana, which represents the path of mastery.

> In classical thought, the four elements earth, water, air, and fire frequently occur; sometimes including a fifth element or quintessence (after "quint" meaning "fifth") called aether in ancient Greece and akasha in India. The concept of the five elements formed a basis of analysis in both Hinduism and Buddhism. In Hinduism, particularly in an esoteric context, the four states-of-matter describe matter, and a fifth element describes that which was beyond the material world.
>
> Similar lists existed in ancient China and Japan. In Buddhism the four great elements, to which two others are sometimes added, are not viewed as substances, but as categories of sensory experience. The ancient Greek belief in five basic elements, these being earth, water, air, fire, and aether, dates from pre–Socratic times and persisted throughout the Middle Ages and into the Renaissance, deeply influencing European thought and culture.
>
> These five elements are sometimes associated with the five platonic solids. Aristotle added a fifth element, aether, as the quintessence, reasoning that whereas fire, earth, air, and water were earthly and corruptible, since no changes had been perceived in the heavenly regions, the stars cannot be made out of any of the four elements but must be made of a different, unchangeable, heavenly substance. [1]

The suits of traditional tarot card decks are analogous to the classical elements, and this is how they are represented in *The Tarot of Creativity*:

---

1   en.wikipedia.org/wiki/Classical_element

Wands= FIRE
Swords = AIR
Cups = WATER
Pentacles = EARTH

In the TOC deck, the suits show the creative process from inspiration (Wands/FIRE) to thought (Swords/AIR) through emotions (Cups/WATER), and then finally entering the material plane (Pentacles/EARTH). Together, they show the path of creative manifestation:

FIRE (Wands)—> AIR (Swords)—> WATER
(Cups)—> EARTH (Pentacles)

This order is not the same one that most tarot scholars follow. My system comes from the insight I had when I wrote my first book, *Parallel Mind, The Art of Creativity*. I was following the genesis of emotions and their role in creating the physical reality.

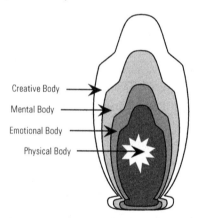

Using my diagram of the four bodies that make up a human being, the creative process is as follows: inspiration from the ethereal creative body becomes a thought when it passes through the mental body; the resultant inspiration is charged with an emotion as it passes through the emotional body; the charged thought coalesces into matter, becoming physical reality.

Notice that the position of the emotional body is the one nearest to the physical body at the center. Its role is to coalesce your creative thoughts from the ethereal creative body into the density of physical form. Emotions are extremely powerful—they can bring us health, happiness, or success in any endeavor; emotions are the most powerful tools in our creative toolbox.

Emotions are the catalyst in the alchemical process of making your thoughts real. You may think that you have to work to manifest your thoughts, but the process is happening all the time without your conscious control. Not many people realize that their emotional life is determining their physical reality. [1]

The suits in *The Tarot of Creativity* trace the same path of creative manifestation, teaching us how to use our power of creativity wisely. In *Parallel Mind, The Art of Creativity*, I stated that we are unconsciously creating all the time.

If that is true, why not become a conscious creator, and create the life of your dreams? To do that you must learn to use your emotions as a guide, a compass to point out the path of your Soul. Eventually, the choice of your emotions can help you find the frequency that matches your desire; this is how to use emotions to consciously create.

Wands/FIRE
Energy: the Super Conscious (Higher Self), inspiration, desire, passion, planning.

Swords/AIR
Thought, self-conscious, the ego, moral principles, communication, reason, the intellect.

Cups/WATER
Emotions, romance, love, creativity, relationships, the Soul, karmic attachments, the past, the subconscious mind.

Pentacles/EARTH
Health, the material world, materialism, the physical body, money, security, the environment, industry, work.

---

1   *Parallel Mind, The Art of Creativity*, Aliyah Marr

The Pip Cards

The pips are the cards numbered from ACE (1)-10. They show current energies that may be hidden from view or that the Querent may not see or want to see.

At the highest level, when correlated with their Arcana numerological equivalent, they show how to apply the higher principles and realizations in the Arcana cards to the issues encountered in daily life. For instance, the Sixes in all the suits are correlated with the Lovers/LOVE card in the Major Arcana; all Sixes are then about the principle of LOVE as expressed through the energy of the suit.

The Court Cards

The court cards trump the lower cards in the suits. The royal figures pictured on the court cards are analogous to those of a modern playing card deck, but the Tarot adds one more card: the Page. The court cards represent creative mastery in each suit. In a departure from traditional tarot decks, the royal cards in the TOC are assigned a number, which aids in interpreting the card's numerological meaning.

11 – PAGE – a message or messenger coming through the suit
12 – KNIGHT – the active agent of the energy of the suit
13 – QUEEN – mastery for the suit expressed as a "female" energy
14 – KING – mastery for the suit expressed as a "male" energy

The Aces

The aces represent the distilled energy—the seed energy or essence of each suit. They are both higher and lower than the court cards, just as in a regular playing deck. Aces are related to their numerical equivalent in the Major Arcana: Key #1, The Magician/ATTENTION, who presents the tools of earthly existence to the newly incarnated Fool. The Ace has no direction of its own; they are filled with raw potential. They are the energy of the suit, ready to be directed by consciousness.

originate/initiate/genesis

The Aces represent raw or initial passion, feelings, thoughts and needs that can be directed into something more. They represent hope, a possibility, an action to take, a future that you can create. The aces demonstrate the promise of the power represented by their respective suit: each suit opens up a path that when used together allow us to create on the material plane.

SPEED READING

As you work with the cards, they will start to accrue new information that you can add to your knowledge of each card. The images start to work as a visual communication device in an ongoing conversation with your intuition and inner guidance.

When I started to study the Tarot. I took a card a day from the Rider Waite Smith deck and memorized its number, image, title, number, and meaning. I held the card in my mind for the entire day. The next day, I memorized another card after I recalled the images and meanings of all the cards from the previous days. Like Alice in Wonderland, I found myself "falling into" each card as the symbols and archetypes on the pictures came alive for me.

Then, after I had thoroughly memorized the deck, I suddenly "saw" the Knight of Swords when I thought of a friend. The image on the card so completely summed up his character at the time that I was startled. The sudden appearance of the card in my mind stopped my train of thought long enough for me to see the connection. From then on, I have a hard time seeing this image without thinking of this type of energy. The Tarot had become a way for my Higher Self to communicate with me by using the images on the card to trigger my intuition.

The cards remained an intriguing mystery to me that I slowly explored as I started to do readings for myself. I recorded each reading in a notebook, in order to track my progress. I read for situations and people that had just entered my life. A couple years later, I found myself suddenly interested in numerology. I realized that the numbers on tarot cards are intrinsic to their meaning.

I recommend that you practice reading tarot first for yourself, before testing your skills on others. If you decide to memorize the cards, it is easier to study all the cards of the same number together; this will allow you to understand how important the number is to the card's meaning, as it assists you in seeing how the energy of the number plays out in the five suits. This book lends itself very well to this technique as all the cards with the same number are grouped together.

Preparing to Read

To read any spread, you must first clear yourself as much as possible of personal agendas, obstructing beliefs, and emotional debris; you must be as blank as possible in order for the cards to work. I like to say that the Higher Self, with whom you are communicating through the medium of the cards, cannot penetrate a wall of personal beliefs or a smoke screen of negative emotions. You must become, as much as possible, a blank slate. The images on the cards are repositories for a great quantity of information. As you work with the cards, you will add more and more information to each card as it accrues meaning for you. Cards will change in meaning according to the reading variables; circumstances such as the meaning of the whole reading, the question asked by the Querent, the position of a card in a reading, and the influence of nearby cards. The Tarot is a tool for your Higher Self; it communicates with you via the symbolic language of the images.

I once had a reading where the Seven of Swords appeared; in this card the traditional interpretation of this card is that the figure is sneaky and duplicitous, taking away the swords from an encampment: the accepted idea is that the 7 of Sword is a thief. Suddenly I saw that the card was telling me that the person who was the subject of my reading was "disarming" or charming. In another reading I read this card as meaning that diplomacy was needed on my part to disarm a potentially contentious situation.

Shuffling

Randomizing the cards can be done in various ways. Standard card shuffling techniques apply. If you do a lot of readings in succession, it may be best to shuffle once and then spread out the deck in a pile and allow the Querent to choose the cards. Alternately you can make a pile of the cards and "mess" them up. The pile of cards can then be easily randomized again for the next client.

Practice Makes Perfect

The hardest reading to do is one that you do for yourself, but this is the best way to practice, since you are always available, and you can verify your results. Keep a log of your readings, and compare your tarot log with your journal to see if your readings are accurate.

I used to do a six-month reading every month, and found that the "predictions," although amazingly accurate, were not necessarily delivered on the time schedule of the reading. In other words, if I saw something was to happen in the month of April when I made the reading in December, it might be delayed or happen earlier by a month or more. The further out the reading, the less accurate the read. This is because psychic awareness taps into potential timelines. A good psychic will read the circumstances with the strongest potential.

Quick Trick for Reading any Card

To understand the cards at a glance, you can see the number of the card as a verb and the suit as the modifying adverb. When you put them together, you have the beginning of a sentence, which can convey a meaning. Thus, you only have to learn the meaning of each suit and of each number to be able to determine what a card means when you get it in a reading. This provides a baseline for the development of your personal lexicon.

Think of the number of the card as the main meaning of the card modified by the suit it is in.

Each suit brings a subtle energy to modify the energy of the number. The suits trace a four step path of manifestation, headed by a Major Arcana card that expresses a more universal principle or natural law. Thus the number Three, which is the number of the Child, and is about childlikeness and creativity, translates as different variants of this base energy in the suits. The Three emerges into its archetypical expression as "IMAGINATION," represented by The Empress, Key #3.

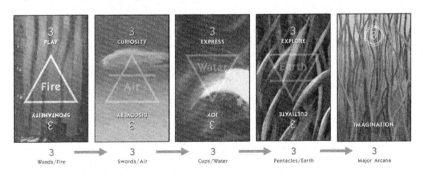

3 of Fire	3 of Air	3 of Water	3 of Earth	3 Major Arcana
Play	Curiosity	Express	Explore	Imagination
Spontaneity	Discovery	Joy	Cultivate	(The Empress)

Using my numerological technique for learning the Tarot, you only have to memorize the meanings for the base numbers, plus the two Master numbers in the deck. Numerology is built upon nine base numbers, plus the Master numbers, which are double number that are all multiples of eleven: 11-99. The Tarot's fifth suit, the Major Arcana, only goes to number 21, but the hidden value for The Fool is the second Master number, 22. If I were starting to learn the Tarot again, I would first memorize the meanings of numbers 0-10 plus the meaning of the Master numbers 11 and 22. The reason that I include number 10 is explained more fully in the section about numerology.

When you memorize the numbers instead of the specific cards, you start to see how the number works through the energy of the suits, and your intuition is given a much broader field in which to play. This book supplies a handy section on numerology at the back of the book, making it easy to study and memorize the meanings of the numbers.

HOW TO USE THIS BOOK

Having the information for both the RWS (Rider Waite Smith) deck and the TOC (*Tarot of Creativity*) on the same page in this book can add depth to your readings. For instance, lets say you have pulled the Five of Pentacles using the RWS deck.

Rider Waite Smith Tarot   Tarot of Creativity

You go to the page for the Fives and you see that the number Five has to primarily do with change and freedom. You know that the Five is the middle of the journey, and it is a kind of portal or gate to the higher energies of the upper numbers of the scale. This gate is guarded by issues that come up in your life, represented by the troublesome Fives.

If you pass the challenge of the energy of the Fives—change, freedom with responsibility—then you can go on to the upper numbers. If you cannot meet the challenge of the Five with equanimity, creativity, and poise, then you will have to go back and repeat the lessons of the lower grades, numbers 1-5.

Now you look at the Rider Waite Smith card meaning. You may find this dismaying: the Five of Pentacles is one of the most potentially negative cards in the deck, meaning financial loss/poverty consciousness/health issues, etc.

The equivalent card in *The Tarot of Creativity* seems to present us with a much more digestible chunk of information: it means "Surrender/Breakthrough." The two words can be taken together, as in "you have to first surrender to what is, before you can have a breakthrough." Or you can look at the energy of the cards in the upright word as the beginning of the energy of the Five of Earth, while the reversed word represents the ending energy of the Five in the Suit of Earth.

So, if you received the card in the reversed position, you know that a breakthrough is imminent once you have surrendered. If you received the card in the upright position, you can take the card's advice, and surrender to "what is" rather than resisting a change that is most likely in your highest good, no matter how it looks now. The two cards both express the meaning of the number Five in the suit: change, chaos, freedom. The Five in the Pentacle/Earth suit is the end of the Five energy—it has worked through the entire process of manifestation that started with the Five of Wands/FIRE, and now you are seeing the energy of the Five as a manifested event or thing. You may realize that you can forestall many "negative" occurrences once you learn the path of creative manifestation shown by the suits in *The Tarot of Creativity*. It is much easier to create from the pure energy of the Fire (Wands) stage than at the solid, hard to change Earth (Pentacles) stage. In the case of the hypothetical reading above, if you had paid attention when this Five energy began in your life as the energy of Fire/Wands, you may have been able to avoid the results of the energy of change, or more effectively deal with it.

The TOC card gives you practical advice that you can use, while the RWS card seems to tell you that you are once again thinking with poverty consciousness. Which card presents you with information that you can use in a positive manner? Reading from two decks gives you valuable insight on the cards. As you keep on reading, you will find that you are slowly adding to an internal lexicon of meanings, imagery, and readings.

Meditation
Next you read the section called "Meditation" to see what insight it can offer for the Five of Earth:

RWS—Do you believe that you deserve health and wealth?
TOC—If you can't surrender you will break, instead of breakthrough.

The Five in the Major Arcana
Finally you can look at the Major Arcana card for information on the Five in the Major Arcana. The Hiierophant/INTUITION card heads up the energy of the Fives. The Hierophant hears the voice of the Higher Self, through his intuition. But first, you must surrender the ego, because the voice of your intuition cannot speak while you are mired in mental confusion or fear.

The herculean task of surrendering at the moment of fear and imminent change takes a lot of courage, but the surrender must presage the breakthrough. In other words, the challenge of the Fives presents you with the price of freedom: courage, which paradoxically can only come when you surrender your ego to the guidance of your Higher Self, and surrender your need to have freedom be what your mind thinks it is.

LEARNING TO READ TAROT

I recommend that you start reading Tarot with only a few cards at first. A one-card reading is a great way to start out, because it allows you to really focus on one card at a time, and this makes it easier to learn the Tarot.

In any reading, your real questions and desires are often buried under superficial concerns. Be careful not to try to mold your reading to those superficial ideas, but allow it to reveal the desires and intentions of your innermost soul. To develop your intuition, it is better to not ask the Tarot questions when you first learn to read; it is much better to open yourself up to whatever comes through. The best way to do this is to empty your mind of all concerns and questions before you lay out the cards. Allow them to speak to you without you trying to assign a meaning or category to them beforehand. By not asking a question, you allow the Higher Self to communicate more clearly with you. When you see the reading, you will naturally know what it is about, because you will see the cards' relevance to your deeper concern.

I often do a Celtic Cross layout for a long reading, but my favorite short reading is a three-card reading. This reading, although simple, can give you oodles of relevant information. Invite the Querent to shuffle, then cut the deck into three pieces, and choose a stack with their non-dominant hand. Then deal out the top three cards in a row. This row can be read in several ways. The most popular way is to read the cards in sequence with the first card as the past, the middle card as the present, and the last card as the future. I sometimes prefer to read the three cards as a sentence. *The Tarot of Creativity* lends to reading this way. First the reading from the Rider Waite Smith deck.

And here are the equivalent cards from *The Tarot of Creativity*.

If you allow the titles on *The Tarot of Creativity*. cards to form a sentence, you get a reading:

Be RECEPTIVE. REMEMBER what you already know (MEMORY).

The High Priestess is a Major Arcana card that indicates deep inner knowledge. The Queen of Swords/AIR means mental mastery and clear discernment. The Seven of Pentacles is a seven, which means that the work indicated by Pentacles is spiritual in nature.

The Summation Reading

One thing that I like to do is sum up the reading in order to get what I call the "meta-meaning." *The Tarot of Creativity* especially lends itself to this practice, as all the cards use Arabic instead of Roman numbers; even the Court cards are assigned numbers. So my reading would sum up like this:

$$2 + 13 + 7 = 22$$

Adding the numbers together returns the sum of twenty-two for the reading, which is a Master number, as well as being the "secret" number of

The Fool. In general, if you arrive at a Master number you stop. A Master number is a double number—they are all multiples of 11, starting with 11: 11, 22, 33, 44, 55, 66, 77, 88, 99. If the sum of the reading is more than 22,

I sum it again to further reduce it. The sum reading tells me that in order

to be RECEPTIVE to the dictates of Spirit, and use my mental abilities to REMEMBER what I already KNOW (Memory), I should allow myself to be fresh to the world (The Fool) and use my INSIGHT (my power of reasoning) as a guide.

If the sum equals twenty-two or lower, I use the corresponding card *and* its sum for enhanced reading. For instance, let's say that your sum of a Celtic card spread is 108; you add these numbers together to get 18—in numerology, you always drop the zero because it has no value—which, in the numerology of the Tarot is The Moon/DREAMING. The 18 is related to the 9 in the Tarot since you can sum the 1 plus the 8 to get 9, The Hermit/EMERGENCE. If the sum of the reading equals the numerical value of one or more of the cards on the table at any point in the reduction process, I look at that card as being more important than the other cards in the reading.

The Six-Month Reading

Another valuable spread is a six-month forecast reading: this spread features six rows of three-card readings stacked vertically. I did this reading once a month when I was learning to read tarot. I recorded all my readings, and found that the monthly readings were very accurate, although the time where a specific energy was predicted to appear might change from month to month.

The first row of cards represents the previous month, the second row reads the current month and the last four rows of readings read the next four months. So if you are doing the reading in February:

ROW 6—4 months ahead (June)
ROW 5—3 months ahead (May)
ROW 4—2 months ahead (April)
ROW 3—next month (March)
ROW 2—current month (February)
ROW 1—last month (January)

Including a reading for the past month and the present month grounds the reading, and lets you check your accuracy, on a month by month basis when you are beginning.

The rule of thumb for all "psychic readings" or intuitive information is that the further out a reading, the less accurate it becomes, since the time period allows for much more change in events, and in the Querent herself.

Reading for Others

Reading tarot for others is a great responsibility. You have to come from a high level of awareness in order to understand what you are seeing, and communicate it to another in a way that is empowering. *The Tarot of Creativity* has this higher awareness built into it. It took me a full year to

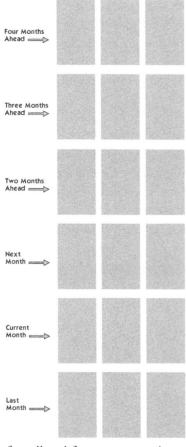

Four Months Ahead ➡️

Three Months Ahead ➡️

Two Months Ahead ➡️

Next Month ➡️

Current Month ➡️

Last Month ➡️

discern the highest possible meaning for each card: I wanted it to be very empowering.

A tarot reader is like a psychologist or a therapist; the client coming to a reader expects to get good advice, and trusts the Reader. Even if you read tarot as a parlor game, you can really hurt other people if you don't take what you are doing seriously.

Then there is the energy of the Tarot itself: like anything that has had that much emotional and mental energy directed at it, it has acquired an innate power of its own over the years. It doesn't matter if you have a new deck straight out of the box or you are reading from your grandmother's deck, the Tarot is a tool that can influence people, and as such should be treated with respect. It is extremely important to give your clients only the highest possible reading you can from the cards; although a reading can foretell and forewarn, a good tarot reader will inform the Querent of how to best approach the upcoming event and get the most out of it, even if it seems to foretell of a disaster.

One time, The Tower card appeared in a RWS reading I gave for a client who had just broken her arm and lost her apartment the previous week. The client knew enough of the Tarot to know that The Tower can foretell of an upcoming disaster, so she gasped when the card appeared. When I saw the card, I heard the phrases: "the other shoe drops" and "trouble comes in threes" so I told her to be cautious and attentive for the third thing that might be coming. A few days later, her car broke down. The reading allowed her to be prepared, so she took this final event in stride.

The Tower is often about the breakdown of the ego's need to control things/events. The appearance of this card was warning my client that her life was about to change in a big way. Of course, as a tarot reader, I did not tell her that her ego was up for a huge fall, just that the Tower indicated a big change was coming. You have to be diplomatic sometimes, and let your client discover some things for themselves.

In other words, telling a client that her ego is in the way isn't a way to advise her if she isn't ready to hear it. Because my client's ego had been holding on to things as they were, desperately working long hours at a job she hated so she could afford her apartment, the break with the old had to be sudden and shocking.

Breaking her arm should have shown her that she had to stop what she was doing, but this was apparently not enough to shake her ego from its hold, so she had to lose her expensive apartment. Finally her car had to break down before she could finally surrender and go a different way.

At the time, the *Tarot of Creativity* deck had not been created, but The Tower's equivalent card in this deck is very illuminating, it is entitled "The Awakening." According to the TOC card title, my client's three-fold disaster was just the prelude to an awakening of her soul; and this turned out to be true: she was on the very cusp of a huge life change; one that was not to her ego's liking.

How to Read Tarot Without a Deck
One day I found myself studying the *Rider Waite Smith Tarot* in earnest. Every day I memorized a card, starting with the Major Arcana and then studying all the cards of the same number together; when I finished I had all the cards so imprinted upon my mind that I could do tarot readings in my head. When I do a reading these days, I can remember all the cards and all their positions in the reading for weeks afterwards because I have memorized all the cards in the deck.

Because of this, I can easily do a reading without a deck. The cards come to me as an auditory message—I "hear" the card titles read to me as if over the phone, and then I form the image of them in my mind's eye. For some odd reason, I often get the cards as their playing card equivalents. For instance, here is a sample of a 3-card reading. The original message using playing card titles: Ace of Clubs—3 of Diamonds—Knight of Spades, which translates to:

Ace of Wands—3 of Pentacles—- Knight of Swords

Looking up the equivalent cards in my deck (you can use this book or *The Tarot of Creativity* deck), I get:

Ace of Fire	3 of Earth	Knight of Air
The Spark	Explore/Cultivate	Engage

The words naturally form a sentence that becomes a reading:

ENGAGE the SPARK of life by EXPLORING
and CULTIVATING your CREATIVITY.

The Summation Reading

Adding these numbers together gives us the summation reading: 1 + 3 + 12 = 16, which reduces to 7. The Tower (16) or The Chariot (7). The Chariot in *The Tarot of Creativity* is titled Adventure. The summation card advises to see the path forward as an adventure.

Quick Start Study

If I was beginning to learn the Tarot today, I would do it the same way, but I would study numerology first, then study all the cards with the same numbers together, seeing how the number is expressed in each suit and in the Major Arcana. This book is designed to make it easy to memorize the deck because it is arranged with all the cards of the same number together, which makes it easy to study the cards; in this way, you could have the entire tarot deck memorized in twenty-two days or less. If you study the Tarot this way, you too could find that you can do readings without a deck, as you can "see" the cards in your mind.

The Tarot Tableau

There is another really interesting way to study the Major Arcana: the Tarot Tableau, which is a way to visualize how the energy of the cards work together by arranging the cards in three rows of seven cards each. The Tarot Tableau and its description is included in the back of this book.

Handling Reversals

When you think about it, learning the Tarot can be a monumental task. After all, there are 78 cards. If you try to learn the reversal meanings at the same time that you learn the upright meanings, you are doubling your task at the very least, and this is just if you believe that all the cards have only one possible meaning in every reading or situation, which is simply not

Rider Waite Smith Tarot   Tarot of Creativity

true. A reversed card, like its upright sibling, never means the same thing in every reading; the meaning adjusts and the card transmutes according to the circumstances and the variables. For this reason, I think it is better to start with the basics before you add complications to the learning process.

When you are learning the Tarot for the first time, I recommend that you only work with upright cards. To do this, simply shuffle the cards so that they remain upright, turn them right side up after dealing, or interpret them upright no matter how they appear in a reading.

Once you have thoroughly learned the upright meanings, you can use your intuition as to what an upside-down card in a particular reading might mean. Remember that just like the upright cards, the reversals will change in meaning according to the circumstances, which could be the question of the Querent or the influence of the nearby cards. Here are a few ideas of what a reversal might mean:

> A hidden energy or influence
> A developing energy
> Blocked energy
> An energy that is waning
> An inner lesson
> An event or influence that has recently passed
> Spiritual information
> A shamanic or spiritual initiation
> The opposite meaning

In general, when a card is upright, its energy is free to manifest; if it is reversed, the energy of the upright card may be blocked, losing power, or not yet fully developed. Many people think that a reversed card means the opposite of the upright card, but this interpretation may be too simplistic once you start really working with the cards, and they start "talking" to you.

Quick Answer Tarot

Reversals are also great for giving yes or no answers to quick questions. The way it works is simple. Pull a card from a randomized deck: if it is upright, the answer is "yes"—if it is reversed, the answer is "no."

THE SEER TAROT SYSTEM

There are many books that offer individual card meanings; most of these books explain the historical roots of the many symbols in the cards.[1] In a tarot card, especially the RWS deck, every detail has a meaning. This can be overwhelming to the new student of the Tarot; in addition, too much information can cause mental confusion, which only impedes the natural flow of intuition. When you add in the fact that these images accrue meaning as you work with them, learning the Tarot can be a truly daunting task. I have a system for understanding the cards that relies on the four elements, just like the Tarot itself. I call this unique way to read the cards the SEER System,™ in a nod to the tradition of using the Tarot as an oracle.

> **S** = S-YMBOLS (Pentacles/EARTH—matter)
> **E** = E-NERGY (Wands/FIRE—intent)
> **E** = E-MOTIONS (Cups/WATER—emotions)
> **R** = NUMBE-R (Swords/AIR—thought)

S = SYMBOLS

A symbol that has universal meaning is called an archetype. The archetypical meaning of the card is explained in a paragraph for each card. In this book, each Major Arcana card lists the major symbols in the RWS card first, followed by the cards with the same number in the four suits. As stated earlier, each card in the Tarot has many symbols embedded in the image. Even color carries a wealth of information. Here is the list of symbols for The Star.

NAKED WOMAN = natural self
8-POINTED CENTRAL STAR = Higher Self
SEVEN STARS = 7 chakras
POOL = universal subconscious
WATER POURING = personal subconscious
LAND = material existence/Earth
JUGS = containers for Spirit/physical body
IBIS = symbol for hope

THE STAR.

---

1 The Glossary of Symbols at the back of this book contains a complete list of symbols and their meanings.

TREE = Tree of Life/Knowledge
YELLOW HAIR = spiritual, consciousness, sun

As you work with the cards, you will absorb the meaning of these symbols; for instance, a figure that is naked often means a natural being, a being restored to its original state of innocence—to its original template. The woman in The Star is naked because she has been stripped of her identification with her ego by the cleansing action of the preceding card, The Tower.[1]

E = ENERGY

This way of looking at the cards comes from my experience as an artist. I read the *composition* and the direction of the lines of the image first. This gives me an idea of not just the meaning of that particular card, but tells me a wordless story through the visual relationships of the cards in the reading.

When I refer to "the lines" of an image, I mean the visible lines and the invisible lines in a composition. The invisible lines are formed by the elements that are composed in such a way as to direct the viewer's gaze. The lines direct my eyes to the important elements, give me the general direction of the card, and provide visual clues as to the overall energy of the image. As an artist, I am always looking at the composition of images; it is a habit to analyze any picture that I see. The cards in the Tarot lend themselves quite well to visual storytelling and composition analysis. However, you don't need to be trained as an artist to read the cards this way; anyone can learn to do this.

Let's look at the Four of Pentacles, which features a man in front of a city with money in his hands, under his feet, on his head, and in front of his chest. The lines of the picture are very static. There is no line leading your eye to the right or to the left of the figure. The only movement here is the strange "yin-yang" circular movement of the arms around the central pentacle. You know that the Pentacles suit represent physical health and wealth, so ask yourself: "if money is represented here by the pentacles, is the energy flowing or not?" You can see that the main "energy" of this

1   A Glossary of Symbols is provided at the back of this book.

card is a holding pattern. This man is holding on to what he has. This is why the card is often called the "miser card."

Now, for comparison, let's look at a very different card, the Knight of Swords. See how the lines of the whole image lead your eye from one side of the card to the other? Notice the jagged clouds in the background.

The Swords suit is about thought, and these clouds have violent and unsettled lines; the energy of thought is moving rapidly, and while the environment is chaotic and windy (referring to the mental state, since the card belongs to the Swords suit), the rider has a definite direction.

The words, "full tilt" come to mind as I look at this card. Depending on the other cards in the reading or on the question asked, this card could represent the Querent's state of mind, or could warn you that "haste makes waste."

I see a self-righteous individual; a social activist, or driven individual; one who may take his beliefs too seriously and may be one who needs to be right at any cost.

E = EMOTIONS (Intuition)

Many people don't know how to access their intuition, but it is one of our most powerful tools. The intuitive person knows how to access their emotions as a subtle guide; they are connoisseurs of emotional nuance. When you

look at a card, access your emotions to tell you the *mood* of the card.

What do you feel when you look at the card on the left? I feel regret and loss. Now check out the card on the right. How does this image make you feel? I feel the energy of happiness

51

and innocence. This card is one of the last cards in the Major Arcana (Key #19), and as such, pertains to a more mature experience, so I would amend these words into a phrase that expresses this image: "The joy of rediscovered innocence." You can see that this card is the emotional polar opposite of the card on the left.

> Why do we have emotions? Are they useful? What is the role that emotions have in the health and functioning of the mind/body system? Not admitting the power—or even the existence—of your emotional life is akin to standing in the middle of a busy highway; you are bound to be hit by the very thing that you deny. Why not admit to this powerful force, not as an enemy that needs to be controlled and conquered, but as a friend who is willing to work for your ultimate benefit, and help you create the life of your dreams? [1]

R = NUMEROLOGY

One of the not-so-secret secrets of the Tarot is its adherence to the ancient art of numerology. This book has detailed information on how numerology works in the Tarot: in addition, all the cards with the same number are in the same section, headed up by the Major Arcana card, and followed by the cards of the same number in the remaining suits. The meaning of the number in each card is explained for each card.[2]

Once you see the cards this way, it will speed your understanding of the Tarot, or if you are experienced, the knowledge will add a new depth to your readings. Numerology can easily be applied to anything in life. And when you combine your knowledge of numerology with the Tarot, you have access to guidance even when you don't have a deck available, which I will explain later.

To understand the cards at a glance, see the number of the card as a noun or a verb and the suit as the adjective or adverb. With this technique, you don't really have to memorize the meanings for any card in the deck, and you don't even have to understand the symbols in the cards; you only have to learn the meaning of each suit and of each number.

---

1   *Parallel Mind, The Art of Creativity,* Aliyah Marr
2   The Numerology section at the back of the book supplies meanings for each number.

The Numerical Relationship of Cards to Each Other

As you start to familiarize yourself with the meanings of each number, you start to see how the cards connect to each other by reduction. The classic reduction example is the card The Devil, which is number 15 in the Major Arcana. Adding the 1 with the 5 returns 6 as the core value.

Number 15, The Devil, is thematically connected to number 6, The Lovers card through numerology. The Devil card demonstrates the misuse of the energy of the base number—Love. The pictures on both of these cards contain the same triadic composition and similar shapes.

All the Minor Arcana cards with the number Six are about love. Each suit reflects a kind of love, because that is the basic energy of the number that joins them. This correlation is the same throughout the deck: all the Twos are about balance, duality, or choice; all the Fives are about change, freedom, or chaos. Once you learn the meaning of the number, the cards start to reveal their innermost secrets.

HOW TO USE THE SEER SYSTEM

Let's try to use the SEER System™ to read a simple spread. I will ask the Tarot to give me a simle three-card reading that will help me demonstrate how to read the Tarot with my technique. Here it is below. You can choose

to read this as the traditional spread of PAST, PRESENT, FUTURE or as a sentence. The TOC works very well with a sentence structure, but I will interpret it as a simple past, present, future reading.

S = SYMBOLS

CARD #1 PAST = 4 of Wands
4 WANDS = foundation
GARLANDS = celebration
CASTLE = security, wealth
WOMEN WITH FLOWERS = celebratory mood, cooperation

CARD #2 PRESENT = 9 of Swords
SWORDS = mental, thought, egoic concerns
BED = rest, dreams, nightmare
HEAD in hands = worry

CARD #3 FUTURE = Queen of Pentacles
GARDEN = abundance, Mother Earth, nature
RABBIT = fertility, sexuality, abundance
MOUNTAINS = mastery, spiritual attainment
ROSES = material desire, sensuality, enjoyment
THRONE = seated in the lap of power and abundance

Look how synchronicity has placed two cards together with the same symbol: the roses on the quilt in the Nine of Swords are also in the garden of the Queen of Pentacles. When you find a symbol or number repeated in a reading, you should pay attention to it. The red rose is a symbol for physical needs and desire. In the case of the Nine, the need is felt as anxiety, while the need is shown as fulfilled in the Queen.

E = ENERGY

In a work of art, the artist intentionally directs they eye of the viewer through the composition. These visible and invisible lines reveal the intention and meaning of the image. The first thing I want to show you is the directional energy that is dominant within each card, indicated by the dark arrows in the first illustration.

Notice that the first card's direction is definitely upward; even the red turret roof on the castle looks like the head of an arrow. In Western culture, we perceive UP to be good and positive, as in "thumbs up." This card is in the PAST position, so this energy is in the past. The middle card, repre-

 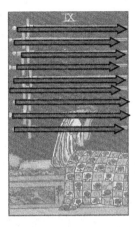 

senting the PRESENT, shows an equally strong direction that leads the eye off the page to the right, towards the card that is in the position of the FUTURE, the Queen of Pentacles, implying that the Querent in the present is worrying about the future. The last card on the right, the Queen of Pentacles, has a distinct "spiral motion" that keeps the eye swirling in the card and keeps the viewer's attention focused on the pentacle that the Queen is holding.

 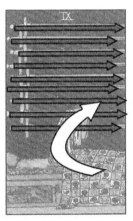 

Now let's add another layer. The white arrows show the direction of the major elements or figures in the cards. The PAST card on the left shows that the energy of the card is trending towards the PRESENT card, which means that the past energy of celebration and great beginnings supports the present. The PRESENT card shows the action of the main figure; she seems to have sat up abruptly, maybe awakening suddenly from a nightmare. She is facing the FUTURE card, which implies that she is anxious about the future. The FUTURE card shows that the main direction of the card is in the gaze of the Queen, looking fondly at the pentacle in her lap. Overall, this is the most important direction or energy in the whole reading: the gaze of the Queen towards the pentacle she cradles like a precious child in her lap. Now let's look at how the ENERGY of these cards work together.

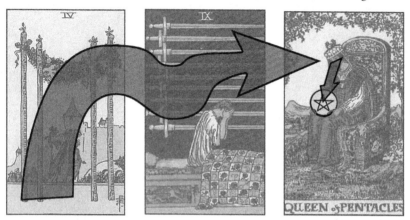

The ENERGY of celebration and good beginnings flows from the PAST, into the PRESENT and towards the FUTURE. The garlands on top of the first card lead the eye towards the next card; although the figure in the PRESENT card seems to be worrying, the flow from the supportive past of good beginnings is maintained. If the figure in the PRESENT card allows herself to remember the PAST and take advice from the Queen, she will be able to relax and allow the flow of abundance to come to her. Now what emotions do you feel when you look at each of the cards?

E = EMOTIONS

The PAST card's mood is CELEBRATORY.
The PRESENT card's emotion reads as ANXIETY.
The FUTURE card's emotions read as COMFORT and WISDOM.

R = NUMBER

PAST CARD = Four of Fire/Wands

Now, let's do the numbers. Four is the number of strong foundations; the number of the Earth; a balanced and stable number. In the TOC the Four of Fire means "stability/structure" which certainly supports the idea of a good foundation.

PRESENT CARD = Nine of Air/Swords

Nine is the number of individual attainment, in this case, since it is in the Suit of Swords/AIR, the card is about thinking. If you think too much, or take the mental path too far without disciplining your mind, you can find yourself worrying about the future or regretting the past.

Your mind's incessant chatter is not allowing you to be present. In the TOC the Nine of Air is "wisdom/lucidity," which shows personal attainment of the path represented by the suit, in this case, mental mastery.

FUTURE CARD = Thirteen: Queen of Earth/Pentacles

In the TOC, this card's title is "Incubate." And, you can see, this is what the Queen is doing in the RWS deck; a woman's lap is a symbol for her womb. The womb is the incubation chamber for physical life. As the second chakra, the womb is the incubation chamber for creative projects: overall it is how we manifest anything on Earth. A woman knows how to incubate a new life in her belly; taking that wisdom to heart shows us that we need to be patient while things are developing.

Summing up the numbers that make up the number 13 returns a 4, which is the number of Mother Earth and not-so-coincidentally, the number of the first card, which only supports the idea of material foundation, grounding and earthly abundance. Now, let's overlay the equivalent TOC cards on top of the RWS cards. You can see that *The Tarot of Creativity* cards can be read as a sentence or advice:

To manifest what you want in the material world, hold a stable vision of the structure of the thing that you desire with the wisdom of patience. Don't worry about when what you desire will manifest: allow proper time for incubation.

The Summation Reading

Now let's combine all the numbers in the reading to get a summation reading: **4 + 9 + 13 = 26, which reduces to an 8**. Keep on reducing the number until it becomes a single digit unless it is a Master number or exceeds twenty-two, the hidden number of the FOOL. Then, pull the corresponding Major Arcana card from both decks.

Rider Waite Smith Tarot   Tarot of Creativity

The STRENGTH in key #8 is not a force of domination but of love. The Woman pictured in the card is your Higher Self who is taming the unruly and wounded ego, represented by the Lion. The

LION is calmed by the love from the Higher Self, and responds by licking her hands. In The Tarot of Creativity card, the word "Mage" is preceded by the powerful pronoun, "I"—this card represents the Querent's ability to IMAGE the world anew. This is true Strength: the ability to focus the ATTENTION of your conscious mind on the higher, more refined aspects of your desire.

The "meta-meaning" of this reading is about manifesting abundance. The cards show us how to focus one's attention properly, not by worrying about the future, but instead, by relaxing into love and trust.

The Queen of Earth/Pentacles knows how to be abundant—she is a Master of Abundance, but since she is a female royal, it is a feminine sort of mastery; she *attracts* abundance—she doesn't need to actively pursue it.

Instead, the Queen rests confidently in her inner knowing; she nurtures—or incubates—abundance inside her, and thus an abundant reality has to eventually manifest around her. She is in a virtual Garden of Eden; she holds the seed of the natural abundance of Mother Earth in her lap.

The Tarot as a Manifestation Machine
You can use the Tarot like flashcards to help you focus your intent, visualize, and then manifest the life you want. This is a very powerful technique that uses the natural structure of the Tarot. The suits of the Tarot reflect all human desires; this makes it very easy to target the area you want to work with at the moment:

Wands/FIRE = intent, energy, success, desire, passion
Swords/AIR = mental discipline, planning, brainstorming
Cups/WATER = love, relationships
Pentacles/EARTH = health, wealth, financial success
MAJOR ARCANA = spiritual laws, spiritual progression

You don't have to memorize the cards, although this helps a lot. If you have memorized all the cards, then you can allow your intuition to bring up a card in your mind. If you are just beginning or have difficulty visualizing the cards, then do this: Separate your deck into suits; put the Major Arcana in numerical order and set it aside for a while. Then choose the category that reflects what you want to manifest and choose the pile of cards of that respective suit (see above). Now choose a single card from your pile in one of three ways:

TECHNIQUE ONE: Randomize the cards in the suit you chose and pick one. This card will be what your intuition and Higher Guidance wants you to focus on.

TECHNIQUE TWO: Look through the cards and see if one really appeals to you.

TECHNIQUE THREE: Put the cards of the suit in a line on the table progressing from the ace and ending at the king. Look at how the cards progress through the suit. Choose the card that most accurately reflects the place you feel you are right now. Now, try one or more of the following:

1. Meditate on your chosen card, choose its equivalent card from *The Tarot of Creativity* or another deck and see how the meaning for this card enhances your understanding. In the case of a card with a seemingly negative meaning, use it to help you resolve the block indicated. Use an equivalent card in another suit or deck to help advise you on how to proceed.

2. If you chose a card with negative implications, choose a contrasting card that best symbolizes what you want to manifest in your life. If the card was positive then keep the card. Memorize the image so you can recall it at will. Visualize this card, bring it up often throughout the day for as many days as seems appropriate. If you can't memorize it, then put the card on a table in your home or on your desk where you can see it many times throughout the day. Feel the emotions and feelings in the card, use the image as a mnemonic device to help you visualize your dream.

3. Find the number in all the suits that match your card's number and line them up to see how to use the power in all of the suits to manifest what you want. If one or more of the cards are "negative" in feel, know that you are merely in a rough spot: use the cards as wise advice to help you correct your course, and ease your transition. Choose another card in the same suit that best epitomizes what you do want and use it as in #2 above.

4. Bring up the Major Arcana card that matches the number of your card for the "meta-meaning" of your cards number. Use this card as wise counsel to advise you on how to best proceed, or how to better understand your situation.

5. Look at the cards in the suit that precede and follow the card you chose (if you chose the Six of Wands, you would be looking at the Five of Wands that precedes your card, and the Seven of Wands that follows it). See how the progression may show you what you need to work on and how to handle what may happen as a result. Alternatively you can use these three cards as a Past, Present, Future reading to gain insight on your path.

How will YOU Read the Cards?

The SEER System™ gives you a great deal of information for each card, and for the reading as a whole. But you don't have to use all four elements of this system in order to benefit from this enhanced reading technique. If you are learning to read the Tarot, you may want to start out with just one of these techniques and then add the others in as you feel ready. On the other hand, you may find that you want to just use your natural intuition to read the cards, without any additional knowledge or techniques. In that case, I recommend getting *The Tarot of Creativity* as your first deck, as it is designed to work directly with your intuition. And finally, you can just read this book like a novel, and allow yourself to absorb the information naturally.

Each number starts a section that then covers all the cards of the same number, starting with the Major Arcana card and ending with the Pentacles/EARTH suit. There is no right or wrong way to read tarot. Strangely enough, a new reader just learning the Tarot may have a slight advantage over an experienced Reader. Like an accomplished artist or like The Fool in the Major Arcana, he is fresh to The World, and can see the cards without prejudice or Judgment.

Hidden in Full View

The originators of the Tarot hid their ancient knowledge in full view, to protect it from those who would keep the average man in ignorance of his true power. The best way to enslave a man is through his mind. The word, "government" means "to rule the mind" (govern-mental).

The Tarot, if read properly, and if its guidance is followed rigorously, can empower the individual to question the status quo, and so evolve his own consciousness. This is why a system of self-realization that allows an individual to tap into their own intuition and guidance is recognized as a threat by the ruling class of any epoch, including this one. Of course, the rulers in any system don't want their constituents to become self-realized; evolved individuals don't need governance, conventions, or traditions; following the dictates of Natural Law. An understanding of the Oneness behind all appearances would not allow these people to hurt one another. Crime would disappear from the Earth. This is what Christ meant when he said, "Whatsoever you do to the least of my people, that you do unto me."

When I first started studying the Tarot, I didn't see the connections that I do now. I was confused by the titles and some of the images, which seemed to present a barrier to my understanding. Realizing that my own preconceptions were the cause I redoubled my efforts to "see beyond" the image into its metaphorical, rather than historical, meaning.

Then I started to see and understand the archetypes in the Major Arcana. The lower cards do not contain the same kind of symbols and imagery. It almost seems as if the Tarot is actually two decks: the Major Arcana and the pip cards. When I focused my intuition on the cards they started to speak to me. But the lower cards continued to mystify me. I wondered, "Is it possible that the lower cards are as meaningful and powerful as the Major Arcana?" When I considered that the Tarot might be an ancient map for the evolution of man, the wisdom of the cards suddenly began to reveal itself to me.

The art of the Tarot is best represented by the Temperance/ALCHEMY card, which demonstrates the magic of creative synthesis and the alchemy of deliberate creation. Reading the Tarot involves a creative synthesis of the Reader's personality, intuition, knowledge, and wisdom, married in a mystical union with the Reader's Higher Self, achieved through the medium of the pictures and numbers of the cards. Whenever we read the Tarot, we are participating in an intriguing tradition of self-discovery, remembrance, and creative envisioning that reaches back into the mists of time, and prepares us for our journey into an empowered future.

KEYWORDS
new beginning
fresh/pure
foolish/wise
innocent/simple
impulsive
leap of faith
ungrounded
need to ground
dreamer/idealist

S = SYMBOLS
CLIFF = descent into life
DOG = socialized consciousness
FEATHER in cap = spiritual support
SUN = divine energy, light
WALLET = tools, possessions
WAND = fire suit, spiritual energy
WHITE FLOWER = pure desire

E = ENERGY
Parallel DIAGONAL lines pointing at the Sun
in the upper right corner.

E = EMOTIONS
Bright, innocent, fresh, new.

R = NUMBER
The ZERO symbolizes Spirit.

THE FOOL

ARCHETYPE

Rider Waite Smith Tarot

SPIRIT IN MATTER—at once both the journey and the seeker of experience. The Fool represents the Spirit who has descended into matter. He is the holy fool who can be either foolish or wise.

Traditionally, The Fool is the only unnumbered card in ancient decks; modern decks assign the value of Zero to this card. One could argue that the Zero is not a number at all, it is a placeholder that has no intrinsic value. However, the Zero as the universal symbol of the circle is an archetypical concept that defines the vast sea of Cosmic Consciousness, the implicate field. A circle is one of the most ancient glyphs worldwide, appearing in every ancient culture on Earth. The symbol of the circle means Spirit, with its center everywhere and circumference nowhere.

The Fool is the most important card in the Tarot; he is said to be traveling through the deck as he travels through life. Ultimately, the Fool represents everyman in his journey through life. The Fool represents the soul of the Querent as it journeys through material existence and learns how to apply the laws and principles of the universe in his life.

Calling this card "The Fool" is a *blind*—an intentionally misleading title, meant to confound the profane seekers of enlightenment, who would not be able to reconcile the "foolishness" of a Fool with goal of wisdom or enlightenment. The Fool stands in for the Hero; a universal archetype that thrives in the mystical arcana of every civilization on Earth.

> A hero ventures forth from the world of common day into a region of supernatural wonder: fabulous forces are there encountered and a decisive victory is won: the hero comes back from this mysterious adventure with the power to bestow boons on his fellow man.[1]

---

1   Joseph Campbell, *The Hero with a Thousand Faces* (1949)

The Hero is in every fable, in every culture. Often he starts out as an outcast or loner. He begins his journey as the underdog in a battle or situation that grossly disfavors him, and proceeds on his quest—suffering one or many dark nights of the Soul—without help from his fellows. He is on his own. Everyone he left behind thinks that he is a Fool. And from their standpoint that is the only thing he can be. Often he wonders if what they think of him is really true, but, although he may waver and doubt himself, he cannot stop his quest once he has started. The Tarot follows the progression of The Fool on his path through life, as he strives to find what he lost; to remember the higher consciousness that he forgot when he was forced into spiritual amnesia by the density of this plane.

The Fool is arguably the most important card in the deck, but this has more to do with the fact that the Fool, as the daring Hero, is a universal archetype. He is a hero because he dares to do what may seem to be dangerous or foolhardy to other souls: come to Earth.

The Fool walks through not just the Major Arcana, which symbolize the "higher" path of spiritual mastery, but through the other cards in the Tarot. He travels through the Minor Arcana, the four suits which each represent a different path of Earth-based mastery. The Fool nears the edge of the cliff but his eyes are on the sky, as if he has a vision of a totally different reality. He is so innocent to physical reality that he doesn't comprehend that he might fall. A little dog that represents socialized consciousness nips at his heels to try to warn him of the dangers of his foolishness. Jumping off a cliff is certainly foolish in the eyes of "normal" people, but the Fool comes from a place where physical, or social rules don't apply. The Fool is looking up, he has a vision.

What is the vision of The Fool? He desires to become The Angel or Perfected Man. His task on Earth is to remember his original, perfected Self while in physical form. He came from a state of perfection, and his job is to "re-member" or reassemble himself back into perfection *while experiencing duality.*

The Fool strides forward into a new world, he is the "holy fool" of the ancient texts. He is the spark of Spirit that decided to come here for the unique experience of limitation and separation that this planet has to offer. He impulsively follows his heart and goes where angels fear to tread. Eyes to the sky, he focuses on his dreams—sometimes at great risk. The realists say that The Fool is foolish to expect that he will succeed, but then those same pundits and naysayers may be surprised at how easily things come to the

Fool. Like a small child, his freshness and openness is his most endearing trait; curiously enough, his innate trust and state of innocence is his shield.

The Fool wears his heart on his sleeve, as he foolishly follows his passions with unrestrained, sheer delight; he lives in the moment, totally engaged and without expectations. Eyes on his dreams and head in the clouds, anyone would think he is about to take a fall. The realists in his life are expecting to laugh when he lands flat on his face, as they are sure he is bound to do, but in most cases the Fool finds himself carried in midair by the sheer lightness of his being.

Or perhaps Spirit just puts an instant bridge magically under his feet as he steps out over the abyss. "How does he do it?" everyone asks, "Anyone can see he has his head in the clouds." Maybe the Fool has The Fool as the hidden card up his sleeve.

When You get This Card in a Reading

Try looking at the world from the Fool's eyes. Until you can see with the eyes of the master who is wise enough to be foolish to the world, you cannot see what needs to change or know how to create anything new.

Meditation

The wisdom of man is foolishness to the gods.

THE FOOL

THE FOOL

The Tarot of Creativity

The Fool is the Holy Fool, the cosmic scout on the rough frontier of consciousness. This card represents the innocence of the pure creative impulse, which desires above all else to infuse Spirit into the density of matter.

The Fool, as representative of the everyman, has four bodies while on Earth. The bodies of man are represented very clearly in the Tarot as the four suits in the lower cards:

1. The Wands/FIRE suit = the Super Conscious/Higher Self
2. The Swords/AIR suit = the mental/egoic body: the self-conscious
3. The Cups Water suit = the emotional body: the subconscious
4. The Pentacles/EARTH suit = the physical body: cellular consciousness

These four suits/elements represent the ordinary paths of The Fool's journey. The final fifth path—the path of the Avatar—is outlined in the twenty-two cards of the Major Arcana.

The hidden number of the Fool is the Master Number Twenty-two, the number of the master builder; it is the second Master number in the Tarot. The number Twenty-two represents the end of the Fool's journey through the Tarot. The Fool is the Alpha and the Omega of the Tarot: he is at once the Zero and the Twenty-two.

When the Fool comes into being, he is the ZERO; he begins his journey through life, and carries little or nothing on his journey. The Fool is the "avatar"—a manifestation of a deity or "ascended soul" in physical form on earth; an incarnate divine teacher. At the end of his journey, he becomes the TWENTY-TWO; he is the "self-realized man," one who remembers the divinity of all things, including himself. The Fool is the scout ship for the Mother Ship of his Higher Self. As the larger Mother Ship cannot "land" on Earth, She has sent a representative on a smaller ship, which is designed for the lower atmosphere of a dense planet. The scout is a physical representation of the Higher Self. He is here for the experience of duality; he comes down to Earth in order to have experiences that the Higher Self cannot have. He is here to report back. As the Fool slowly remembers the vibration of "home," the vibrational state of his body gets closer and closer to the rarified atmosphere of the Mother Ship, and it becomes easier and easier for him to communicate with his Higher Self. This communication marks the beginning of a new partnership of consciousness for the Fool: the divine triad of the integrated self.

The path delineated by the Tarot tells you how to purify thoughts and emotions, and how to maintain the proper coordination of your self-conscious and your subconscious by aligning your lower self, the creative, mental, emotional, and physical self with the desires of the Higher Self—the greater part of your consciousness. In order to do this you have to raise the frequency of each of your four bodies to better match that of your Higher Self, which lives in a state of oneness, outside the physical plane.

The secret of the Fool is his innocence and simplicity, he trusts in his journey, and thus he carries nothing with him: his spirit is unburdened and light. As the Fool travels through the Tarot he discovers the principles and laws of existence. He seeks to clear his thoughts and emotions so that he is a clear conduit for Spirit; he seeks to achieve enlightenment. This state is indicated in the final Major Arcana card, The World/TRANSCEND, a card that shows that the Fool has completed his journey through life. He has succeeded in becoming self-aware while existing in the dense realm of physical reality.

When You get This Card in a Reading
Know that you can look at life as the perennial beginner, and this freshness to life—without memory of hardship, victimization, humiliation, or blocks—is the real secret to creativity. Do the opposite of what you always do, break some rules—risk being foolish.

Meditation
Fools rush in where angels fear to tread.

KEYWORDS
attention/focus
direction/misdirection
magic/illusion
teaching/manifestation
communication/speaking
divination/channeling
showing/telling

S = SYMBOLS
FLOWERS = incarnation, manifestation
LEMNISCATE = infinity, the Higher Self
OUROBORUS belt = infinity, Spirit, life
TABLE = field of awareness, the Earth
TOOLS = paths to self-awareness

E = ENERGY
Diagonal line of The Magician's arms lead the eye from his upraised arm with the wand pointing at the sky to his other hand pointing at the Earth.

E = EMOTIONS
Mysterious, hints at esoteric knowledge.

R = NUMBER
THE ONE IS INDEPENDENT—the number One is the Male or Yang principle—he who goes forth, initiating, taking action. The number One is the "I" in "I am."

THE MAGICIAN

ARCHETYPE

Rider Waite Smith Tarot

The Magician is the first teacher that the Fool encounters on his path to spiritual enlightenment. This figure or universal archetype is related to the principle of consciousness symbolized by (the Greek god) Hermes.

THE MAGICIAN.

Hermes is a god of transitions and boundaries. He is quick and cunning, and moves freely between the worlds of the mortal and divine, as emissary and messenger of the gods, intercessor between mortals and the divine, and conductor of souls into the afterlife. He is protector and patron of travelers, herdsmen, thieves, orators and wit, literature and poets, athletics and sports, invention and trade. In some myths he is a trickster, and outwits other gods for his own satisfaction or the sake of humankind.[1]

Mercury was the Roman equivalent of the Greek god Hermes. He wore winged shoes and a winged hat and carried the caduceus, a herald's staff with two entwined snakes that was Apollo's gift to Hermes. Mercury was known as the "keeper of boundaries," referring to his role as bridge between the upper and lower worlds, and he was also the guide of souls to the underworld. The Magician's main symbol is a rod, similar to Mercury's caduceus.

The Magician is a man who knows how to use the tools of creative thought and action on the physical plane. As such, he might be a master of illusion, however, at the higher level, the Magician does not deal in illusion but in real magic—transforming a creative inspiration into a physical manifestation. Either way, he is the master of attention: in the case of the illusionist, he knows how to misdirect the attention of others, in the case of the enlightened individual, he knows how to use the power of his focus and attention consciously. He is surrounded by a lush garden, which represents his perfect relationship with Mother Earth and his alignment with the

1 en.wikipedia.org/wiki/Hermes

forces of nature. He knows how to use the tools of directed consciousness on the earthly plane.

The Magician has taken the bag off the shoulder of The Fool and spread out the contents on the table. The Fool has been carrying these items in his pack since he left the realm of spirit, but he hasn't known the content of the sack until this moment. The items on the table seem to be symbols or tools. What do they mean? The Magician is showing the Fool a map of how to manifest desire into matter—the rules of the game, so to speak. Each symbol on the table is a suit in the Tarot, a tool in life, but the Fool must learn how to use them, and especially the proper order in which to use them. The Magician uses the tools of consciousness represented by the elements on the foursquare table of awareness; the field of attention in which the Magician is embedded while on Earth.

The Magician is holding aloft one of these tools: the wand. He is using the wand like a lightning rod to attract the pure energy of creation that this symbol represents. His other hand points at the ground. He demonstrates how to use your body as a "lightning rod" to conduct energy, and transform it into matter: he literally brings Spirit down to Earth. He uses the power of his attention to bring Spirit into matter. Thus, he demonstrates the Hermetic axiom: "As above, so below." This is how the creative impulse works on the material plane.

As the bringer of the element of Fire to man, The Magician is the archetype god-teacher Prometheus or Thor who shows us how to create using Spirit within the system of duality. The items on the Magician's table represent the Aces in the deck, each a path of creative mastery. The order of the tools on the table—significantly at the level of the Magician's midsection or solar plexus, the chakra of personal will—shows the order in which they must be used in order to achieve the four-step MAGIC trick of bringing something from the infinite field of Spirit into the expressed state of matter:

1. Pure Energy (Fire/Wands)
2. Thought (Air/Swords)
3. Emotions (Water/Cups)
4. Matter (Earth/Pentacles).

This is the path of creative manifestation. The creative act is the result of a lifetime of focused will. "Will" is not to be confused with willpower, dreams, prayers, or wishful thinking; instead, it is a surrender to the will of the Super Conscious. Directed will is symbolized by the Magician's raising of the Wand. He uses the Wand like a lightening rod, to bring energy down to earth, infusing matter with Spirit (bringing a higher consciousness into the earth plane).

The mastery of personal will is not to be confused with the direction of the body's desires, nor with the infantile, objectified desires of the ego. The alignment of The Magician's will with universal Will allows the creation of things that serve higher desires—intent—to channel through him.

You can see this idea represented in the position of The Magician's arms; the energy from above channels through the arm with the wand held aloft to the other arm, which points to the ground. Thus, the Magician achieves the alchemist's goal of transmuting his own body/mind complex into a rarefied form of matter; he is a liberated being, a form that is vibrating at an entirely new level while still in material form.

The Magician as a creative master has learned to channel and nurture the energy of his thoughts and emotions. He knows that he doesn't really create anything, he simply transforms it, respecting the primary law that energy cannot be created or destroyed; it can only change its state or form. He has come to respect the raw energy of his subconscious as a powerful force that can be channeled by conscious intent in order to create a physical form, transforming a wave into a particle and back again.

The Magician shows the Fool everything he needs to know about how to use the principles of consciousness on the physical plane, but can the Fool understand what he is teaching him?

When You get This Card in a Reading
You or someone else is the Magician in your life. Is the Magician misdirecting your attention or showing you true magic?

Meditation
What is the function of a lightning rod and how does it work?

THE MAGICIAN

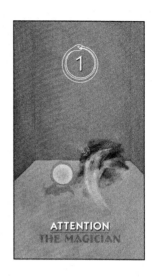

ATTENTION

The Tarot of Creativity

ATTENTION is the main skill of the Magician; he has learned how to direct his focus in order to create consciously. In *The Tarot of Creativity*, the Magician represents the power of will and directed attention in the ancient path of self-mastery. All esoteric paths of self-realization require an initiation on the part of the student. This initiation always involves a regimen of rigorous discipline in order to pass to the next level. The Magician knows how to use the elements of his world in order to create a reality or an illusion. There is no ethical basis for his power; he has simply learned to use the tools of creativity in order to create what he wants.

Regardless of whether he is merely a performer or an accomplished Mage (wise master), he is the master of directed attention or focus. An illusionist intentionally misdirects the attention of the audience, so that they cannot see how he performs his tricks. Thus a politician or businessman might be a Magician and use his ability to trick his audience into believing what he wants them to believe. He has gained the power of their ATTENTION; the collective agreement of his audience helps him reinforce and grow his power over them. He is the director of their consciousness; he uses the energetic mass of their agreement in order to manifest what he wants. A true Mage ("mage" is the root of the words "image" and "imagination") on the other hand, knows that he creates the appearance of his outer world from the inner direction or focus of his thoughts and emotions.

When the Magician gains higher awareness, he has no need of social ethics, because he is *conscious*, and realizes the interconnectedness of all things. "What you do to the least of my creatures, you do to me," to paraphrase Christ. What is outside is inside; it cannot be otherwise. In the consciousness of Oneness, there is no need for external social rules, as you are now living within the natural laws of the universe: from this level, greed, cruelty, and hatred cannot exist in you. The initiate on the path of enlightenment eventually learns that misdirected attention creates an ugly world, missing the key ingredients of the Garden of Eden: fairness, equality, abundance for all and most especially, Love. Unconscious thoughts and emotions create hell on Earth; conscious directed attention creates Heaven.

The Magician on this card is a Mage, not an illusionist or trickster, although a less disciplined adept may master the Magician's superficial skills. He is the master of attention: he knows that he is the creator of his reality through the direction of his thoughts and the energy of his emotions. Like a master artist, the Magician has learned to create by using the focus of his attention; he directs his thoughts consciously. As the first card in the Arcana, the Magician is new to the world; like Aries, the first sign in the Zodiac, he may be a bit brash and rough around the edges. But as he steps into the mastery of ATTENTION, he remembers the art of magic from his Spiritual recognition of himself as pure energy, and recognizes the gifts around him, the earthly tools of his trade, represented in the four paths of the suits in the Tarot. As an adept at the alchemy of creative magic, he wields these tools just as a master artist wields paint and brushes: Fire for raw passion and intent, Air for inspiration and thought, Water for emotions, and Earth as the canvas on which he expresses the energy of his desire in a material form. The Magician strives his entire life to understand and align himself with the direction of his Higher Self, or Super Conscious. He tries to understand how to align himself with the force of *intent*; he seeks to surrender the smaller egoic self to the larger Self that directs him.

ATTENTION directs the flow of your energy, and you are creating more of what you pay attention to. Be careful to choose your thoughts and emotions very carefully, and be diligent and consistent in how your direct your attention. Then what you create will seem like magic to others.

When You get This Card in a Reading
Take a moment to think about where your attention has been recently. Are you paying attention to what you want or to what you don't want?

Meditation
You energize (bring life to) whatever you pay attention to.

Related to
Wheel of Fortune/ACCELERATION (Key #10)
The Sun/CREATIVITY (Key #19)

ACE—WANDS

S = SYMBOLS
HAND from clouds = divine message
LANDSCAPE = springtime
WAND sprouting leaves = new life/energy

E = ENERGY
UPRIGHT line pointing up, as in "thumbs up."

E = EMOTIONS
Vitality. Potency. Approval.

R = NUMBER
The Ace as a One shows a promising direction or path.

Rider Waite Smith Tarot
A hand holding a wand emerges from the clouds. The wand is sprouting leaves. This card shows a powerful image of a wand or staff suddenly sprouting leaves. The hand that holds the wand emerges from a cloud like an omen of good tidings. The hand emits light rays, as if it is the Sun coming out from a cloud.

KEYWORDS
new direction
new project
potency/viriity
new opportunity
a great direction
a good idea
approval
"thumbs up"
good time to start
go forward now

This card is an augur of good beginnings; the energy of pure intent is flowing in a positive direction. The Wands are the beginning of the manifestation energy, so it is too soon to see anything in form; the leaves sprouting on the wand tell of the coming spring, summer and eventual harvest.

When You get This Card in a Reading
This a "thumbs up" sign from your Higher Self/Spirit for a new direction you are considering taking.

Meditation
Spring has sprung from dead wood like sparks of fire. A beginning energy; a new, positive direction.

ACE—FIRE

THE SPARK

The Tarot of Creativity

The Ace of Fire represents the power of pure intent. As a spark is to a flame, this card indicates the direction of the energy, the beginning of a new path—it doesn't illuminate the whole path.

The Fire suit marks the beginning of creative manifestation; this process must always begin with the energy of intent. All the cards of the Wands/FIRE suits are about direction or intention. Nothing is yet in physical form, there is only a current of energy that you can choose to follow like a light in the darkness.

When You get This Card in a Reading

Your creative project is about to burst into life; all you need is the spark of passion.

Meditation

The spark is the beginning of the flame.

ACE—SWORDS

S = SYMBOLS
CROWN = victorious
HAND = inspiration
MOUNTAINS = hard-won discipline
SWORD = mental body
YOD = divine blessing

E = ENERGY
UPRIGHT line pointing up: approved or victorious.

E = EMOTIONS
Success. Triumph after difficulty.

R = NUMBER
The Ace of Swords/AIR expresses the number One as in "the best and the brightest."

KEYWORDS
victory/success
bound for success
divine inspiration
good idea/approval
potency/potential
new opportunity
new idea

Rider Waite Smith Tarot
A sword surmounted by a crown and laurels emerges from a cloud. The RWS card shows a sword crowned with laurels and a gold crown. It signifies a victory, a great idea, a divine inspiration. The suit of Swords is about mental processes. As an Ace of Swords, this card augurs well for any new idea that involves the intellect: ideation, brainstorming, strategy, planning, branding, or direction.

When You get This Card in a Reading
The Ace of Swords is an omen of spiritual approbation; the appearance of this card in a reading indicates the approval of an idea or direction.

Meditation
Great ideas require faith in order to carry them out.

ACE—AIR

INSPIRATION

The Tarot of Creativity

"Inspiration" means the "breath of spirit." You breathe in Spirit when you inhale, and when you breathe out Spirit breathes you in.

Your experiences on this plane of duality and separation are what Spirit wants from you; every time you breathe out, the information that you gathered as a Scout on the physical plane is inhaled by Spirit. When you breathe in, you breathe in the breath of Spirit; thus you become "inspired."

The Suit of Air is about mental mastery, so this card has to do with the power of the intellect. It represents a good idea, an inspiration for a project, or a new direction.

When You get This Card in a Reading

A new idea has been placed in your mind by your Higher Self, which your brain receives as an inspiration "that comes out of the blue." Go forward, act on your inspiration, and you will do well.

Meditation

INSPIRATION: (the act of breathing in) + (divine guidance) = the "breath of Spirit." Feel Spirit breathing in you as you consider your new direction.

ACE—CUPS

ACE ⚭ CUPS.

S = SYMBOLS
CUP = abundance
DOVE = Holy Spirit, divinity
EQUILATERAL CROSS = Earth
POND = collective conscious
POURING WATER = abundance, emotional release
WAFER = Communion, Spirit as food for the Soul WATER LILIES = good fortune

E = ENERGY
FLOWING lines to pond from cup.

E = EMOTIONS
Abundance. Flowing. Emotional release. Joy. Inner peace.

R = NUMBER
The Ace of Cups/WATER shows the promise indicated by the number One as a dream or a vision of plenitude.

KEYWORDS
fulfillment/love/support
abundance/gushing
emotional response
crying/release
healing/renewal
your dreams come true
a state of grace

Rider Waite Smith Tarot
A cup overflowing with water, a white bird descends with a wafer. The ACE of Cups shows a "divine hand" emerging from a cloud, holding a cup that is overflowing. The dove descending towards the liquid in the cup represents the Holy Spirit, or Sophia.

> *Sophia is identified by some as the wisdom imparting Holy Spirit of the Christian Trinity, whose names in Hebrew—Ruach and Shekhinah—are both feminine, and whose symbol of the dove was commonly associated in the Ancient Near East with the figure of the Mother Goddess. The dove was also sacred to the Goddess Isis.*[1]

---

1 en.wikipedia.org/wiki/Goddess

Inscribed on the wafer the dove holds in its beak is an equilateral cross, which is an ancient symbol for the Earth and physical manifestation. As the dove descends into Earth, Spirit descends into matter, symbolizing the way that higher consciousness transforms lower consciousness—this is called the "state of grace" by many mystics.This card is the "Holy Grail" card. The search for the Holy Grail is the search for the memory of the divine Self, for the realization of the divinity of all things. The search for the sacred in the "profane" cannot be concluded as long as you are searching for anything outside yourself. Nothing is there. The Grail that the seeker quests is inside himself all the time. The Grail is the divine Chalice of the Soul, the Heart of man. It represents what the ancients called a "state of grace."

When You get This Card in a Reading
Your heart tells you whether you are on the right path or not.

Meditation
If the Holy Grail is still on Earth, where would you look for it?

ACE—WATER

THE CHALICE

The Tarot of Creativity
The Ace of Water symbolizes the ever-present potential for the realization of natural abundance. You start creating from the primordial *feeling* of desire, the SPARK in the Fire suit; this deep intent from your Higher Self came into your mind as an INSPIRATION—as seen in the last card, the Ace of Air—but your personal emotions about your desire is what will give it life, and thus we arrive at the Ace of Water. THE CHALICE of the Soul is filled with emotions; as you fulfill your desires, you come to realize that what is important isn't what you create, or what you want to create, but the *feeling* about what you are creating.

The trick isn't in changing anything, you only have to change how you *feel* about what has already been created. The Ace of Water poses a difficult truth: in order to experience a new world, you have to first accept and love the world that you see. This is the meaning of the word, "fulfillment." The Ace of Water shows us what happens when we align our personal emotions with the intent of our Higher Self: the amazing emotional fulfillment of coming home, returning, remembering our natural self, the amazing, pure energy that came to Earth in order to experience form.

When You get This Card in a Reading
Pay attention to the wisdom of your heart and you can't go wrong.

Meditation
The heart is a Chalice that fills with love.

ACE—PENTACLES

S = SYMBOLS
DOOR in hedge = door to the future
HAND in clouds. = divine approval
LILIES = purified desire
PENTACLE = health/wealth

E = ENERGY
Primary STATIC circular line follows the pentacle's shape. Secondary line: the eye is led down the path towards the door in the hedge.

E = EMOTIONS
Hope. Assurance of good future.

KEYWORDS
hope/promise
a solid offer
a new direction
new health/wealth
ideas coming into form
manifestation

R = NUMBER
The Ace of Pentacles/EARTH suit expresses the promise of the number One manifested into form.

Rider Waite Smith Tarot

A hand emerging from a cloud holds out a pentacle like an offering. Following the path of the Aces in the Tarot, we come finally to the Ace of Pentacles. It is the last element in the progression of the path of manifestation of a new potential.

The intent of a new beginning shown in the Ace of Pentacles became an idea with great potential for success in the Ace of Swords; it was infused with the energy of emotions in the Ace of Cups and now, in the Ace of Pentacles, it finally manifests in the physical.

Meditation

An offer is before you. Will you take it?

When You get This Card in a Reading

If you get this card in a reading, know that whatever you have been working on is ready to manifest. This card is a good sign that you are well on your way.

ACE—EARTH

THE SEED

The Tarot of Creativity

The seed of intent and thought has taken root. The energy you started as THE SPARK in the Fire suit, became an INSPIRATION in the Air suit and THE CHALICE of hope in the Water suit, now starts to manifest in the Earth suit as THE SEED of a physical opportunity.

When You get This Card in a Reading

Everything worthwhile started from the seed of an idea. Take time to nurture the seed and the plant will naturally grow: it is Law.

Meditation

The tree is hidden in the seed.

S = SYMBOLS

B & J = Boaz & Jakin
CROWN = Egyptian goddess, Isis
CUBE throne = rules the physical plane
EQUILATERAL CROSS = the Earth
MOON = subconscious, dreams, psychic
PILLARS = duality, opposites, balance
BOOK = universal law
POMEGRANATES = quantum implicate

E = ENERGY

STATIC figure of the High Priestess; her dress FLOWS like water over her lap.

E = EMOTIONS

Mysterious, secretive, enigmatic; unfathomable depths, unexpressed power, pure potential.

R = NUMBER

THE TWO SEEKS BALANCE—the Two represents the mystery and power of duality; the divine marriage of opposites, the Akashic records, and the infinite potential of the quantum implicate.

THE HIGH PRIESTESS

ARCHETYPE

Rider Waite Smith Tarot

The High Priestess is the goddess energy; some say she is the ancient Goddess Isis. She symbolizes a primordial principle of consciousness; the vast sea of potential, that which exists before the expression of matter. She is the unknown, and the unknowable, the remembered original, undivided Self without name or form. She represents the womb of creation, the dark, empty potential of all

THE HIGH PRIESTESS

things—the quantum implicate. She is the pure, unexpressed energy of the universe waiting for conscious direction through the ATTENTION of The Magician.

The High Priestess represents Cosmic Consciousness, the quantum implicate, pure potential waiting to be expressed into form by the direction of focused intent. She sits serenely upon a throne that is an unadorned simple cube. The cube is one of the oldest symbols for the physical plane: the Pharaoh sat upon a cube throne in ancient Egypt. In India deities are often shown with a cube under each foot.

When salt forms crystals, they are cubic in form. Salt could be said to be one of the most important elements for developing the first life on Earth. The ancients understood the cube as the symbol for the Earth; to put a ruler on a throne shaped like a cube meant that they ruled the Earth, and in this card, the cube throne conveys the idea that the Source rules and supplies the world of form.

Duality is like a room with two mirrors on opposite walls that repeat a central image verbatim ad infinitum. The system of duality is automatic; without conscious direction it will keep on reproducing the same thing faithfully and endlessly, just like a room with facing mirrors. The High Priestess sits in perfect equilibrium between two pillars that represent duality. On the pillars—one black and the other white—are written the initials "B" and "J." B stands for "Boaz," which means "Intellect." J stands for "Jakin" which means "Spirit."

Spirit and Intellect oppose each other; The High Priestess gives them equal emphasis and thus brings them into a perfect balance that resembles the Oneness that She represents. She is the ONE that symbolizes the I AM PRESENCE sitting between the TWO of duality in perfect, eternal equilibrium.

We are challenged by this image to imitate The High Priestess by expressing balance and poise in all that we do. As She reflects perfect balance, so we should practice detachment from unconscious thoughts and emotions. We should realize that the Source of all, the quantum implicate, is waiting for our input. We can use this power unconsciously and thus manifest monsters, or we can use our conscious intent to direct this power to manifest a positive reality. Either way, She is here at our command. Through Her we are wise magicians who can manipulate reality, or we can remain as unconscious slaves to our lower consciousness.

Don't be deceived by this book's use of terms such as "god" or "goddess"—the words simply represent a principle of consciousness, a force of the natural world, not a personality or even a being. The force here is very impersonal, more of a law or system that can be understood and then utilized. Just as the game of tennis could not be properly played without the law of gravity, so the system of duality cannot be mastered without understanding the rules of the game—without mastering the underlying laws of the universe.

The trick of existing in a manifested reality—of being a god inside your own creation—is to realize your innate power and clear the smoke from the mirror. Duality is a simple binary system; it does not operate in the same way as the game of oneness, although the rules of oneness underlies all the rules of duality, as the greater, higher reality. Duality is balanced upon a simple principle of polarity. The system of duality as a TWO is always seeking balance; not only is balance its natural state, but it must be balanced or cease to exist. A pendulum that swings wildly is just as balanced as one that doesn't swing or hardly swings at all. Oneness is static, creation is not. Creation requires the element of change, so in a system that is more complex than oneness—duality—change is a constant; change is one of the governing principles of the binary system of duality. Without change, you have no movement, and the system then would have to collapse back down into the underlying state of oneness. Game over.

Going back to oneness cannot be the intention of the spiritual seeker or the goal of the game of life. The Toltecs call the game of duality, the "smoky mirror." We don't realize that we are generating the image in the mirror, and that it is us. The "smokiness" is induced by the parameters of the game; our amnesia is produced by the density and slowness of the space-time continuum. Duality works on a basic, impersonal principal of *reflection* (the MOON symbols in the High Priestess card). The goddess Isis in this image shows her perfect reflection. She perfectly reflects us; she mirrors back our consciousness. In Her mirror, we see either darkly or clearly. She shows us either the "smoky mirror" of our reactive thoughts and unconscious emotions or the clear reflection of our innate divinity.

The mirror is "smoky" only when we cloud it with unconscious thoughts and negative, reactive emotions; it is smoky because we don't see the connection between what we witness and what we have thought or felt. The quantum implicate—Source/the quantum field—creates whatever we are prepared to see; She creates reality according to how we command Her. Her body is the reflection that we see in everything around us and in our very physical bodies.

The High Priestess shows us that we are in command of All That Is; that we are creators of what we see. Or rather, we direct Her to create, by the direction and flow of our consciousness. This is not to mean that we are above or superior to Her, it is just the way that things work in the system in which we are embedded.

In order to change things on the physical plane, we have to access our divine right to choose; the power of choice comes from the attainment of personal power by determining your own direction or intent. In order to access this wisdom, you have to transcend the ego's lower desires and needs.

You have to exercise the power of conscious choice in order to have the power to choose. Like a body builder, you have to first make the decision to change yourself through conscious discipline, and then build your muscles by exercising your power to choose. You build personal power through conscious choice. There is no way to achieve consciousness through unconscious behavior or habits. You can't sleep through the process of waking up.

When You get This Card in a Reading
Know that you have enormous resources. Tap into these now.

Meditation
The subconscious is a vast, deep sea; what you think of as you is only a wave on the surface.

THE HIGH PRIESTESS

MEMORY

The Tarot of Creativity

MEMORY is the attribute of The High
Priestess. As the principle of the universal sea
of consciousness, She re-members all potentials; through her you can access the Akashic
records: the quantum file that contains all
potential, timelines, and manifestations. She
reflects the commands and viewpoint of the
Higher Self, and represents the universal sea of
awareness, as well as the collective conscious

of all beings. She is the impartial witness; she holds no emotions of her
own. She is the mysterious infinite that perfectly reflects the light of higher
consciousness. She poses the riddle: What does the moon in the water of a
lake reflect?

The High Priestess/MEMORY card represents the female principle
of receptivity; it symbolizes the womb of creation, Zero Point; she is the
Divine Void, the black hole that the universe exists within. This card represents the creative power that avails itself willingly in every moment to our
every thought and emotion. We can choose to use this energy or we can be
washed down the stream of collective thoughts and agreements. The use of
MEMORY is important for the path of the creative master. Are you a victim
of your past? Or do you let the burden of old thoughts and emotions shed
from you as a snake sheds last year's skin?

While the traditional name of this card is The High Priestess, it would
be more accurate to call it The Goddess card. The energy represented here
is the non-judgmental and loving Divine Feminine, who witnesses all of
creation and all of the acts of mankind with the unconditional love of a
mother or a goddess.

The myth of Isis is a parable about the restorative nature of love, and
the essential balance between the two polarities of order and disorder. Set,
the god of destruction, violence, and chaos murders his brother the wise
king Osiris (representing order). In an effort to utterly destroy him, he cuts
the body of the ruler into pieces and scatters them to the winds. Isis as the

goddess of life, finds the pieces, reassembles the parts, and then magically restores him back to life.

The Goddess Isis brought Osiris back from the dead; her magic was that she was able to re-member him with love. This myth tells us that only the power of LOVE can bring us back to life. This is the meaning of the phrase, "the quick and the dead." If you are not in unconditional love with life, you are in effect, dead; you are dead to life. You are alive if you know how to generate and receive love.

When You get This Card in a Reading
This card represents the well of creative energy that is available to us all.

Meditation
Everything you will ever need to know is already inside you.

Related to
Justice/REVERSAL (Key #11)
Judgement/THE EPIPHANY (Key #20)

2

2—WANDS

S = SYMBOLS
LILY = pure (spiritual) desire
LAKE = calm, future potential
MOUNTAINS = goals, attainments
ROSE = physical desire
WANDS = balanced energy
WORLD = the future, goals

E = ENERGY
UPRIGHT lines of the wands dominate this image.

E = EMOTIONS
Established. Solid.

R = NUMBER
The Two is a stable number; stability is good, but too much stability can result in stagnation.

KEYWORDS
stability/balance
waiting/planning
decision to be made
strategy/authority
good foundation
ready to go forward

Rider Waite Smith Tarot
A man tries to foresee the future in a world that he holds like a crystal ball. The man here is a successful merchant, or entrepreneur who has invested the energy of the Wands into the direction indicated by the Ace of Wands. Now he has stepped back and he is evaluating his position. He holds the world as a globe in his hand, indicating that he is aware of the law of balance. In the system of duality, balance is always obtained, one way or another. The Two of Wands represents the balance of a good foundation, but the energy is not moving forward yet; it is waiting for you to choose your direction and set your intent.

When You get This Card in a Reading
Follow your highest excitement at all times and you cannot go wrong.

Meditation
A bird in the hand may be worth two in the bush.

2—FIRE

EQUAL • DIFFERENT

The Tarot of Creativity

The Two of Fire, like all the Twos, is about duality and balance. Equality doesn't have anything to do with valuation. Valuation and imbalance are false concepts that go against natural law. They are concepts that belong only to a lower consciousness that is based upon the key supporting concepts of separation and survival. A being in survival mentality must make distinctions and evaluate his world all the time. He cannot understand the concept of true equality, because he only has experienced separation and valuation. He is convinced that certain things are more valuable than others; that more of something is better than less of it.

When you have an understanding of the oneness and equality that underlies the illusion of duality, you start to act and think holistically. A person with a higher consciousness is able to hold two apparently contradictory concepts in their mind at the same time. When someone is able to understand the concepts of "equal" and "different" at the same time, it means that they have evolved their understanding to the higher level of oneness that underlies the system of duality.

All systems seek balance, or rather, all systems naturally balance themselves. If they didn't, they would not exist at all. Any system more complex than Oneness requires evolution, which is just a form of change. The natural evolution of the inhabitants of any system is towards an overview of the system, called "transcendence" (The World/TRANSCEND) otherwise known as "enlightenment."

Those who transcend duality are able to see Oneness while experiencing a world seemingly defined by separation. This ability to hold several paradoxical "truths" in mind at the same time is crucial to being able to transcend any system. These truths do not cancel each other out, nor does one disprove the other. In fact, one truth is not even better than any other one.

One of the first realizations a child has at the beginning of his life is that other people are *different* from him. At first, a child does not see separation: he and his mother are one. As he grows, he starts to lose this awareness. As he becomes socialized, he begins to echo the valuation system of the human world. He sees that some children are raised above others and recognized as superior in some way, which establishes an artificial valuation system in the child that will influence his entire life. Thus he starts to experience inequality as natural. He has forgotten the natural Law of Equality that is found in the original experience of Oneness.

This is the path for most of us. We are the Holy Fools who came from Oneness and have to experience the fullness and creativity of separation, polarization, and duality before we can return home. The challenge is not to return to the nirvana of non-existence where Oneness is natural, but to have the realization of Oneness while in the system of duality.

When You get This Card in a Reading
Only when everything is equal can you finally make an informed decision. In order to make an informed, non-emotional choice, you have to be able to discern the difference between your options.

Meditation
An enlightened man listens to the counsel of his heart.

2—SWORDS

S = SYMBOLS
BLINDFOLD = not seeing, blinded, intuition
CROSSED SWORDS = equal choice, undecided
LAKE or SEA = calm emotions

E = ENERGY
CROSSED lines over the woman's breast. Crossroads. A choice.

E = EMOTIONS
Indecisive. Unsure.

R = NUMBER
The Two in this suit tells you to weigh your choices. A branching path is ahead.

KEYWORDS
decision/indecision
discerning/impartial
balanced/immobile
choice point/equilibrium

2

Rider Waite Smith Tarot
A blindfolded woman holds two swords before a becalmed lake. The woman here is unable to see her way forward. Unable to judge which direction is better, she sits blindfolded before a lake holding two swords aloft: each sword represents an idea, a direction, a belief, a path or way forward. The swords are crossed over the woman's breast, indicating that her decision must come from the heart. She has suspended her thoughts or beliefs. Her blindfold signifies she is listening to her inner voice, her intuition. She knows she has a decision to make, and that decision, like all decisions has the power to change her life. There are three ways of making a decision:

1. choose the lesser of two evils
2. choose the greater of two opportunities
3. choose what most excites you; follow your heart

The first two reflect a mind bound by the social structure based upon inequality and valuation. The third one shows how a heart that is free, bound only to the guidance of the Higher Self, navigates through life.

When You get This Card in a Reading

The Two of Swords represents a pause to reflect, or indecision.

Meditation

What weighs more: a pound of feathers or a pound of lead?

2—AIR

JUNCTURE • CHOICE

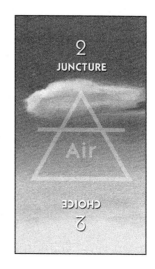

The Tarot of Creativity

The Two of Air represents a crossroads in thought, a juncture or choice. People who procrastinate cannot make up their minds. This is because they can't choose which option they prefer. It may be because they are limiting their field of choices from the outset to things that they believe are possible, and thus don't see anything they want, or it may be because the choices seem the same; they can't discern the difference or feel a preference for one or the other.

Ultimately, we all want things that feel good in our lives and find ways to avoid things that feel bad. But when our thoughts—represented by the Air suit—include beliefs about lack, separation, inequality, and valuation, our minds become clouded, and our thoughts unclear. Without clear vision, it is hard to make up your mind, or even know what you want.

When You get This Card in a Reading

You have come to a juncture in your life, a crossroads. You get to choose; will you be guided by your mind or by your heart?

Meditation

The path splits before you. You must make a choice in order to go forward.

2—CUPS

S = SYMBOLS
CADUCEUS = health/healing
COUPLE = animus/anima, partnership, balance
CUPS = sharing/partnership
WINGED LION = desire taken to a higher level

E = ENERGY
The lines formed by the arms and gaze of the couple form a BRIDGE in the shape of a lemniscate.

E = EMOTIONS
Equality. Sharing. Harmony.

R = NUMBER
The Two represents balance, equality, partnership.

KEYWORDS
partnership/equality
balance/relationship
love/friendship
healing/reunion
diplomacy/cooperation
synergetic/symbiotic

Rider Waite Smith Tarot
A caduceus and a red-winged lion blesses a couple. This image symbolizes a healing, a relationship, a union of opposites, or a partnership of equals. The Two of Cups signals emotional balance, a desire for true partnership. A mature person who is ready for love in his life is ready to give love freely without operating from the level of his needs; in fact, he has no need for anyone else to fulfill.

Someone who is willing to love doesn't see love as an investment. He doesn't look for someone to fill his needs or occupy a role in his life. He is ready to love you for who you are, not for who you are for him. Your point of power is in the awareness of the relationship; the balance, action, and accord between polar opposites.

When You get This Card in a Reading
A healing, a relationship, a union of opposites, or a partnership of equals.

Meditation

A marriage of opposites, an accord reached.

2—WATER

RELATIONSHIP • DIPLOMACY

The Tarot of Creativity

The Twos are about balance; for a partnership or relationship to succeed each partner must feel supported and nourished. Each has to respect the other as an equal. Diplomacy, a natural outgrowth of the emotion of compassion, is a necessity for the success of the relationship.

Many people think that relationships are an investment of time and energy. But relationships of this kind are really an investment in unprocessed expectations. We have all seen the comical way a baby bird pursues its exhausted parents long after it has grown large enough to provide for itself. If you are concerned with getting your needs met, you can only have a needy relationship.

When You get This Card in a Reading

What do relationships mean to you? Do you feel that you have to give up something or compromise in order to have a relationship? Are you ready to give without expectations?

Meditation

A marriage of opposites is duality in action. Duality is the playing field of creation.

2—PENTACLES

S = SYMBOLS
JUGGLER = juggling potentials/resources
LEMNISCATE = infinity, cyclical fortune
SEA = up and down motion
SHIPS = enterprise, possessions

E = ENERGY
SWIRLING figure eight in shape of lemniscate or Yin-Yang.

E = EMOTIONS
Insecure. Unbalanced. Pay attention.

R = NUMBER
The Twos are about balance: juggling is balance in motion.

KEYWORDS
juggling resources
exchange/transfer
prudence/fluctuation
adaptability/management

2

Rider Waite Smith Tarot
A man juggles two pentacles in front of a heaving ocean that tosses ships wildly on its waves. Everything in this picture is going up and down, like the heaving waves of the turbulent ocean in the background behind the figure. Nothing is grounded or stable. Everything is in flux, and the man has to be a juggler in order to keep all his projects aloft, and maintain the balance of his resources. Behind him, the ships, representing his efforts and investments, are having difficulty staying afloat in a stormy sea.

The Two of Pentacles shows what happens if the stasis and indecision of the previous Twos are carried too far: not coming to a decision in the Two of Wands or in the Two of Swords, and not cementing an equal partnership in the Two of Cups, leaves you juggling resources on your own. Alternatively, this card may be telling you to shake things up a little, don't take your situation too seriously. Play a little with the way you do things and see if it makes a difference. The static balance of the Two's is starting to move. You don't want to be caught flatfooted when it moves into the creative energy of the Threes.

The balance in this card is moving instead of static, but the movement of juggling doesn't carry the juggler forward; it is another way to stay in the same place. As a Pentacle/Earth suit, it is the last in the energy of the Two; thus the juggling in this card is preparing you for the creative movement in the next number, the Three. Ride the imbalance out and allow the movement to prepare you for the next event in your life, like a runner warming up his muscles by running in place.

When You get This Card in a Reading
You might be in a precarious balance right now, but this is not necessarily a bad sign. Juggle your resources. Play a little bit with the balance and don't take things too seriously.

Meditation
Sometimes balance can be achieved by juggling what you have.

2—EARTH

COMMUNION • PARTNERSHIP

The Tarot of Creativity
The Twos are expressed in the physical as balance and equality—communion and partnership between equals. Your partnership may require a bit of juggling before it settles down, or it may need constant adjustment to work for all parties concerned. You may need to be a juggler to make your life work.

When You get This Card in a Reading
In order to achieve a fair partnership, equality has to exist first. Communion requires honesty and communication.

Meditation
What do the words equality and respect mean to you? Can you give as well as receive?

2

S = SYMBOLS
FLOWERS = Mother Nature, creativity
GRAIN = fertility, abundance
HEART SHIELD = love
CROWN = zodiac, 12 states of consciousness
STAFF = rules physical nature
VENUS SYMBOL = sexuality, sensuality

E = ENERGY
S-SHAPE of the figure indicates a feeling of flow, nature and femininity.

E = EMOTIONS
Sensuous. Natural. Abundant. Maternal.

R = NUMBER
THE THREE EXPRESSES—the number Three represents the combination of the Divine Masculine, the ONE, with the Divine Feminine, the Two, producing the Divine Child, represented here as the principle of IMAGINATION.

THE EMPRESS

ARCHETYPE

Rider Waite Smith Tarot

The Empress symbolizes MOTHER NATURE. This is the Mother Earth card: Gaia, matter—the quantum *explicate*. She represents fertility, creativity, nurturing, abundance, and sexuality.

The Empress is the energy of unconditional love translated into matter. The implicate field (The High Priestess) holds an impersonal energy; implied but not expressed—it is the boundless field that contains all potential, all timelines, all possible forms and realities. The Empress card shows us how this energy expresses itself on the physical plane.

The implicate field is unconditional love, as it enters the field of expression, or the physical plane, it changes into a form that reflects as closely as possible the original energy that engendered it. Energy is the progenitor— the mother of all form. Creation is an energy to matter conversion machine.

The Empress, as the symbol of the physical plane, shows us the secret to the physical reality we experience, but more importantly, she hints at our role in creation—our consciousness directs the machine of creation. When we create unconsciously, we create by default whatever lies in our subconscious. When we learn how to create deliberately, we create new worlds. The maternal figure on this card seems to be pregnant. She is pregnant with the energy of creation which is about to come into form. Her headdress of 12 stars represents the zodiac, and the 12 states of consciousness. Her staff is surmounted by a globe that symbolizes Earth, and shows us that she rules the plane of matter.

The Empress sits comfortably in the Garden of Eden, inside the expression of her love, shown in this image as the grain, the trees, and the fruit. She demonstrates how to bridge Spirit to matter, how to bring the reality of love into the physical plane; it is symbolized by the shield that seems to support her throne. The heart-shaped shield is engraved with the symbol of Venus, the feminine goddess of love. This unconditional love is unlike any earthly love; it is a higher love, a love that is the Source energy of the universe. The bridge between Spirit and matter, between our Higher Self and our Self-conscious/Subconscious is our Heart. But it is not our physical heart, or even our emotions; it is what the mystics call the High Heart. The High Heart (thymus gland) is what the ancients referred to as the "seat of the soul."

If you look at the seven chakra system in the human energy body, you can see that the fourth chakra stands squarely in the middle: the fourth chakra is the bridge. Each chakra has a non-evolved and an evolved version. The evolved version of the fourth chakra is the High Heart. The bridge of the Heart is what brings Spirit into the physical. And while nothing can exist without the energy of Spirit, the goal of the ascetic is to bring a higher consciousness into the physical.

The Empress represents the archetype of the Goddess CERES, symbolizing Earthly existence: the expression of the abundant and fecund Mother Nature, the creative explicate that mirrors the underlying implicate order. Encouraging and nurturing the growth and development of all things, she responds to your self-conscious, creating according to the images you send her. If you believe in evil, she responds to your images of evil, disease, and unhappiness that you send her and mirrors back a fearsome landscape, populated with the monsters that you first created in your imagination. If you focus instead on images—thoughts and feelings—of love, vitality, and health, she faithfully responds with a reality that fulfills your commands.

She represents the Soul, the physical body, the Earth, and the personal subconscious, because she is the agent that fulfills the images that you send her in all these forms of physical reality. She is the archetype of abundance in all its forms. She loves you unconditionally.

When You get This Card in a Reading
The Empress as a symbol for the archetype of Mother Nature rules the state of matter, and your physical body. Work with Nature instead of against her.

Meditation
What if the Garden of Eden is still here? Where, then, would it be?

THE EMPRESS

IMAGINATION

IMAGINATION

The Tarot of Creativity

IMAGINATION is the attribute of The Empress. She is pregnant with new worlds, limited only by your imagination and by the boundaries of your desire. The Empress represents both your body, and Mother Nature/Mother Earth; she is yours to command, not to control.

She is a willing, equal partner in the joy of physical existence. In order to manifest anything on the physical plane you have to deal with the power of your imagination. She is in love with you. As your body, she listens to you, and in absolute adoration, executes your commands: your thoughts and emotions. If you are not consciously in partnership with Her, or if you try to dominate Her, you are sending images of death and destruction that can only wreak havoc on your body and on the Earth. Unconscious emotions and thoughts create demons and monsters, while conscious thoughts and emotions have the power to create Heaven on Earth. You are what your emotional images are; and these images create the reality that you think of as "out there" as well.

Where would we be without imagination? This card is both the profoundly fertile feminine source of creativity, and the playful and joyous child of that same creative source. The playful child of imagination is the result of combining the first two principles of creative consciousness: the One and the Two, the Magician and the High Priestess. When you direct your thoughts and emotions with ATTENTION, and use your power of MEMORY as a free and abundant resource, you have access to unbridled IMAGINATION.

Remember that the creative principle of imagination can be misused in misdirected fantasy; your imagination can be like an infinitely powerful, wild horse; it can easily run away with you, and you can end up bruised and scratched in the brambles of the dark forest of your subconscious. Or, you can use it like a child does, for pure creative enjoyment.

When You get This Card in a Reading

You can create consciously with your imagination, or create from your conditioning or your fears. Either way, you have to live with the results.

Meditation

Emotional reactivity brings you into a future that can only mirror your conditioning. Creative (conscious) imagination brings you into a future of your choice.

Related to

The Hanged Man/REVERSAL (Key #12)
The World/TRANSCEND (Key #21)

3—WANDS

S = SYMBOLS
BAG on shoulder = ready to travel
CLIFF = ready to leap
OCEAN = future, potentials
SHIPS = enterprise, ideas launched
WANDS behind him = foundation/research
WAND in his hand = idea for the future
YELLOW SKY & SEA = personal power, will

E = ENERGY
UPRIGHT lines pointing up, as in "thumbs up."

E = EMOTIONS
Strength. Power. Preparation. Confidence in the face of the future.

R = NUMBER
The stability of the Two gives you a good platform for a leap of faith represented by the creative Three.

KEYWORDS
foresight/vision
leadership/authority
expansion/the future
dominion/strategy
premonition/envisioning

Rider Waite Smith Tarot
A man looks to the horizon, contemplating ships out at sea. The man on this card has his cloak on and a pack on his back. He is standing on a hill overlooking an ocean of potential, considering which way he will go. The decision he made in the Two of Wands has been made. He is about to take off. The Three of Wands represents an attitude of competence, a person willing to take a calculated risk in a new direction, one that he has been preparing for.

Since it is a card in the Wands suit, you are in the beginning of the creative process reflected by the number Three: if you try too hard to plan things out at this preliminary, brainstorming phase, you might find yourself boggled down with details, or you might kill off your idea.

The path of your highest excitement is most often illuminated by your "small desires"—things that can be easily accomplished, things that are right in front of you. While you may not yet know your highest purpose, you can get to this information by following the "breadcrumb trail" left for you to find by your Higher Self.

When You get This Card in a Reading
Consider a new direction. This is not yet a big plan or detailed strategy for the future. That is for later.

Meditation
With a solid base behind you, look to create your future.

3—FIRE

PLAY • SPONTANEITY

Tarot of Creativity
The Three of Fire shows the creative nature symbolized by the number Three beginning to show in the natural creative urge for spontaneity and play.

The Suit of Fire is about *feelings*, as opposed to emotions (represented by the Water suit). Emotions are how you *react* to what you have created so far, while feelings are a frequency that you project in order to create. Attitude is everything. You cannot create something positive from a negative mood, or visa versa.

The Suit of Fire kicks off your creative process with a conscious intention, meaning that you are committed to holding a consistent vibrational frequency that matches the frequency of what you desire—this frequency is felt in the body as a mood. A light mood creates a world of ease and light; a gloomy mood creates dark and fearful things.

Allow yourself to partake in small pleasures, and your mind will naturally open. Stretching, taking a walk, eating a good meal, anything that allows you to experience pleasure and joy might be the best thing right now. The main thing is to clear your mind to receive the intuition coming from your Higher Self. The Higher Self often speaks in a quiet voice. It is communicating with your heart, so don't allow your mind to interfere at this stage. In a world governed largely by left-brain values and activities, it may be difficult to justify "extracurricular" activities, but learning to follow your intuition takes time and practice.

When You get This Card in a Reading
When you get this card, consider what direction you can take now that best reflects your highest excitement. Play with it for a while, try it out. Don't be serious: allow yourself to respond spontaneously.

Meditation
Play is the wisdom of the child.

3—SWORDS

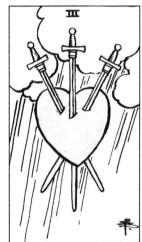

S = SYMBOLS
CLOUDS = overwhelming emotions, sadness
HEART = emotions/passion
RAIN = release of emotions
SWORDS piercing heart = harsh words

E = ENERGY
CROSSED swords meet at center of the heart.

E = EMOTIONS
Betrayal. Grief. Sadness. Jealousy.

R = NUMBER
The mental creative energy of the Three can be misused by thinking too much.

KEYWORDS
gossip/criticism
grief/loss/guilt
emotional reaction
negative response
heartbreak/betrayal
pain/separation

Rider Waite Smith Tarot
Three swords pierce a heart. In the background a storm rages. The Three of Swords shows what might happen if you take the natural creative power of the Three too far: gossip, harsh words, jealousy, betrayal. A misuse of the creative aspect of the mind is indicated in this card; imagining negative occurrences, slanders and slights.

The clouds indicate a dark mood brought on by emotional blocks and mental anguish. However, the rain indicates that the worst has already happened, symbolizing a healthy cleansing brought on by the release of long-suppressed emotions.

When You get This Card in a Reading

If you get this card in a reading, don't be dismayed; the worst has already happened. But if this still bothers you think about how your beliefs about what others think or may think are limiting you.

Meditation

What are you afraid of? Only your ego can be hurt.

3—AIR

CURIOSITY • DISCOVERY

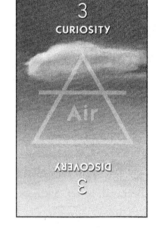

Tarot of Creativity

There is a great pressure on us to conform; life in modern society requires us to meet the expectations of others, and strive to not to make waves. Fear prevents us from exploring, and discovering. Many of us are creatively blocked. All creative blocks are limitations set by fear.

The only difference between an "average person" and a creative genius is the openness of their mind. Inspiration and revelation cannot happen in a closed and fearful mind. All great discoveries were made by people driven by their curiosity to explore.

When You get This Card in a Reading

The mental creative power of the Three of Air is expressed positively in a mood of curiosity which naturally leads to new discoveries.

Meditation

"I do not seek. I find."—Pablo Picasso

3—CUPS

S = SYMBOLS
CUPS UPRAISED = celebration
DANCING = celebration/partnership
FRUIT = harvest, fall, bounty, abundance
GARDEN = abundance/sharing

E = ENERGY
DANCING lines.

E = EMOTIONS
Happiness. Sharing. Jubilance. Success.

R = NUMBER
The Three is the number of the creative spirit: the Child.

KEYWORDS
abundance/celebration
creativity/expression
joy/success
reunion/coming home

Rider Waite Smith Tarot
Three women dance in a circle, raising their cups in a mutual salute. The Three of Cups shows us how the natural creativity of the Three can be used to create a true partnership among equals. Three women raise their cups, showing a communion of spirit, a reason to celebrate.

When You get This Card in a Reading
If you get this card in a reading, it is a time to celebrate what you have; celebrate the people in your life.

Meditation
As you bring a mood of appreciation for everything in your life, more and more things appear for you to celebrate.

3—WATER

EXPRESS • JOY

Tarot of Creativity
The Three of Water shows us how the creative force expresses itself in the physical plane as the emotion of joy. When you allow yourself to experience joy, life becomes easy and fun. You are in the flow of a fervently creative time.

When You get This Card in a Reading
The number Three is a light-hearted child who only needs to play.

Meditation
Joy is the natural product of creative expression.

3—PENTACLES

S = SYMBOLS
CATHEDRAL = social structure
CRAFTSMAN = expertise, talent, genius
MONKS = patronage, respect, social approval
PENTACLES = wealth/talent

E = ENERGY
Strong vertical line of center column points to a Triskele pentacle design. The spiral motion of pentacles attracts the viewer's attention.

E = EMOTIONS
New work. Creativity. A good commission.

R = NUMBER
The Three is a creative number; an active number. In the suit of Pentacles/EARTH, the creativity of the Three has manifested into form.

KEYWORDS
craftsmanship
excellence/planning
talent/skills/financing
mastery/success
satisfaction/teamwork
support/patronage

3

Rider Waite Smith Tarot
A craftsman consults with his patrons about a building. The man featured here is the stone mason. In the Dark Ages, the stone mason employed to raise a cathedral was the equivalent of the modern architect, engineer, and building contractor all rolled into one. He was often also the artist in charge of producing the sculptures for the building. A cathedral usually took generations of skilled craftsmen and artists to produce.

The pentacles are symbols embedded in the structure that supports the cathedral, symbolizing that the creative power of the Three is what supports all physical form—creativity is the energy behind all expressions in the physical world, whether man-made or natural.

This card shows you the final building of the creative vision first conceptualized in the Three of Wands. When we get to the Pentacles/EARTH stage of creative manifestation, we have to handle details well. After all, if you don't put the precise measurements into an architectural plan, the whole thing may fall down. This is due to the density of this plane which operates by certain laws; gravity doesn't exist at "lighter levels," such as the level of intent represented by the Wands suit or the level of thought represented by the Swords suit. The suit of Pentacles, as the suit of the material, is very practical.

When You get This Card in a Reading
Your work and skills inspire confidence. You attract attention from potential patrons and supporters. Teamwork becomes easier now. Abundance starts to flow.

Meditation
You are well prepared to go forward. Your hard work has paid off.

3—EARTH

EXPLORE • CULTIVATE

Tarot of Creativity

It is time to explore and cultivate your ideas. The Three of Earth expresses what happens when you have followed the path of creative manifestation through the number Three.

What was easy to start in the Three of Fire may be a bit harder when you get to the Three of Earth. The manifestation process is easier to influence at the beginning in the Fire stage than in the manifestation stage represented by the Earth suit. But if you are conscious of all aspects of yourself, and the proper way to create, represented by the four suits of the Tarot, you can direct change in a conscious way.

When You get This Card in a Reading

Spend some time with your creative muse. Don't plan anything, just play and brainstorm for a while without any mental or emotional constraints.

Meditation

Time to explore and cultivate your creative ideas.

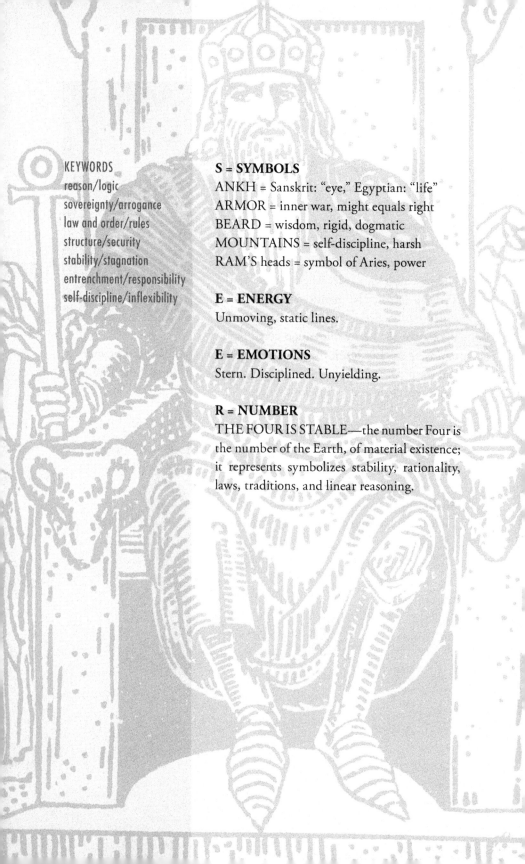

S = SYMBOLS
ANKH = Sanskrit: "eye," Egyptian: "life"
ARMOR = inner war, might equals right
BEARD = wisdom, rigid, dogmatic
MOUNTAINS = self-discipline, harsh
RAM'S heads = symbol of Aries, power

E = ENERGY
Unmoving, static lines.

E = EMOTIONS
Stern. Disciplined. Unyielding.

R = NUMBER
THE FOUR IS STABLE—the number Four is the number of the Earth, of material existence; it represents symbolizes stability, rationality, laws, traditions, and linear reasoning.

THE EMPEROR

ARCHETYPE

Rider Waite Smith Tarot

THE EMPEROR.

The traditional keyword for this card is "reason." This card represents the development and ascendency of the power of logic and self-discipline, which can be taken too far, to the point of rigid beliefs, methods, and dogmatic stubbornness.

Within the castle of reason that the Emperor has carved out for himself, he rules supreme. If a bit austere in his approach, he regards himself as the ultimate source of wisdom and sustenance for his people: he provides all within his purview a structure and stability that is necessary for growth. He provides a stable environment for the Empress to nurture her young. However, he is unimaginative, and resists change.

The Emperor is an ascetic who has learned that emotions can be energetically wasteful, and thus has emphasized the use of logic and learning in his left brain at the exclusion of everything else. He is the father figure who rules with an iron fist, for the good of his people, and because he knows he is always right. The rocky, barren landscape behind him shows the results of the war he wages upon himself, and upon Nature. The Emperor battles his natural instincts and impulses; he rules himself with the force of his will and his logic. He is a master of self-discipline, reason, and asceticism.

The Emperor can be rigid in his beliefs, and can be especially suspicious of any emotional awareness, or creative activity. He is a scientist that relies only on what is proven, and only accepts proofs that his left brain can acknowledge. Anything else reeks of emotionalism or superstition to him. The Emperor is a disciplined being who lives exclusively in his mind; he can't see the present, nor can he imagine a different future. His vision is limited to the past he remembers and to a future that can only repeat the past.

Logic can only go so far; it is not creative, and the Emperor, locked within the stone walls of reason, cannot see how the dominance of his left brain commits him and those he rules to a harsh existence. Life lived this way, without the chaos of creativity and the unpredictability of change, is consigned to a dry, harsh existence without magic or miracles. The Emperor represents the left brain, seeing only reason, logic, and learning; he wants to rule not because he is the best for the job, but because he can't imagine anything else. A good Emperor rules with reason and logic; his lack of emotions allow him to access his insight. With clear-headed logic, he can build the structures of a fair and just society, but he is the "establishment" that we all must overcome if we are to build anything truly new.

When You get This Card in a Reading

If this card shows up in a reading, step back from what you are creating, whether it is a painting or a business, and examine what you have started in a rational, emotionally-detached manner. Is your thinking sound? Analyze it objectively.

Meditation

The quiet voice of the heart can be heard only when the mind is calm and the emotions are still.

THE EMPEROR

INSIGHT

Tarot of Creativity

The number of this card is Four, a very stable number. It is the number of the Earth, the four directions, the number of the elements, and is often traditionally represented by a square. It stands for the clear sight of reason. Reason is actually the precursor to INTUITION (the next card) because only a clear, uncluttered mind is capable of higher INSIGHT. If the mind is preoccupied by fear, anxiety, and egotistical concerns, the higher creative functions of the brain are not accessible.

The number Four stands for the heart chakra, but the lesson of this card applies to the higher understanding of this chakra. The heart is the bridge of our "higher" chakras with our "lower" ones. The heart chakra, or Higher

Heart, contrary to what you might think, isn't connected to the emotional body, but to that function which reason provides: the faculty of choice. The power of choice is directly attributable to the development of rationality and reason. In order to have the clear insight indicated by this card, the heart must not be blocked with unconscious emotions or beliefs.

There is a stage of creativity where the organization and structure represented by the number Four is necessary. The pure creative energy of MEMORY (The High Priestess) is directed by ATTENTION (The Magician), and the inspiration supplied by IMAGINATION (The Empress) comes down to Earth squarely in the number Four, landing in the clear structure of The Emperor/INSIGHT.

This card is the card of the rationalist, symbolized by the often overdeveloped left-brain bias of Western society. And all this structure and analysis can go too far, all too easily: rationalism can become rigid, structure can become a prison, and reason can become a petty argument for limited thinking. To release the true magic of this card, you have to have learned to apply the discipline of INSIGHT to the principles represented by the preceding cards, ATTENTION, MEMORY, and IMAGINATION appropriately and with finesse. If your emotions are running rampant, you cannot achieve a higher consciousness. Only with the application of personal discipline can you obtain the clarity of the mind that the heart needs.

A proper ruler is fair, rational, and rules with detachment. The Emperor represents the self-conscious and the logical function of the left brain. When The Emperor sits squarely on his four-cornered throne (the Earth/physical plane), he rules with the clarity of INSIGHT, which is a quality of the heart when it is empowered and supported by a clear and sober mind.

When You get This Card in a Reading
Calm your emotions, observe quietly from the standpoint of a mind that has been stilled. Allow yourself to transcend your beliefs and social conditioning.

Meditation
Insight is the gift of a sober mind.

Related to
Death/METAMORPHOSIS (Key #13)

4—WANDS

S = SYMBOLS
CASTLE = security/success
GARLANDS = celebration
FLOWERS = hope
WANDS = good beginning/foundation (4)
WOMEN = celebratory mood/cooperation

E = ENERGY
VERTICAL lines of the wands signify hope for a better future.

E = EMOTIONS
Celebratory. Lighthearted.

R = NUMBER
The Four is the number of the Earth; this number in the Wands/FIRE suit indicates a good energetic foundation.

KEYWORDS
celebration/happiness
good energy/harmony
new beginnings
pleasure/hedonism
good will/marriage
family/community

Rider Waite Smith Tarot
Four wands festooned with garlands, a celebration in front of a castle. Four is the number of strong foundations; the number of the Earth; a balanced and stable number. The energetic foundation has been laid for the future structure. You and your partners have taken off some time to celebrate how far you have come. The Four of Wands shows the foundation of good energy, potential for success. This card means that the energy is supportive for building something new.

When You get This Card in a Reading
Your plans have been approved. Your proposal has been accepted.

Meditation
Celebrate what you have built so far and the plans you have for the future.

4—FIRE

STABILITY • STRUCTURE

Tarot of Creativity
This card is titled *stability/structure*. Since this is the Fire suit, the stability and structure indicated by the Four is expressed as energy and potential. This is the card of good beginnings, harmony, and good will.

When You get This Card in a Reading
A sound foundation needs stable elements.

Meditation
A rational approach provides stability and structure for whatever you build.

4—SWORDS

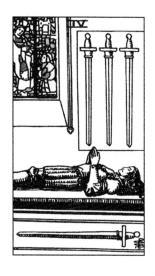

S = SYMBOLS
STAINED GLASS = vision, sacred window
SWORDS = thought, clarity, precision, judgment
TOMB = rest, contemplation

E = ENERGY
The UPRIGHT lines of four swords point at the man lying below, who has his hands in prayer, indicating an inner listening. The fourth sword lies below him at rest (horizontal line).

E = EMOTIONS
Contemplation. Stillness. Meditation. Rest. Quietude.

R = NUMBER
The Four of Swords represents mental contemplation and rest

KEYWORDS
contemplation/rest
meditation/focus
withdrawal/hiding
delay/suspension
recuperation/healing

Rider Waite Smith Tarot
A knight rests beneath three swords, the fourth sword underneath him. Although the primary lines on this image are vertical which generally indicate wakefulness, the three swords are gray, and therefore are de-emphasized, indicating the kind of alertness to an inner voice as one would experience in the state of contemplation. The figure here is not dead, and the slab below him is not his coffin. He is merely resting or perhaps he is meditating; a good practice for anyone from the Suit of Swords. Meditate, rest your mind, clear your head and suspend your ego.

When You get This Card in a Reading
Use this time of rest wisely; contemplate or meditate.

Meditation
Meditation is not focused attention but awareness without thought.

4—AIR

REASON • BELIEF

Tarot of Creativity

All the Fours are about stability and the physical plane. Four is the number of the Earth. Modified by the Suit of Air, which represents the mental body, the stability of the Four is expressed as *reason/belief.*

A belief is an energetic vortex: Psychiatrist David Shainberg and quantum physicist David Bohm believe that our thoughts are vortices in the river of our energy bodies. They tell us that a vortex is a particularly stable phenomenon; the stability of this energy configuration explains how our attitudes and beliefs can be so resistant to change:

"A particularly powerful vortex can dominate our behavior and inhibit our ability to assimilate new ideas and information. It can cause us to become repetitious, create blockages in the creative flow of our consciousness, keep us from seeing the wholeness of ourselves, and make us feel disconnected from our species … when we allow the same vortices to take form repeatedly the (psychiatrist David Shainberg) feels we are erecting a barrier between ourselves and the endless positive and novel interactions we could be having with this infinite source of all being."

A person with left-brain dominance will often resist the idea that the reality they see may be based upon their belief system. For them truth is a self-evident absolute; they forget that their truth might have started as a thought in someone's mind. The thought has become an apparent truth through repetition and agreement.

Those who believed that the world was flat had plenty of agreement from everyone around them, in fact, no one in history had ever questioned the basis of this belief, nor requested proof of it. The artist questions everything, he nurtures a state of inquiry, and explores everything in his environment. That is the value of the artist—he is a scout on the frontier of thought.[1]

This card is like a Greek drama mask: one side is laughing and the other is crying, but the two sides express the same energy. On the one side, you can use your reason in a positive way in order to cut through emotional reactivity, on the other side, your logic may have solidified into a belief that only serves to limit you. Taking your powers of logic and reason too far drains all the magic from the world.

When You get This Card in a Reading
Take time to pause and reflect on yourself, on your beliefs and on how you feel about what you are doing. Question all your beliefs.

Meditation
Just because you believe it doesn't mean it is true.

4—CUPS

S = SYMBOLS
CUPS = potentials, offering
HAND in clouds = divine force, inspiration
TREE = Tree of Life, Tree of Knowledge

E = ENERGY
UPRIGHT line pointing up from seated man up into the tree, echoed in the upright cups. Hand comes in from the left, pointing at man's head, who gazes at the cups before him.

E = EMOTIONS
Contemplation.   Meditation.   Stillness. Reflection.

KEYWORDS
offering/intuition
contemplation
meditation/consideration
reevaluation

R = NUMBER
In Swords/AIR the Four means mental rest.

1   *Parallel Mind, The Art of Creativity,* Aliyah Marr

Rider Waite Smith Tarot

A page sits below the tree of wisdom and life. He contemplates three cups before him: one cup is offered by a hand coming out of a cloud. Three cups stand before the figure as potentials, the fourth is presented to his intuition from the Higher Self. He has his back to the cup, and seems to be solely focused on the cups in front of him. Will he ignore the gift offered to him?

This card is reminiscent eof the story of Buddha and how he achieved enlightenment after meditating for 49 days (7 weeks: 7x7) under the Bodhi tree, or Tree of Life; it was there that he discovered the answer to his question, and formulated the Four Noble Truths, which are the four cornerstones of the Buddhist philosophy.

When You get This Card in a Reading

Quiet your emotions so you can hear the small, quiet voice of intuition.

Meditation

A mind too focused on tangible reality cannot hear the voice of intuition.

4—WATER

STILLNESS • EASE

Tarot of Creativity

The Four of Water tells us that would be wise now to rest and be still. When we stop the incessant spinning of our minds we gain peace of mind. When our emotions are calm and still, a sense of ease permeates our body and mind.

When You get This Card in a Reading

The only way to make proper decisions is to first cultivate a mood of stillness and ease.

Meditation

Only when your emotions are still can you feel the ease and confidence you need to go forward.

4—PENTACLES

S = SYMBOLS
CITY = material success, social standing
CROWN = mental sovereignty, intelligence
PENTACLES = health, wealth

E = ENERGY
STATIC image.

E = EMOTIONS
Guarding/protecting resources. Saving for rainy day. Greed. Miserliness.

R = NUMBER
The Four symbolizes material security.

KEYWORDS
possessiveness/security
anxiety/fear
greed/insecurity
defensiveness/protection

Rider Waite Smith Tarot
A man with a crown sits in front of a cityscape with a pentacle on his head, and two pentacles under his feet; he holds the fourth in his arms over his heart. The lines of the picture are very static. There is no line leading your eye to the right or to the left of the figure. The only movement here is the strange "yin-yang" circular movement of the arms around the central pentacle. The man holds his pentacle "close to his chest," covering, protecting, or hiding his heart.

The suit of Pentacles/EARTH represents physical health and wealth. You can see that the main "energy" of this card is a "holding pattern." This man is holding on to what he has. This is why the card is often called the "miser card."

When You get This Card in a Reading
This card is often called "the miser card," but it may merely mean that you are conserving (or should conserve) resources. Most readings have to do with fear, which is really the fear of loss. This card expresses the ego's need for protection in a world that seems to be dangerous.

Meditation
Be careful that your possessions do not possess you.

4—EARTH

GROUND • FOUNDATION

Tarot of Creativity

The Earth suit expresses the stability of the Four in the material realm. You have to be grounded in order to experience the stability of a strong foundation.

When You get This Card in a Reading

If you get this card in a reading, pay attention to what gives you a feeling of connection and strength. This helps you create a strong foundation for whatever you want to build.

Meditation

Ground yourself in goodness and abundance.

S = SYMBOLS

ACOLYTES = students of enlightenment
SCEPTER = spiritual trinity
CROWN = opened pineal gland
KEYS at feet = keys to the kingdom
PILLARS = social order vs. personal liberty
POPE = intermediary, dogma

E = ENERGY

The primary DIRECTION is upwards from the gaze of the two acolyte monks towards the Hierophant and back down again, showing the flow of information (teaching/speaking). The right hand of the Hierophant points up.

E = EMOTIONS

Listening. Teaching. Learning.

R = NUMBER

THE FIVE LOVES FREEDOM—the number Five is the number of man; the number of his physical senses and the number of his limbs and head. Five symbolizes change and freedom.

THE HIEROPHANT

ARCHETYPE

Rider Waite Smith Tarot

Five is the number of change. Change often involves loss, since the stability/stagnation of the Fours must often be broken before change can happen. The Five expresses the role of the fifth chakra, the channel of INTUITION that impels us to speak our truth.

"Hierophant" literally means "the one who teaches holy things;" this card is the number of the ancient oracle or clairvoyant mystic. The Hierophant is a scribe or translator for the messages of Spirit; he listens and channels this wisdom directly, and considers it his job to teach and enlighten others. The Hierophant is seen seated on a throne between two pillars symbolizing Law and Liberty or Obedience and Disobedience, according to different interpretations.

> A hierophant is a person who brings religious congregants into the presence of that which is deemed holy. The word comes from Ancient Greece, where it was constructed from the combination of ta hiera, "'the holy,' and phainein, 'to show.' In Attica it was the title of the chief priest at the Eleusinian Mysteries. A hierophant is an interpreter of sacred mysteries and arcane principles.[1]

So what has happened between the rational mastery represented by the preceding card, The Emperor, and this card? The adept has opened his pineal gland. This pea-sized gland sits in the center of the head, and is one of the master glands of the whole body, in charge of our circadian rhythms and regulating the production of melatonin which affects the emotional body.

The word "pineal" stems from the Latin word, "pinea," for "pinecone." The symbol of the pinecone seems to be ancient and universal, appearing in Sumerian, Greek, and Roman cultures. Mystical traditions identified the pineal gland as the third eye, and the "Temple of the Soul." The tiara on

1   en.wikipedia.org/wiki/Hierophant

the head of The Hierophant symbolizes this inner temple; it is in the shape of a pine cone, which is the ancient symbol for the awakened pineal gland.

By adulthood, most people's pineal glands are obscured by a layer of calcium, and the natural functions of the gland are more or less blocked. When the pineal gland is covered by this layer of calcium, the gland cannot function properly, disabling the gland from its potential function.

When you have cleared the pineal gland, it is free to function normally. The biological system undergoes a "rejuvenation" owing to the restoration of the normal biological function of the pineal gland. For those individuals who take this further and meditate with their eyes focused on the position of the pineal gland—the geographic center of their brain—the eventual result is that the pineal gland returns to its full function. Now they are able to "see" with their awakened third eye, which restores their natural ability to communicate with their Higher Self. This is why enlightened individuals were often called "seers." When the pineal gland is restored to full functioning state, the person is said to be "awakened" or "enlightened," and capable of inner sight.

The Hierophant in the RWS card wears a triple crown that resembles a pine cone, the esoteric symbol of the opened pineal gland. The keys to Heaven are at his feet. The yellow tabs behind his ears symbolize that the Hierophant is listening to the wisdom or INTUITION from his Higher Self, and teaching what he has learned to others, shown as acolytes at his feet. The Hierophant can be a representative of a belief system if he still believes that power is outside himself; as this is his experience of the divine through his ability to channel his Higher Self. Sometimes this card represents dogma rather than enlightenment, as The Hierophant's power may be conferred on him by society, without first coming from his own personal experience and self-discipline. In that case, he is more of a political figure on the social plane. And on the personal plane, the intuition of The Hierophant has to be rigorously examined for traces of his ego, in order for it to be accepted as wisdom indeed.

When You get This Card in a Reading
Listen to the small inner voice of your intuition; the information coming from your Higher Self.

Meditation
Quiet your mind so you can hear the gentle voice of your intuition.

THE HIEROPHANT

INTUITION

Tarot of Creativity

The number Five lies in the middle of the sequence numbers as we travel the path of numerology; it represents a portal or gate to the higher energies of the upper numbers of the scale. This gate is guarded by issues that come up in your life, represented by the troublesome Fives. If you pass the challenge of the energy of the Fives—change, freedom that comes with responsibility—then you can go on to the upper numbers. If you cannot meet the test of the Five with equanimity, creativity, and poise, then you will have to go back and repeat the lessons of the lower grades, numbers 1-5.

The Hierophant has opened his fifth chakra, and so can speak to others as he channels the wisdom coming from his Higher Self. He has transcended the rigidity of the logic and reason of The Emperor, by opening up to the voice of his Higher Self, which comes through his intuition. INTUITION, as a function of the right brain is holistic in nature, and comes in like a channeled message, often surprising in its wisdom and scope.

Card number Five of the Major Arcana, The Hierophant, represents the fifth chakra, the throat, which symbolically means speaking and, more important, listening; an intense listening to the inner voice of intuition. As the Hierophant, you become the scribe for information coming from your Higher Self. The information comes in the form of INTUITION, and it can be heard only when you quiet the egoic mind (sacrifice the lower needs and desires for the higher).

This card tells us that we should use our intuition to see with the eyes of the Higher Self; this gives us a much broader and more empowered perspective. Intuition is one of the best tools of the conscious creative. Learning to listen to your intuition is key to creative thinking. Creative inspiration through the medium of developed intuition naturally flows to an individual with an open mind and engaged heart.

Intuition can only function when beliefs and emotions are cleared; one must be in an open, detached state in order to hear the voice of intuition, which is coming from your Higher Self. The reason that people often think that an agent outside of them is giving them this information is because they are still functioning from the level of reason, which can only comprehend linear realities, not multidimensional ones. And from the level of the limited left brain, they cannot imagine that they have access to an infinite, ever-ready storehouse of information without any effort on their part, except maintaining an open and detached mind.

The Hierophant shows us how to listen to the Higher Self and how to access the incredible resource of INTUITION; it tells us how to use intuition to see "the forest and the trees"—the holistic vision, and the details at the same time. To hold a creative vision in the face of a different reality is what it means to be a "visionary." The Hierophant is encouraging us to use and integrate both sides of the brain: the left brain that "sees the trees" and the right brain that "sees the forest."

We cannot quiet our minds down to listen to our intuition if we haven't done the work of clearing our beliefs and emotional reactions. The best way to cut down mind chatter is to make the ego feel safe. Strangely enough, the ego only feels safe once it feels love.

Nothing in the left brain—the center of logic and reason—can make you feel safety or love. Love can only come in with "faith"—love has to be discovered, or rather, rediscovered as the true nature of reality, while fear has to be recognized as a false program. Once the mind/ego is quiet, you can feel a current of information flowing in through your ears and into your mind. Get ready to take notes!

When You get This Card in a Reading
If you get this card in a reading, remember that you have access to an infinite source of information via your intuition; all you have to do is learn to quiet your mind.

Meditation
Your intuition never needs acknowledgement or validation from others. What is good for you is good for you alone. Your path is unique, and as valid as any other.

Related to
Temperance/ALCHEMY (Key #14)

5—WANDS

S = SYMBOLS
MEN = young, masculine energy
WANDS = energy

E = ENERGY
LINES pointing in all directions.

E = EMOTIONS
Competition. Chaotic. Fighting.
Disharmonious. Disorganized. Non-aligned.

R = NUMBER
The image of the five men with wands on this
card introduces the energy of the Fives, as the
undirected, chaotic energy of change.

KEYWORDS
disorder/disorganized
misaligned/non-aligned
lack of cooperation
dissension/argument
debate/quarreling
competition/challenge
argumentative/excited

Rider Waite Smith Tarot
*Five men battle, compete, or play with five
wands.* The image shows a frenetic energy,
perhaps a friendly competition, or a war. In
any event, it is obvious that non of the partici-
pants are interested in going the same way, or cooperating. Sometimes
competition is good, but if everyone is fighting to be first, no one wins. To
work together, there has to be a solid foundation and rules to fairly govern
participation and partnership.

When You get This Card in a Reading
Change is afoot and it is coming in as disorganization, chaos, or disharmony.
Energy moves in many different directions, nothing solid can be established.

Meditation
Too many chiefs and not enough Indians.
Too many cooks spoil the stew.

5—FIRE

UNEXPECTED • OPPORTUNITY

Tarot of Creativity

The number Five is the middle of the numbers 1-9, and as such it is a portal or gateway. The Fives are the turning point, and the Fire suit are the beginning of the energy of the Five. You can feel the static electricity of the storm as it approaches: can you weather the coming change?

When the tsunami breaks will you cling to the roof of your house as the rains flood the streets? It is a more constructive idea to take to a boat and float with the change than trying to fight the storm and maintain old structures.

Even if you wanted things to change we all experience a bit of resistance when change finally comes. We are not ready to recognize the shape that change comes in, and if we cannot see it for what it is, we are in danger of missing an opportunity.

When You get This Card in a Reading

In *The Tarot of Creativity*, the change represented by the number Five in the Suit of Fire is expressed as an unexpected opportunity; pay close attention to see if you can recognize the opportunity in the chaos of change.

Meditation

Be prepared to see an unexpected opportunity in the chaos of change.

5—SWORDS

S = SYMBOLS
CLOUDS = turbulence, disorder
LAKE = emotions, subconscious
MAN with three swords = victorious
MEN walking away = giving up, letting go
SWORDS = mental, the ego

E = ENERGY
JAGGED DIAGONAL lines of clouds give a stormy, turbulent feel to this image. The gaze of the man in the foreground leads the eye directly to the defeated men walking away in the distance.

E = EMOTIONS
Victory at any cost. Taking advantage. Over zealousness. Very combative. Gloating.

R = NUMBER
The Five here represents sudden, possibly violent change.

KEYWORDS
disorder/disorganized
lack of cooperation
dissension/argument
debate/quarreling
competition/challenge
argumentative/excited

Rider Waite Smith Tarot
A man holds three swords and watches his opponents or companions turn away, ignoring the remaining swords on the ground. It appears that a battle has been fought and one side was defeated. The victor has all the swords; the opposition threw their swords on the ground, unwilling to fight anymore.

When You get This Card in a Reading
Are you prepared for what you might lose if you are set to win at all costs?

Meditation
What does "surrender" mean to you?

5—AIR

RISK • FREEDOM

Tarot of Creativity
The two words on the TOC card are "risk" and "freedom." The choice is always to see the words on *The Tarot of Creativity* cards separately or read them together as a phrase.

This card expresses the energy of the Five as an exciting proposition. Change comes at a cost, but the cost may be that you are going to lose something that is actually inhibiting your forward movement.

When You get This Card in a Reading
Is freedom ever not worth the risk?

Meditation
Is there anything in the concept of "freedom" that scares you?

5—CUPS

S = SYMBOLS
BLACK cloak = color of mourning
BRIDGE = emotional connection
CASTLE = distant success/plans
CUPS = spilled water (emotions)
STREAM = emotions, subconscious

E = ENERGY
VERTICAL line of figure in black cloak directs the eye towards the figure's head. The eye then follows the man's gaze to the three spilled cups on the ground.

E = EMOTIONS
Regret. Loss. Mourning.

R = NUMBER
The Fives are about one of the essential laws of life: change. In the case of the Cups/Water suit, it is about our emotional reaction to change.

KEYWORDS
loss/grief
longing/separation
setback/defeat
regret/surrender

5

Rider Waite Smith Tarot
A cloaked figure seems to mourn the spilled cups before him. The figure ignores the full cups behind him and focuses gloomily on the spilled cups before him. He is not aware that the way forward represented by the spilled cups is only one path, and that path seems to have just ended. If he would just turn around he would see that there is another way, another direction he can take that will be emotionally fulfilling. But as long as he is focused on what is gone, he is stuck where he is, and can't move forward in any direction. He sees the loss that comes with the change that the Five represents, but not the freedom that might come next.

One day, as I was contemplating the concept of dropping personal history, I found a piece of graffiti stenciled on the sidewalk: it said, "Drop the Rock." Like a message dropped from the sky just for me, it was a metaphor for how our personal history—our story and the emotions connected to it—is like a heavy rock that we are carrying on our shoulders.

There is a saying in the South, "He is as serious as a heart attack." Most of us are fighting the gravity of our thoughts, represented in the size of that invisible rock we are carrying. Often we do not want to release our attachment to our personal burden and drop the rock, but when it finally happens, the effect is incredible.

Q: When do we get to drop the rock?
A: When we stop gripping it so hard.

When heavy concern for the self is gone, your thoughts and emotions are free to guide you towards your natural preferences, and towards the fulfillment of your dreams. Suddenly the world becomes crystal clear and perfect: it feels as if you have just flipped your view outward instead of inward.

The box in which you were living suddenly turns inside out, and you are an observer in a beautiful, immensely interesting world. It is as if you have walked into the real world, after having lived your entire life inside a flat black and white photo. Colors are more intense, space seems somehow more 3D than before; everything is truly perfect; there is a wonderful variety, taste, color, texture, and tone to everything.

Because you are no longer comparing what you see to any ideal of perfection or to what you think it should be, beauty exists in every nook and cranny, even in what you may have formerly considered ugly.

This is the essence of the artistic experience.[1]

When You get This Card in a Reading
Are you missing an opportunity because you are focused on what you have lost?

Meditation
Is your cup half-full or half-empty?

---

1 *Parallel Mind, The Art of Creativity*, Aliyah Marr

5—WATER

EXCITEMENT • EXPANSION

Tarot of Creativity

The Water Suit of the TOC expresses the change brought by the number Five as the emotion of excitement and the resulting feeling of expansion. This means that you always have the choice to interpret your emotions differently, and experience a different reality as a result.

The Buddhists say that there are skillful and unskillful emotions: conscious and unconscious emotions. To decide to translate the energy of an emotion in a more empowered manner is a mark of emotional maturity. This does not mean you suppress or deny your emotions. You simply refuse to be a victim of them. When you move from a knee-jerk reaction to your thoughts and emotions to a considered response, you have achieved detachment. Detachment is the prerequisite for the attainment of personal freedom, otherwise called "enlightenment."

When You get This Card in a Reading

Excitement leads to a feeling of expansion, an empowered feeling that can only lead to your best future. Follow the trail of your innermost feelings.

Meditation

In order to feel the nature of your true being, you must relax and soften your ideas of who you are.

5—PENTACLES

S = SYMBOLS
CRUTCHES = disability
RAGS = poverty, hardship
SNOW = "out in the cold," unprotected,
STAINED GLASS = the light of consciousness

E = ENERGY
Two figures trudging in the snow from LEFT
to RIGHT.

E = EMOTIONS
Poverty. Disinheritance. Disenfranchised.
Unloved. Unsupported.

R = NUMBER
The energy of the Five reaches its full
expression in the Suit of Pentacles/EARTH,
as a change that is now in form.

KEYWORDS
difficulty/lack
financial troubles
poverty consciousness
struggle/ill health
physical neglect
rejection/unsupported
excluded/judged

Rider Waite Smith Tarot
*Two impoverished and crippled figures walk by
a cheerily-lit stained glass window in the snow.* In this image, the attention
of the viewer is caught and held by the beautiful stained glass window.
The contrast between the light of the window and the darkness of the
night outside emphasize the message of this card: separation, isolation,
deprivation.

The Querent may not have paid enough attention to the messages of
the Five in the earlier cards, and now pays the price of sudden, possibly
catastrophic change. If he had listened to his intuition back when he felt the
wind of the coming change in the Five of Wands or taken the temporary
defeat of the Five of Swords to heart, he might have avoided this eventuality.

When You get This Card in a Reading
Ask yourself, "What am I resisting?" If you feel resistance, then you are in
separation consciousness, and negative emotional reactions are the result.

Try "turning yourself around" and focus instead on things that bring you joy: this produces the polar opposite of resistance: unity consciousness.

Meditation
Do you believe that you deserve health and wealth? Then choose the thoughts and emotions which make up the vibrational reality that supports your dreams. You can't be experiencing a reality that is vibrationally different from your emotional reality.

5—EARTH

SURRENDER • BREAKTHROUGH

Tarot of Creativity
This card tells you that fighting change is like swimming upstream. Surrender instead, and you may find yourself suddenly at a breakthrough.

The two words on the TOC card can be taken together, as in "you have to first surrender, before you can have a breakthrough," or you can see the upright word as the beginning of the energy of the card, while the reversed word represents the ending energy of it. Or you may simply choose to only read the word in the upright position as the meaning of the card.

When You get This Card in a Reading
A breakthrough is often preceded by some kind of surrender. What are you holding on to that you could let go of?

Meditation
If you can't surrender you will break, instead of break through.

equality/difference
attraction/connection
desire/detachment
love/passion
healing/inclusion
integration/marriage
cooperation/collaboration

S = SYMBOLS

ADAM & EVE = marriage of opposites
ANGEL = archangel Raphael/healing
CLOUDS = spiritual goal, heaven
MOUNTAIN = attainment, wisdom
SNAKE = Kundalini, renewal, healing, DNA
SUN = happiness, life, Source, element of Fire
TREE of Knowledge= inner knowledge
TREE of Life = "burning bush," Spirit as a force

E = ENERGY

RADIATING lines of the Sun dominate the image.

E = EMOTIONS

Balance. Healing. Equality.

R = NUMBER

THE SIX EXPLORES LOVE—the number Six is the number of healing, balance and harmony.

THE LOVERS

ARCHETYPE

Rider Waite Smith Tarot

THE LOVERS.

The esoteric keyword for this card is "discrimination" which means "the recognition and understanding of the difference between one thing and another." The Self, on its journey through the stages of life, now becomes aware of an Other, a separate sex, a separate person, a feeling of distinction and separateness. This is the power of discrimination in its most basic form.

But this card means much more: it show the right partnership between the elements of the Triadic Self: the male side of the Self—the mental/egoic body—with the intuitive/emotional/physical body; both in partnership with the Higher Self. The male figure looks to the female, who looks, not at him, but at the Angel—the Higher Self, or Super Conscious—for guidance. This triad shows that the mental/egoic body cannot direct the whole self, and in fact, must work through the subconscious self, as this is how the Higher Self gives its information.

Archangel Raphael steps down the energy of the light from the Sun and distributes it equally to both the man and the woman, who represent the two parts of duality. The energy of Spirit represented here by the light and the heat of the Sun underlies and supports the fabric of duality. Raphael holds his hands above each of their heads in the sign of a benediction, blessing or in the action of healing, or rather, "wholing;" the action he takes is one of reunification—the recognition of the wholeness of duality, or what I call the "divinity in the duality."

The Tree of Life is behind the man, bearing twelve fruits, and the Tree of Knowledge is behind the woman, a serpent twined around it. The snake present in this image represents self-knowledge. In ancient cultures snakes were often seen as a symbol for life and revered, as was all life. In a strange archetypical way, the symbol for the strands of twisted DNA resembles the shape that a snake takes when it moves around a branch. The snake in the Garden of Eden curled itself—embracing life and self-knowledge—around the Tree of Life (in this card, around the Tree of Knowledge). This is a symbol for the lifelong journey of the Seeker towards total self-knowledge: the task of bringing the consciousness of the identity of the individuated Self into the experience of life or matter.

The story of the Fall is the story of how we lost our connection with the bliss of a higher dimensional Earth. We created an extreme state of separation, and this became what we call "evil." This lower, negative state caused us to disconnect with the state of Nirvana in the Garden of Eden, and to be rejected from the higher state of bliss/oneness by our lowered vibrations. The Garden of Eden is always there for us when we reconnect with all parts of ourselves; in fact, the Garden of Eden is only a frequency away. The symbol of the snake in the story is an unmistakable reference to Eastern esoteric knowledge:

> Kundalini stems from yogic philosophy as a form of shakti or "corporeal energy." Kundalini is described within Eastern religious, or spiritual tradition as an indwelling spiritual energy that can be awakened in order to purify the subtle system and ultimately to bestow the state of Yoga, or divine union upon the seeker of truth. The Yoga Upanishads describe Kundalini as lying "coiled" at the base of the spine, represented as either a goddess or sleeping serpent waiting to be awakened.[1]

The journey of the Self started with undifferentiated consciousness: humans and animals in the Garden of Eden lived side-by-side in a state of total harmony and bliss. Once humans made a choice to pursue individuation in the search of self-knowledge—by choosing the apple, which has the sacred symbol of the pentacle, the number of man, at its heart—they had to leave the garden of bliss, and journey through lower forms of consciousness.

The self-conscious is the newest kid on the block in the story of evolution; no animal has the kind of brain that seeks to know itself. Our nature forces us to be self-reflective. Self-reflection is how the cosmic mind experiences ego (individuation). Once we integrate the new self-conscious with our total self, we will once again find ourselves in the Garden of Eden, because we will have rediscovered Oneness inside the experience of individuation. We will have come to recognize the divinity inside duality.

If you ask the Higher Self any question with the right mindset, you will get a totally honest and often surprising answer. I once asked, "What is

1 en.wikipedia.org/wiki/Kundalini

the purpose of emotions?" I got this answer: "Emotions are the gateway to intuition."[1] You can see this in this card: imagine yourself standing as the man (the mental/egoic self) in this card, asking a question. The question is answered by the Higher Self but it has to be funneled through the emotions and subconscious—through the intuitive Heart represented by the woman in this picture: the result is an answer that comes into the mind as a vision, through words, or as an intuitive feeling.

Traditionally, The Lovers card meant "discrimination" or "choice;" as in *wise choice*. Choosing the higher version of everything: relationships as true partnerships, respect for difference, the understanding of true equality. Only an immature individual wants a relationship of dependency. An adult understands the nature of equality, and stands in their own independence and sovereignty while respecting that of others.

At the highest level, love is expressed as unconditional LOVE, which is respect for difference; the recognition of the equality of all things, and the recognition of the divinity inside all form, as all form is just an expression of the energy of love.

6

When You get This Card in a Reading

When you get this card in a reading, take time to think about whether your thoughts and emotions are aligned with your highest creative intention. What does the term "unconditional love" mean to you? Does it apply to how others treat you, or to how you view others?

Meditation

The Garden of Eden isn't a location; it doesn't exist in time or space—it is an energy, the energy of unconditional love. Eden is only a frequency away.

---

1   Read my book, *Parallel Mind, The Art of Creativity* for more on how to creatively use emotions.

THE LOVERS

LOVE

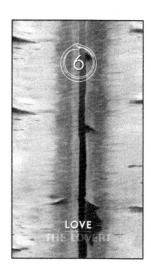

Tarot of Creativity

LOVE is the title of The Lovers card in *The Tarot of Creativity*, but this is not the imperfect love of the spiritually immature; the love referenced here is *unconditional love*.

This card has integrated the independence of the Five and turns then to recognizing the Divine Other, a being that is the equal of the personality, but whose personality is so different as to be impenetrable at times. Realizing the difference and the divinity of the other is crucial to understanding the nature of duality.

When you can see the sacred in all things you have surrendered the ego's need to control; now the ego—the man in this image—stands in the proper position in the Triad of the Self, no longer in control. The ego (mental body) is now the personal assistant of the Higher Self, responding to the direction and guidance of the Higher Self through the intuition of the emotional/physical body, represented by the woman in the picture.

The Lovers/LOVE card shows us how to deal with Duality at the highest level, that of non-judgmental acceptance, which is actually unconditional love. This is the card of the "Divine Other," the recognition of how to reconcile the state of duality into a working partnership. Which duality? Essentially, that which is inside ourselves. Superficially, this is the *Anima* (female) inside the male, and the *Animus* (male) inside the female, but the meaning of this Tarot card goes much further than Jungian psychology.

The Love card refers to the ability to see the divinity and sacredness of the Divine Other, the other half of the androgynous Soul. Like the Yin/Yang symbol, a tiny bit of the female portion exists within the male and visa versa.

Most people are looking for love outside themselves. They are looking for another to reflect their beauty and value back to them. This narcissistic tendency is a cover for the insecurity of a maladjusted ego: an immature self-conscious.

An unhealthy ego is one that lives in separation and seeking. It doesn't admit to the existence of anything outside its own narrow definition of self and doesn't admit to the possibility of a bigger world outside the reality defined by its own thoughts. Without the respect of universal LOVE the ego is alone in a desert of inherited beliefs and dry facts, no matter how many people are actually around. So the self-conscious goes on a quest to find the perfect lover, the LOVE that it intuits must exist but cannot feel.

The ego doesn't recognize that it has always had the perfect lover already. LOVE is not a projection or a statement, or even a desire. You cannot search for LOVE in the world reflected by your ego; the ego can only mirror the emptiness and despair of its own loneliness.

The lesson of the Lovers/LOVE card in the Tarot is this: to teach you how to balance the egoic self and the personal subconscious. This is the object of all holistic spiritual traditions: to regain the natural equality between the high heart and the head. You can only discover, or more appropriately, uncover, the source of LOVE in the core of your being. She is there, and has been there all the time.

This card signifies the recognition of the power and beauty of the subconscious, which in the Tarot is represented by the female figure, as the self-conscious is the male. The subconscious is here to serve our thoughts and desires. She fulfills every wish and command of the self-conscious, without question. If you send this personal powerhouse unconscious thoughts, the universal subconscious fulfills them, and mirrors to you the substance and emotional reality of those thoughts. If instead, you send your subconscious conscious thoughts, she will construct the hologram of reality to reflect those thoughts.

The subconscious is a master of attentive listening, and listens to you day and night to fulfill the command of your thoughts and emotions. It never makes a mistake, and if you think that you are giving her directed thoughts but have a conflicting belief or emotion underlying that thought, she will respond to the emotion, since she sees this as your true command, taking your stronger emotion before your weaker thought or belief as your true desire.

The subconscious reflects you, and you see this reflection as your reality. She is in direct communication with your Higher Self, represented by the Angel in the RWS Tarot. Until you have disciplined your ATTENTION by focusing your thoughts and by choosing your emotions, you can only reach the Higher Self through the subconscious, since an undisciplined mind cannot directly access the Higher Self.

The Lovers card could be seen as depicting the mechanics of the Law of Attraction in action. In the TOC card, we see two birch trees. They pose the riddle, "What is equal, but different?" In their reflection of each other they show you how your thoughts and emotions are unfailingly reflected in the hologram of your outer reality. This is the meaning of the traditional keyword, "discrimination," the ability to discriminate accurately is to be able to see both the similarities and the differences. It takes an attentive mind to see similarities where the average man sees only differences, and differences where others see only similarities. When you can perceive similarities, LOVE can then heal the world (Archangel Raphael); to see differences allows the free will of individuality to exist. And so, creativity resolves the riddle of "What is equal, but different?" A creative individual is the perfect lover of his world, because he has the vision given to him by his refined discrimination.

A person who understands equality and respect for all things is someone who practices unconditional love. The lesson here is one of respect and attention (card #1, The Magician). Show respect and LOVE to your subconscious by sending her conscious, carefully directed thoughts. Use your emotions to support those thoughts, and she will help you manifest your dreams.

When You get This Card in a Reading
Treat everything around you with LOVE—and you will see LOVE reflected in everything around you.

Meditation
Can you see the divinity in duality?

Related to
The Devil/THE SHADOW (Key #15)

6—WANDS

S = SYMBOLS
HORSE = power, virility, motion, nobility
LAURELS = recognition, success
WANDS = energy, element of Fire
WREATH = victory, accomplishment

E = ENERGY
UPRIGHT lines of wands all pointing up, as in "thumbs up."

E = EMOTIONS
Confidence. Success. Approval. Accolades.

R = NUMBER
The Six of Wands shows harmony and happiness in acknowledged accomplishment.

Rider Waite Smith Tarot
A man crowned with the laurel leaves of victory and holding a wand crowned with a wreath marches in a procession before an adoring crowd. The numbers in the Tarot are always best represented by the Major Arcana card; the cards in the lower cards show the way the number is translated in the suit, but they are also a fragment or one-dimensional example of the base energy of the number. The image on this card shows a triumphal march, a common theme in the Renaissance. The number SIX symbolizes harmony and love. In the suit of Wands, the love signified by the number Six is expressed as recognition or adulation.

In contemporary life, this is like the experience of stardom. The fans "love" the movie star or music star, and idolize him or her; they want to identify with the object of their adoration. This adulation is heady stuff for the object of their affections, because the star is really not much different from his fan base. The danger is that he may believe that he is the image that his fans are projecting, a two-dimensional version of whatever they believe he is, or rather, what they want him to be.

KEYWORDS
success/vindication
triumph/acclaim
accolades/victory
acknowledgment
accomplishment
self-importance
worthiness/self-esteem

6

When You get This Card in a Reading

What do the words "success" and "victory" mean to you? How do these words feel in your body?

Meditation

To be successful you have to first allow yourself to *feel* successful; the feeling is the first stage in the creative process (Wands/FIRE) that eventually creates the reality (Pentacles/EARTH).

6—FIRE

ATTRACTION • ATTACHMENT

Tarot of Creativity

All love starts with attraction. You are magnetically drawn to that which you love by the natural power of attraction. Attraction leads creative desire; desire creates forward movement. Attraction helps us see the path to our dreams, and encourages us to take action and move in the direction of what we desire. Attraction's alter ego, attachment, stops forward motion towards your desires.

Attraction is activated by desire. Most of us have experienced both attraction and desire; like the polar ends of a magnet, it can be said that a kind of energy flows from the attractor to the desirer and back again. We are energetic beings in an ocean of energy. Any time there is a strong feeling there is energy, and all energy can be used however we want. Without wants or desires, we would never move anywhere, we would not feel a need to do anything—we would be like a rudderless boat floating in a bland sea of indifference.[1]

---

1 *Parallel Mind, The Art of Creativity*, Aliyah Marr

When You get This Card in a Reading

Attraction is a creative force. When we become aware of our attraction we have the power to create in a conscious direction. Otherwise, we can become unwittingly attached to the object of our attraction.

Meditation

Be careful that a healthy attraction doesn't become an unhealthy attachment.

6—SWORDS

S = SYMBOLS

BOAT = freedom, voyage
CHILD = the inner child, Spirit
LAKE = emotions, subconscious
MAN = guide, psychopomp
STAFF = authority, rule, mastery, guide
WAVES = emotional turbulence
WOMAN = the subconscious, the body

E = ENERGY

Strong DIAGONAL line of man's staff. Another strong DIAGONAL line in the lines of the boat.

E = EMOTIONS

The calm after a storm. Acceptance. Peace. Harmony. Leaving the past behind.

R = NUMBER

The Six in the Suit of Swords represents thoughts of peace and harmony.

KEYWORDS
letting go/moving on
positive movement
renunciation/regret
depression/sadness
need for change
changing location
new direction

Rider Waite Smith Tarot

A man guides a boat with a woman and a child huddled in the bottom from troubled waters into a calm sea. After the battle and apparent defeat of the preceding card, the Five of Swords, peace and harmony are welcome. The energy of the number Six modified by the Suit of Swords, becomes the peace or lull after the storm. The woman in this picture may symbolize the subconscious, the physical body, or the emotional body. The child she shelters is the inner child. Swords represent thought and the ego; by and large, the Swords suit, representing the mental body, is the most negative suit in the Tarot, due to the undisciplined nature of the average person's mental state.

A strong DIAGONAL line is formed by the man's staff as he poles the boat away from the turbulence of the river into the calm waters of the lake. Diagonal lines are very active lines. Another strong DIAGONAL line is formed by the body of the boat, going forward into a better future.

The figure of the man resembles the archetype of the PSYCHOPOMP, who is the guide to the underworld, the region of reality beyond time-space. He steers the boat of humanity over the river Styx, which formed the boundary between the Earth and the underworld.

> The psychopomp, which literally means the "guide of souls" are creatures, spirits, angels, or deities in many religions whose responsibility is to escort newly deceased souls from Earth to the afterlife. Their role is not to judge the deceased, but simply to provide safe passage.
>
> In Jungian psychology, the psychopomp is a mediator between the unconscious and conscious realms. It is symbolically personified in dreams as a wise man or woman, or sometimes as a helpful animal. In many cultures, the shaman also fulfills the role of the psychopomp. This may include not only accompanying the soul of the dead, but also vice versa: to help at birth, to introduce the newborn child's soul to the world.[1]

The woman in this picture symbolizes the subconscious, the physical body, or the emotional body. The child she shelters is the inner child. Swords represent thought and the ego; by and large, the Swords suit, representing the mental body, is the most negative suit in the Tarot, due to the undisciplined nature of the average person's mental state.

---

1 en.wikipedia.org/wiki/Psychopomp

When You get This Card in a Reading

The peace represented by this card seems hard-won, and perhaps temporary. Peace and harmony cannot happen in the world until it is cultivated first in your mind. Let go of what doesn't work, calm waters up ahead.

Meditation

What if life isn't a battle, but a love story?

6—AIR

SIMPLICITY • OPENNESS

Tarot of Creativity

Remember the last card in the suit: the words on that card were *risk/freedom*. This card assumes that you took the risk, and you now know that you are safe; thus you can open up. In order to create you have to cultivate a mood that allows new ideas to germinate; this card shows you the way to do that by advising you to adopt a mental attitude of simplicity and openness.

When You get This Card in a Reading

The energy of the Six encourages you to be childlike and approach everything with an attitude of openness.

Meditation

A creative master cultivates an attitude of simplicity and openness

6—CUPS

S = SYMBOLS
CASTLE = foundation, shelter, protection
CHILDREN = innocence, love
HOUSE = home, comfort, family, lineage
WHITE FLOWERS = pure love, spiritual

E = ENERGY
The image is mostly STATIC. The only directional line runs from the gaze of the boy to the girl.

E = EMOTIONS
Nostalgic. Sentimental. Innocent.

R = NUMBER
The Sixes are always about love. The Cups/ WATER suit expresses love as an emotion.

KEYWORDS
innocence/unworldliness
gratitude/good will
giving/receiving
nostalgia/playfulness
simplicity/goodness
contentment/ease
appreciation/love

Rider Waite Smith Tarot
A figure hands a cup with flowers to a smaller figure. Because this card is in the Cups suits, it is about the *emotion* of love. This image conveys a sense of sentimentalism, romance, nostalgia, and/or innocence; but this card suggests that it refers to a memory or dream: something that isn't real or present.

The past doesn't exist except as a memory in our brains. Memory is like a hologram: it is non-local. There is not one place that it exists, all parts of it are in the whole and the whole is reflected in all the parts. If you are too attached to the past, it can prevent you from going forward. Do you look on your past with love and understanding, or do you have negative feelings or regrets? Nostalgia, like its apparent polar opposite—regret—keeps you from living in the present.

When You get This Card in a Reading
Spend some time appreciating what you have. This card appears when you might need to appreciate the little things in your relationships. This refers to

all relationships, even the one you have with yourself, or with your memory of the past. The past is what you make it.

Meditation
Home is where the heart is.

6—WATER

ALLOW • BALANCE

Tarot of Creativity
The Six of Water in the TOC shows the proper way to address the emotional content of love. While the RWS card shows an immature form of love that clings to the past—nostalgia— the TOC demonstrates that love can reach a higher level that does not cling to the beloved, resist change, or lose one's identity in another, instead it allows the water of emotions to reach its natural level.

You are being asked to examine your emotions, and to drop the ballast of old, dense memories that don't serve you; then you will rise naturally on the high of emotional balance.

When You get This Card in a Reading
If you get this card in a reading, remember that life becomes easier if you allow it to balance itself out naturally instead of trying to force things or make something happen. You don't have to do much except to get out of the way by dropping whatever doesn't serve you.

Meditation
Emotional mastery does not mean suppression or even control, it is a matter of flow, allowing, and choice.

6—PENTACLES

S = SYMBOLS
PENTACLES. = health, wealth
SCALES = balance, fairness, investment
RAGS = poverty consciousness, disease, lack

E = ENERGY
The dominant shape in this image is the invisible TRIANGLE formed by the direction of the gazes and hands of the three figures.

E = EMOTIONS
Beneficence. Generosity. Charity. Healing. Fairness.

R = NUMBER
The Six in this suit is about how the energy of LOVE expresses in the physical as security and abundance.

KEYWORDS
giving/receiving
benefactor/generosity
teaching/learning
dominion/submission
valuation/measuring
benevolence/investment

Rider Waite Smith Tarot
A wealthy benefactor hands coins to beggars with one hand, and weighs his money with scales in the other. The wealthy man looks to the beggar on his right to whom he is distributing money. His hand points at the beggar, while the beggar's outstretched hands point to the other beggar, who, in turn, gazes up at the wealthy man.

This card shows what happens when you take the attributes of the number Six—love and equality—into the material plane. Does this card really represent the true spirit of these qualities? The scales in the hand of the benefactor hover over the head of the second beggar like a benediction or a judgment. The scales could mean justice and fairness or they could indicate the parsimonious nature of the wealthy man who counts the pennies even as he gives them away to the poor.

When You get This Card in a Reading
If you get this card in a reading, think about what you are investing your energy in and why.

Meditation

True abundance: the relationship between the giver and the receiver when they understand that they are one and the same. They are an equation that balances duality and fulfills the Law of Karma.

6—EARTH

APPRECIATE • DISCRIMINATE

Tarot of Creativity

One of the original, traditional keywords for the Six in the Major Arcana, The Lovers, is "discriminate." Modern usage of this word is a bit negative, but the more neutral meaning—*to note or observe a difference; to distinguish accurately*—is closer to the meaning of unconditional LOVE.

To love doesn't mean that you are blind to difference, in fact, romantic love often focuses on difference. The higher form of love, unconditional love, also observes difference, but it celebrates it. To discriminate means that you recognize the divine other, or the oneness that underlies duality. The power of discrimination allows you to recognize and appreciate others for what they are, not for what you want them to be.

When You get This Card in a Reading

Appreciation makes things grow; discrimination allows you to choose wisely.

Meditation

Whatever you pay attention to gets bigger.

KEYWORDS
travel/success
challenge/adventure
control/responsibilities
paradox/steadfastness
movement/stillness
knowledge/wisdom
spirituality/consciousness
study/analyze
drive/determination

S = SYMBOLS

8-POINTED STAR = Higher Self
CASTLE = attainment
CHARIOT = the "Merkaba"
MOON epaulets = power over subconscious
SPHINXES = duality drawing the chariot
SQUARE = the heart's dominion on Earth
STARS on canopy = the universe, the zodiac
WAND = brings Spirit into matter
WINGS on Sun = freedom, spiritual

E = ENERGY

A dominant shape of a TRIANGLE is formed by the two sphinxes and the charioteer; a STATIC image in which nothing is moving.

E = EMOTIONS

Mysterious, hints at esoteric knowledge.

R = NUMBER

THE SEVEN SEEKS THE UNSEEN—the Seven is the number of the spiritual seeker, the mystic, and the scientist.

THE CHARIOT

ARCHETYPE

Rider Waite Smith Tarot

This image presents a paradox; it seems to be about travel, yet nothing is moving. The analysis of the picture's composition reveals a hidden triangle.

The triangle is one of the ancient symbols for the Higher Self or God. It is a very stable shape, and although the title of the card, The Chariot, suggests motion, the image imparts a very calm, centered feeling. Even the sphinxes have their paws folded. This means that the movement suggested by the card is *inner* movement.

The number of this card, seven, is often called "the first spiritual number" and it correlates (as all the first eight cards do) with a chakra, in this case, the crown chakra. In the RWS Tarot one often sees crowns in the images on the cards; the crown signifies intelligence. This card presents an image of the right use of your intelligence; it shows you how to use your intelligence to govern your thoughts and your emotions. Seven is the divine marriage of the Three and the Four, the marriage of the number of nature/ IMAGINATION with the number of Earth or matter. The Seven is the number of divinity; the recognition and partnership with the divine triad: the mind/ego, the emotions/body, and the Higher Self.

This card could be called the first "conscious" card of the individual, as the preceding cards represent the principles of consciousness and the laws of the universe that the initiate has to master. The Chariot is the culmination of the first tier of cards in the Tarot Tableau[1] representing the laws of consciousness/the universe. By mastering the principles in the preceding cards you attain the spiritual mastery represented by this card.

This image pictures the Higher Self as the Charioteer whose goal is to descend more fully into material form, represented by the chariot—the physical body. The Chariot on this card is the personal "Merkaba," the body which you have prepared to use as the vehicle for your Soul on Earth. In Ancient Egypt, the word "Merkaba" was actually constructed from three

---

1 See the Tarot Tableau in the Back of this book for more information.

smaller words: MER meant a "rotating light," KA signified "Spirit," and BA was a word for the human body. The Merkaba is the vehicle of ascension; esoterically, it is the process wherein the physical body is transformed into a vehicle for Spirit. Alternatively, the Merkaba can be seen as the "energy body"—or Spiritual body that resides in all forms. In the human being, it can be "remembered" and thus activated, or rather reactivated. The Star Tetrahedron, also known as "The Star of David" is the sacred geometrical form that is the Merkaba. It is comprised of two opposing tetrahedrons that are spinning in opposite directions.

As the body "ascends" in frequency, the Spirit can "descend" into physical form; thus the two meet in the middle, at the level of the (high) heart; on the physical body, this chakra is the thymus gland. The key to the ascension process is not the mind, or the beliefs, or even the emotions of the aspirant, but the heart. The fourth chakra stands in the middle of the body chakras; on the physical body, this chakra is the thymus gland. Its function is to bridge the higher chakras with the lower chakras.

The Merkaba, as the "vehicle" of ascension is a way for the timeless, formless, limitless Spirit to enter the experience of limitation, otherwise known as 3D or physical existence. When Spirit first came into human form on Earth, it experienced amnesia, and became crucified on the cross of Space-Time.[1] The act of ascension restores the original MEMORY of divinity (Key #2) and INTUITION (Key #5); the combination of these two principles of consciousness returns the number Seven—the Chariot. The process of the transmutation of energy to matter—the reciprocal movement of implicate to explicate and back again—is constantly at play in the created universe, but the challenge is to awaken Spirit in Matter, to awaken consciousness *inside* the dream of material existence.

> I once spent a couple of hours with Credo Mutwa, the spiritual leader of the Zulu tribe in Africa. He explained to me that Merkaba (one word) was a Zulu word meaning a space/time/ dimension vehicle. He told me that according to Zulu legend his entire tribe had come from another dimension here to Earth using the Merkaba.[2]

---

1   Key #12, The Hanged Man/REVERSAL
2   Drunvalo Melchizedek

By understanding the wisdom in the preceding cards, you are now capable of refining your thoughts and emotions to the point of "rising" in consciousness. This rise prepares the body to allow your Soul to "descend" more into your physical body; ascension of your physical/mental/emotional form to meet your Higher Self as it descends into the physical. The integration of more light into the physical causes the lightening of the physical form, and thus you "ascend." The only way the Higher Self can do this is when you have purified your mind and emotions of the heavier thoughts and emotions. We have to make ourselves receptive to the Higher Self, and so the real meaning of this card is learning to surrender limitations to a higher purpose—the intent or Will of the Higher Self.

The word "chariot" is found 44 times in the Masonic Bible; 44 is a Master number. The vision of Ezekiel in the Bible spoke of a chariot of FOUR wheels drawn by FOUR living creatures, each with FOUR wings and the FOUR faces of a lion, man, eagle, and ox. These creatures represent the fixed astrological signs, the elements, and the suits in the Tarot. The "wheel" of the chariot is shown in the Major Arcana card, #10, The Wheel of Fortune.

The letter associated with this card is "Cheth," which means "fence" or "limitation" in Hebrew. The card is also assigned to the sign of Cancer, who, with his protective shell and defensive claws, resists change. In order to ascend, you have to transcend the limitations of your beliefs (mental body) and unconscious emotions (the subconscious). This card, with its triangular composition, hints at the rewards of ascension while in the body, and this is what the "ascended masters" did: they ascended past the barriers of old, denser consciousness. They achieved what the shamans did when they traveled in their Merkaba, by assembling all of their energetic totality in their energy body. They traveled not in the physical world, but through dimensions.

The Fool has gained wisdom from the archetypes in the first six cards: from The Magician he has learned how to focus his ATTENTION, from The High Priestess, he knows that all he needs for his journey is residing in his own MEMORY—the universal Akashic records of the implicate order. The Empress showed him the richness and the creative potential of his IMAGINATION, while The Emperor demonstrated how to master his mind and control his emotional impulses with reason. This new rationality gave the Fool emotional detachment and mental INSIGHT. The Hierophant taught him how to access the wisdom of his Higher Self through his INTUITION, and finally, The Lovers showed him the powers of discrimination and choice that come with unconditional LOVE.

The Chariot represents the FOOL's body/mind/emotional self that has been purified by the discipline of the preceding cards; he has rid himself of most of his heaviest emotions and limiting beliefs, but most importantly, he has surrendered to the wisdom of his Higher Self. His hold on this realization is mostly mental, so it is tenuous at best, but he realizes that he has to practice surrender on a constant basis. His main opponent is his ego, which wants to take over the reins and drive the chariot of the Self. This, however, can never be.

The charioteer steers the chariot of his Soul through conscious choice; he directs all his energy—physical, emotional, mental—along the road laid out by the intent of his Higher Self. Like a good parent, he treats the children of his self-conscious and subconscious (his beliefs, thoughts, and emotions) with gentle firmness, compassion, and kindness.

When You get This Card in a Reading

You are going forward, but you don't seem to be moving yet. Everything is underneath the surface.

Meditation

"Circumstances don't matter, only state of being matters." ~ Bashar

THE CHARIOT

ADVENTURE

Tarot of Creativity

Up until Key #7, The Chariot/ADVENTURE, we experienced a separate existence, with very little interference from the Higher Self. When we make the bid for the freedom of higher awareness represented by this card, we let the Higher Self know that we are ready for a more aligned partnership with it; meaning that at this stage, we are open to the voice of the Higher Self.

When you pull this card in a reading, it often means victory, freedom, travel, or success, but a deeper study of the card reveals much information for the conscious creative. In the Chariot/ADVENTURE card, you are learning dominion over duality by disciplining your mind and emotions. This card is the card of choice and intent: the choice represented by your personal free will, and intent of your Higher Self. You can choose not to do this and remain unconscious, victimized by fate, or you can take the reins of the Chariot of your body/mind complex and choose the higher road of personal enlightenment. Once you make this choice, you can never go back; you can never forget what you know. If we want to go forward on our path, there is really only one choice we can make, and that is to blend with the higher Will of Spirit.

Dominion is not to be confused with domination, nor is self-discipline ever to become punishment or chastisement. The Charioteer is the master of his fate, and controls the duality of his nature: his self-conscious and subconscious with the Love and respect that he has learned from the preceding card #6, The Lovers/LOVE.

This card represents the reconciliation of opposites: the balance of limitation with freedom, the balance of personal responsibility with the spirit of adventure. Only someone who has learned to choose their thoughts and emotions can achieve this supreme balance and personal mastery. In numerology, we use reductionism to derive the meanings from any set of numbers. The Seven can come from three different combinations, and thus we can see three paths that show how the adept can arrive at this mastery:

1 + 6: The Magician/ATTENTION plus The Lovers/LOVE: Be ATTENTIVE to your unconscious thoughts/emotions and apply DISCRIMINATION/LOVE: keep the ones you want and discard whatever is unnecessary.

2 + 5: The High Priestess/MEMORY plus The Hierophant/ INTUITION: Use your EGOIC MEMORY to discover all your unconscious thoughts and emotions, and your SOUL MEMORY to remember your original self. Your INTUITION will guide you which ones you should keep and which you should discard.

3 + 4: The Empress/IMAGINATION plus The Emperor/ INSIGHT: Use your REASON to help you keep your IMAGINATION from running amok and creating a reality that you don't want. This combination of root numbers is the balance of polarities: male/female, left/right brain, nature/ mind, reason/heart, Heaven/Earth.

The task of the number Seven is to "learn to remember." When the adept achieves the aim of this card in the Major Arcana, he has prepared his body to receive more light. The preparation is the "learning" while the task of "remembering" is achieved by the cooperation of the cells of your body and your Higher Soul in bringing in this higher Light into your consciousness. Running the lighter consciousness of the Higher Self through the physical form activates the Merkaba, the counter-rotating tetrahedrons of male and female polarity, achieving the act known as "ascension."

In *The Tarot of Creativity*, the figure is speeding towards an almost invisible line on the left, representing another plane of existence. He is committed to taking the leap of faith even though he is not sure where or how he is going to land. As he flies through space in the last moment on this side of consciousness, numbers fall to the ground below him, like moments in time. He has transcended all old descriptions, thoughts and unconscious emotions, and is heading full-tilt into a new way of being: a way that integrates his three selves—the subconscious/body, self-conscious/ mind, and the super-conscious/Higher Self—into one fully-aligned being. The new level of awareness that the charioteer has achieved is a true ADVENTURE; like any adventure, it carries with it a feeling of excitement and insecurity at the same time. When we walk, we must first experience the uncertainty of imbalance so we can step forward. The Seven is the first divine number, and it is not in balance, it is not static; it moves forward in a grand leap, the leap of faith that we all must take when we truly want to go forward. Just like a child taking his first steps, you must be brave in the face of the unknown.

This grand adventure called life is not an armchair excursion; it takes courage, self-discipline, and perseverance. In The Chariot/ADVENTURE card, The Higher Self has descended more into the physical world, into your life, into the physical vehicle—the Merkaba of your body. This *movement in stillness* requires a determined and persistent effort from us as we learn to exercise our personal will and inner focus, as we learn lessons of vibrational maintenance and ultimately, of creative manifestation. Since the movement is an inner advance, the adept has to wait for evidence to appear on the outer reality.

The aspirant has to wait in faith, and learn to discern the frequency of what she desires, then take inner action to consistently transmit this frequency as a way to beckon the lines of the universe that match that frequency. This is spiritual movement, inner movement. To the casual observer, the adept isn't moving or doing anything, but she is following the lines of her intent, walking an inner path. Just as an individual bird follows the general intent of the flock, she stays in the channel of her desired frequency: she *becomes* the frequency, and thus the world changes around her, turning like a wheel around the axis of her focused attention.

The ancient, universal symbol for the Creator, or Cosmic Consciousness, is a circle (or wheel) with a dot at the center. The perimeter of the circle conceptually defines the void at the heart of the implicate. The point at the center of the symbol is the abstract representation of the *attention* of the creator being. When the spiritual seeker remembers her innate power, it automatically puts her at the center of this circle, right at the Zero Point of creation. Thus, her attention is her point of power.

As the adept steps into her own power, she knows that she must center herself with her attention, which she learned at the beginning of her journey from The Magician. At this card, The Chariot/ADVENTURE, she is putting into practice what she has learned from all the previous cards. When she focuses her attention (The Magician) to align with the intent of Spirit is sober (The Emperor) and focused on unconditional love (The Lovers), she can use her intuition (The Hierophant) to access the intent of her Higher Self. This ignites the power of the infinite creative potential that surrounds her (The High Priestess), allowing her to create in material form—in cooperation with nature (The Empress).

Unconscious behavior and thinking will be shed from your mind and body and fall to the ground as you take the courageous leap of faith into the adventure that lies before you. And, while it may seem to the casual observer that you have not even moved a muscle or traveled an inch, you have traversed miles over the desert of belief, and cleared a vast ocean of emotion in your flight.

When You get This Card in a Reading

If you get this card in a reading, know that you can achieve personal mastery only when you are choosing your thoughts and emotions. Success is not defined by the achievement of any material goals; success is the ability to be happy, no matter the circumstances.

Meditation

"For me there is only the traveling on paths that have heart, on any path that may have heart, and the only worthwhile challenge is to traverse its full length—and there I travel looking, looking breathlessly." ~ Don Juan, Carlos Castaneda, *The Teachings of Don Juan: A Yaqui Way of Knowledge*

Related to

The Tower/AWAKENING (Key #16)

7—WANDS

S = SYMBOLS
HILL = attainment, success against the odds
WAND = magic, energy

E = ENERGY
This cards shows two very strong directions: the six VERTICAL wands or staffs that seem to be trying to defeat the man, and the DIAGONAL direction of the wand that he is using to fight them off.

E = EMOTIONS
Defense. Holding one's own.

R = NUMBER
The Wands are about energy; combined with the spiritual number Seven, this card means spiritual intent or direction.

Rider Waite Smith Tarot
A man holds a hill with his staff against six other wands. The man in the picture seems to be just barely holding his own against the opposition. "One against many" may be the slogan of the hero, the iconoclast, the social activist, and the rugged individual.

KEYWORDS
proactive/taking action
taking responsibility
taking advantage
seize the moment
defending yourself
resistance/integrity
opposition/challenge
conviction/resolute

Heroism is exhausting work. The strange thing is that the true heroes of life are often unnoticed and unrewarded. As a Seven, this card is about the mental/egoic attributes of the seventh chakra (the head), as well as about the spiritual aspects of the number Seven, and about the energy/intent of the Wands suit.

This card at one level tells us that the "work" of the figure in the card has to do with holding intent against social pressure to conform, while at another level it warns us that the ego of the individual is also involved. Maybe they need to win or prove themselves. As the seventh chakra is one of the head chakras, they may need to be recognized among their peers or in their field. But a need to establish one's superiority is an attribute of a lower consciousness, and this attitude carries a heavy price.

When You get This Card in a Reading

The energy you are currently expending is the subject of this card. Consider whether it is worth continuing to expend energy in this direction. What is the underlying intent of your actions: are you doing what you are doing because of potential rewards? Or would you do what you are doing without any recognition or rewards?

Meditation

The phrase, "King of the Hill" comes to mind with this image. Are you fighting yourself or others unnecessarily?

7—FIRE

ALIGNMENT • FOCUS

Tarot of Creativity

Seven is the first spiritual number while Fire is the first suit in the path of creative manifestation; this card shows us how the energy of the Seven begins. The seventh chakra is one of the two chakras that represent the mind. This chakra represents the connection with the Higher Self and the faculty of the pituitary gland (some believe it is the pineal gland) to receive information from "higher" dimensions.

In most people the pineal and pituitary glands are shut down to a greater or lesser degree. These two glands are natural partners, and must be "opened" in order to experience enlightenment—which means that they become fully functional. In order to "wake up" the normal functions of these two glands, you have to align yourself with the intent of your Higher Self and learn how to focus your mind and your energy in a direction of your choice. When these two glands are fully open, the third eye is opened, and the reality of Eden is finally seen.

When You get This Card in a Reading
The Fire suit is about energy, intent, and alignment. Ask yourself if you are using your energy wisely, are you choosing your intent and focus, or are you reacting unconsciously to what you think is around you. This card reminds you to have steadfast persistence, be alert to your environment, and hold fast to your intent.

Meditation
Align yourself with your Higher Self; choose your focus carefully.

7—SWORDS

S = SYMBOLS
ENCAMPMENT = army, civilization, society
SWORD = thought, clarity, judgement

E = ENERGY
A strong DIAGONAL line formed by the four swords in the figure's hands directs the eye towards the gaze of the man who is staring back over his shoulder at the camp he left.

E = EMOTIONS
Sneaky. Duplicitous. Diplomacy. Disarming.

R = NUMBER
The Swords/AIR suit represents thought, and the number Seven is about intellectual achievement. This card refers to mental action; diplomacy, a speech, or clever words.

KEYWORDS
diplomacy/disarmament
disarming/charming
deception/sneakiness
avoidance/procrastination
anti-social/independent
manipulative/secretive

Rider Waite Smith Tarot
A man seems to be sneaking away with the majority of the swords from an encampment. This figure could equally be a diplomat or a thief. It may indicate a charming—a literally *disarming*—personality. Of course, the meaning of this card depends upon the context of the reading, the Querent's question, and the other cards in the reading. The figure on this card could

be the iconoclast who defies societal norms and breaks all the rules. In that case, he is actually a tool of evolution since organizations tend to prevent individual expression and inhibit progressive movement.

When You get This Card in a Reading

If you get this card in a reading, consider whether it indicates a hidden agenda, or a need to be covert. Alternatively, this card could mean cleverness or diplomacy.

Meditation

Words can be swords or shields, but at a higher level swords and shields are not needed at all.

7—AIR

HIDDEN • INTENT

Tarot of Creativity

The Seven seeks what is hidden; *intent* is the spiritual force that is behind all that manifests on the physical plane. Or, the words on this card could be taken together as a phrase: *hidden intent*—which describes quite accurately the feeling of the sneaky character in the equivalent RWS card.

The secret message of this card encourages you to discover the channel of intent in your life. It is hidden underneath your daily concerns, and cannot show until you seek it out by changing your focus from daily life to your spiritual guidance.

When You get This Card in a Reading

What is hidden and what is in the open?

Meditation

You can see what is hidden by understanding the intent below the surface.

7—CUPS

S = SYMBOLS

CLOUDS = inspiration, confusion, illusion

CUPS = emotions, subconscious

ITEMS in cups = fantasies, wishes, potentials

E = ENERGY

HOVERING energy of the cups in the clouds.

E = EMOTIONS

Imagination. Ideas. Fantasy. Confusion. Illusion.

R = NUMBER

Seven in the suit of Cups/WATER results in a card that reflects the emotional values of spiritual desires.

Rider Waite Smith Tarot

A silhouetted figure is amazed by a vision of cups with diverse offerings in each one. The figure silhouetted in the foreground appears to have emotional attachments to his visions, so most or all of them are probably fantasies coming from the egoic mind. One of them even contains a hidden face in the design of the cup, which seems to indicate that following the fantasy of worldly renown might be a path with ultimately negative results. The big question is, what does the covered figure represent? It could be the only spiritual choice in the field of attention, or it could symbolize a deeper illusion.

Seven is usually a number that means spiritual or intellectual attainment, but the figure here seems to be presented with too many possibilities or dreams. This card only makes sense when you consider the suit, and realize that these visions may be emotional fantasies that only seem to be spiritual in nature. The Seven of Cups offer seven fantasies in the cloud before the figure in the foreground. Which one should he choose? Are they just figments of an overactive imagination?

KEYWORDS

fantasies/illusions

dreams/wishes

options/alternatives

many choices

too many choices

overindulgence

dissipation/excess

confusion/overwhelming

When You get This Card in a Reading

Be aware that emotions can cloud your vision and create illusions. The imagination is a powerful tool, but the misuse of the power of emotions may keep you looking in the wrong place for the materialization of your dreams.

Meditation

Your visions may be grand but they may be ungrounded fantasies at this time.

7—WATER

DETACHMENT • DISCERNMENT

Tarot of Creativity

Just like a mirage of water on a desert might appear to a thirsty pilgrim, the energy that supports your illusions is not your thoughts, but the emotions that surround your thoughts. A thought hasn't any power unless it has an emotion accompanying it.

Use detachment and discernment to see which are emotional fantasies and which are true opportunities. Detachment helps to remove the emotional charge, and discernment helps you to determine which is the right path for you.

When You get This Card in a Reading

The energy of the number Seven as applied to the Suit of Water results in emotional sobriety through the action of detachment and discernment.

Meditation

Mental clarity is the result of emotional detachment.

7—PENTACLES

S = SYMBOLS
GRAPEVINE = fertility, abundance
HOE = work, harvest
PENTACLE = talent, wealth, health, skills

E = ENERGY
VERTICAL line of hoe points to head of farmer, and the gaze of the man directs the eye towards the seven pentacles.

E = EMOTIONS
Satisfaction. Patience. Waiting for the proper time to harvest the fruits of your labor.

R = NUMBER
One of the meanings of the number Seven is "patience" and another is "timing."

Rider Waite Smith Tarot
A man with a hoe contemplates a harvest of pentacles ripe on his vines. The image in the RWS card shows a farmer taking a rest, leaning on his hoe, looking at a harvest of pentacles growing on the vine like huge grapes. He seems to be measuring the growth of his crop.

KEYWORDS
wise investments
appreciation
hidden money
consider/evaluate
review/take stock
harvest/payoff
strategize/plan
crossroads/milestone
reflect/pause/meditate

As a Pentacle, this card's theme is about health and wealth. In both, the idea of appreciation is paramount. In the stock market or in real estate, an investment "appreciates" over time. One of the meanings of the number Seven is *timing* and another is *hidden*. When you take these two together with the theme of the suit you come up with the meaning of this card. Depending upon your concerns, this card may mean that the way forward is to appreciate what you have rather than focusing on any lack in your life.

In the area of health, look to nurturing yourself and spending time talking to your body in terms that encourage it towards the original and natural state of wellbeing: as you change your internal dialogue, your body will naturally respond with the manifestation of perfect health. In the area of wealth, look to what you have, and allow it time to grow.

You create health and wealth in your emotional body first—and the way to access the source of the creative power in your subconscious is in how you feed it with your conscious thoughts. The farmer in this picture is looking at the fruits of his labor—if he has correctly nourished the vines of his subconscious, it will produce the healthy crop that he envisioned. But if he fed the plant poison, the fruit would be unhealthy and poisonous as well. The water that he gave the plant—water represents emotions—is what determines the outcome. The subconscious can only reflect your conscious thoughts and emotions. The emotions you feel today are indicators as to how you have programmed your subconscious up until now.

The best way to change your reality is to change what is in your subconscious, by dropping your resistance to your experience—to what you have already manifested—and appreciate it instead. As you appreciate what is, your health and wealth appreciates in like measure.

Alternatively, the "hidden" nature of the Seven may point out that you have overlooked something good, or that you are about to discover hidden resources.

When You get This Card in a Reading

If you get this card in a reading, take time to evaluate the fruits of your labor and what you have achieved up until this point.

Meditation

Timing is everything.

7—EARTH

RECEPTIVITY • WILL

Tarot of Creativity

The traditional keyword phrase for the Major Arcana card of the same number, The Chariot, *receptivity-will*, is used as the words for this card.

The meaning of the card in the TOC is very similar to its counterpart in the RWS; you have to be patient in order to be able to be receptive, and you have to have a sense of timing in order to be able to properly apply your personal will. In a higher sense, this card expresses the ego's surrender (receptivity) of the individual's will to the will of Spirit.

Following the path of the Sevens through the suits, you have achieved the following: (Wands/FIRE) you *aligned/focused* your intent and energy; (Swords/AIR) you saw through to the *hidden/intent;* (Cups/WATER) you learned how to emotionally *detach* and *discern* your way through the forest of illusions. Now you are at the final manifestation of the spiritual Seven energy, and this card asks you if you are ready to take the next step.

Receptivity is one of the attributes of a creative mind, which is open and yet directed at the same time. If you were only receptive and completely open, you would be mad, not conscious. Like window shutters that open in one direction at a time, the self-conscious directs the mind through selective receptivity.

When You get This Card in a Reading

See yourself in a partnership with your Higher Self; be receptive to its will by listening to your intuition.

Meditation

A good farmer doesn't pull up the new seed to see if it has sprouted. Have faith in the growth of your creative project.

self-control
self-determination
patience/compassion
unconditional love
serenity/inner strength
kindness/patience
comprehension/perseverance
moderation/composure

S = SYMBOLS

CROWN OF LEAVES = allied with nature
LION = the ego/fear-based consciousness
LION'S MOUTH = needs of the ego
LEMNISCATE = Higher Self, wholeness
ROSES = taming passion with beauty, love
WOMAN = the Soul/Higher Self

E = ENERGY

DIAGONAL LINE going from the woman to the lion and back again in a figure-eight pattern that echoes the lemniscate above her head.

E = EMOTIONS

Love. Healing. Gentle discipline.

R = NUMBER

THE EIGHT BUILDS POWER—The Eight is the only number besides the Zero that you can draw and over again without picking up the pen from the paper. The EIGHT is the number of the builder. As the number of the Earth doubled, the Eight is the number of karma and manifestation; the universal law of cause and effect.

STRENGTH

ARCHETYPE

Rider Waite Smith Tarot

The Lion in this card represents the wounded ego, and the woman is the Higher Self, who tames the Lion with love. She teaches the ego that its desires are a poor substitute for what the ego really wants; the security and richness provided by the experience of love.

This card demonstrates how the wisdom of LOVE can surmount all problems by taking them out of the realm of unconscious desire and suffering into a higher space of compassion and understanding. The Strength card, as an Eight, represents the astrological sign of Leo, which symbolizes the stage of individuation in the progress of the evolution of consciousness, individual and collective.

> In Jungian psychology, also called analytical psychology, [individuation] expresses the process in which the individual self develops out of an undifferentiated unconscious. It is a developmental psychic process during which innate elements of personality, the components of the immature psyche, and the experiences of the person's life become integrated over time into a well-functioning whole.[1]

The self-conscious or ego is the new kid on the block of consciousness; it is the state represented by Aries and by The Magician card in the Tarot. When the Fool gets to the Strength card, he sees what happens when the ego evolves to the next octave.

The evolution of consciousness can be traced through the Major Arcana which not-so-coincidentally also corresponds to astrology. Cards #1 through #7 show the struggle to emerge into awareness. Card #7, The Chariot, is analogous to the sign of Cancer, which represents the care and protection of a mother's love. At card #8, and at the sign of Leo, the child discovers that he is separate from his mother; this is the process of individuation, and it

---

1 en.wikipedia.org/wiki/Individuation

is the reason that the ego develops. The perception of an objective reality is important only at one brief stage of evolution; when the Self becomes self-aware—when it recognizes that it is separate from the world around it. The Strength card could be said to be the part of the Tarot that best represents where humanity is at this point in our evolution.

Card #8 of the Major Arcana shows a lion—the ego, or self-conscious—being tamed by a woman dressed in white who represents the Higher Self. When the seeker, as represented by The Fool, gets to the Strength card he is at the point of understanding that the totality of the Self is a partnership of three parts: the self-conscious or ego-mind, the Higher Self, and the subconscious.

The number eight is the ancient symbol of the lemniscate turned 90 degrees; it was first used in the Tarot card, above the head of The Magician—then known as the Juggler or Magus—in the 1700s. The lemniscate is a mathematical symbol representing the concept of infinity, the idea of *limit-lessness*. If you take a Zero and twist one end 180 degrees, you end up with a lemniscate. The figure-eight shape that defines the lemniscate is also the cross-section of the inner surface of a torus: the torus is believed to be the new shape of the energy field of an evolved man. In esoteric terms, the symbol of the lemniscate stands for wholeness and completion. The symbol of the lemniscate is suggested in three ways in this card: in the number eight, in the figure above the woman, and in the hidden shape indicated by the composition of the image.

In this image, the lemniscate represents the presence of the Higher Self, in the symbol above the woman's head and in the invisible lines of the image's composition. You can trace an invisible figure eight starting from the head of the woman down to the feet of the lion, crossing in the middle where the lion and the woman intersect: at the mouth of the lion and the caressing hands of the woman. This image conveys the partnership of the divine triad:

TOP—Higher Self symbolized as the lemniscate above the head of the woman

MIDDLE—self-conscious at the point of intersection of the lion's mouth (the mental body/egoic needs) and woman's hands

BOTTOM—physical body/subconscious: the feet of the lion

True strength is quiet and unassuming. It conquers fear with love. Key #8/STRENGTH is the beginning of the second tier of cards in the Tarot Tableau representing how you can apply the first seven principles, represented by the first seven cards in the Tarot, in order to master life.

The WOMAN in white is the Soul of the Querent, in its purified form, transformed by the alchemy of The Chariot, which merged the Higher Self with the physical body, and by the purified ATTENTION of The Magician. The Fool learned to use his reason properly through The Emperor/INSIGHT card: he became aware of and quelled the passions and needs of the ego, so that his mind would not be sending unconscious images to his body/subconscious.

Many people think that emotions are impossible to control, and this is certainly true if you listen only to your mind. This card tells us how to hear the voice of the Higher Self by convincing the ego or mental body to quiet down its incessant chatter of judgments, value systems, and concerns.

This is why one of the first efforts of any spiritual adept is to find a way to de-identify with the ego. Many people think that they have to kill their ego in order to end its domination, but this doesn't work. Since the ego thinks it is you, it thinks that if it dies, you die too. Any attempt to kill the ego will result in making it feel threatened. It reacts by going into overdrive in order to survive.

The ego thinks that it is protecting you somehow by worrying and planning. It assumes that it is all you are. The only way to get the ego to let go is to let it know that it is safe to let go. The ego can only be quiet when it feels safe. The Tarot is not encouraging you to kill the ego, instead, it shows you how to integrate the ego into the whole self, by giving it tasks to which it is better suited. The trick is to find ways to assure it that it is safe to let go of worry and concern. Once the ego feels safe, it can understand that it no longer needs to be in control, and now it is safe to let the wisdom of the Higher Self in.

The ego thinks that it is protecting you when it controls you, but it has gone from being your guardian to being your guard. The only way to make the ego feel safe is to love it, and appreciate it for what it does well. This card shows you how to give your ego a new job description, one that serves the total self instead of just the egoic self. In effect, you change its job from CEO of your company to the personal assistant of your Higher Self.

The LION in this card represents the fear-based ego; a consciousness that is based upon a false idea of separation. As long as your limiting beliefs and fear place you *outside* the light of LOVE, you cannot be healed *through* LOVE. The conscious individual has learned how to choose his thoughts and emotions—he chooses his vibrational frequency. Once his emotions are conscious and his thoughts are no longer hidden from himself, he has achieved personal power—enlightenment.

This card shows the proper partnership of the three elements of the Self. The WOMAN in white is the evolved version of the subconscious in the card The Empress. She is Mother Nature/the personal subconscious/ the eternal Soul. She receives instructions and vision from the Higher Self, represented by the LEMNISCATE above her head. This figure, which looks like an eight on its side, shows us the way that creative energy naturally flows into form and back again into Spirit.

We can see this same figure-eight shape if we trace the energy that flows from the woman to the lion and back up again. This is the way unconditional love flows: from the giver to the receiver and back again; from the observer to the observed, and back again; whereupon the observed becomes the observer and the observer becomes the observed. The particle collapses into the wave and the wave coalesces back into a particle, ad infinitum, as the observer comes to realize his complicity and personal part in the never-ending flow of creation.

The ego was gravely wounded at the moment of incarnation; the moment when the individual became a separate awareness in a body on Earth. The LION as a separate ego has had to endure and survive a harsh existence, outside of LOVE. Even though he has made himself king of all the animals, nothing in the world of the mind or body can satisfy his eternal hunger and thirst; he is never fulfilled and is always wanting.

As the lion cries out from the pain of his Incarnation Wound, a beautiful WOMAN comes to him, unafraid. At first, the LION responds by roaring louder. Does this being not know he is the king of the Earth, and that he could kill her with one swipe of his huge paw? Then he hears her angelic voice—tones of such ethereal beauty that he lays down at her feet. She reaches down and gently closes his mouth—suddenly he is no longer hungry: his stomach is magically full. He has no needs or hungry desires. The roses from around her waist fall gently on him as she looks tenderly at him. He licks her hand in love, surrender, and adoration.

The Higher Self tames the passions and needs of the wounded ego/ LION with love. She eases his hunger, heals him, and calms his fears. She closes his mouth, and shows him the tenderness of love. The LION responds by licking her hand. The Wound of Incarnation—the pain of separation—is now healed through the power of Divine Love.

The two circles of the figure eight that were unnaturally separated by the descent into matter, are now rejoined; the energy of Spirit now flows freely into the physical body and the experiences of the individual now flow towards the Higher Self to be integrated. The healed ego no longer has a need for superficial, material things, as it was only a way to fill the hole left by the pain of separation from his Higher Self. The LION will then lie down with the lamb; the ego no longer needs to conquer or dominate once he has the only thing that he has ever needed: LOVE.

When You get This Card in a Reading
You are the originator of the reality you perceive.

Meditation
As you sow, so you will reap.

8

STRENGTH

I-MAGE

Tarot of Creativity

The brain cannot perceive directly. It perceives according to its belief system, according to previous experiences that it has catalogued. Actual experiences or fantasies are experienced by the mind as real and of equal value.

In *The Tarot of Creativity*, the idea of creating by generating a conscious image is conveyed by using the hyphenated word, I-MAGE. The hyphen separates the "I" from the word "mage;" like the phrase "I am," it implies that you are a *conscious creator*. As a wise mage, you are deliberately sending conscious images to your subconscious, and thus creating your reality. You choose what you want to create by mastering INTENT, the skill demonstrated by The Magician (1). As you apply your personal WILL (1) to a SPIRITUAL (7) concern, you combine Keys one with seven and achieve eight, the number of material manifestation.

The number Eight symbolizes descent of the Spirit more fully (consciously) into matter. The eighth chakra is the chakra of the Higher Self, sometimes called the Seat of the Soul; it sits about two feet above the top of the head, and carries the attributes of Christ Consciousness: selflessness, spiritual awareness, unconditional love, and community awareness.

The figure eight is two Zeros connected by a bridge or passageway. The Eight symbolizes the relationship of the divine triad of the Self: the Higher Self resides at the top of the figure eight, the body-emotions or physical plane is at the bottom of the figure, while the self-conscious is the bridge or passageway where the two lines cross in the middle.

The traditional keyword of the Strength card is "suggestion." We are thought forms created by our Higher Self, but we have been gifted with the right of self-determination. The Higher Self will not violate the Law of Free Will by dominating us. In the I-MAGE card, the self-conscious, or the egoic self, has surrendered to the direction of the Higher Self. It has accepted the intent of the Higher Self as its own: it emits a higher vibration than it did when it was unconscious. As a result, the ego (mental body) and the emotional body of the lower self have stopped being a block between the suggestions (the intent) of the Higher Self. Thus, things that are chosen by the Self are now able to manifest freely, because the energy of the entire Self is flowing and whole; no longer separated by limiting beliefs or unprocessed emotions.

We are scouts on the frontier of awareness: we have ventured boldly into a very dense plane of existence. But now, with Key #8, Strength, we have surrendered to the direction of our Higher Self, so we are now using more of the energy and direction from our Higher Selves. In our previous existence as beings of lower consciousness, we had to get our energy from other people or animals—we had to hunt and exploit others for their energy. Thus, the ongoing drama and karma of 3D existence.

The self-conscious was created by the Higher Self as a thought form, and bestowed with the gifts of intelligence and free will. In the motion created by the focused intent of the Higher Self, the thought form evolves into a creative and autonomous being, governing its own form and determining its own reality. Ultimately, it becomes a creator in its own right, sending out thought forms that, in turn, evolve into individuated consciousness with free will of their own. The whole structure of the creative process resembles a fractal where each piece is an exact copy of the whole form, replicating itself ad infinitum.

Once we absorb the wisdom of this card, we no longer experience life from a purely materialistic/dualistic view. We now understand that there is no such thing as random occurrences; and while we still cannot see anything but the tip of the iceberg, we know that a greater reality lies underneath. We see beyond the superficial and know that random things such as disease or accidents cannot happen anymore to us, as there is no longer any reason for Spirit to use these things as motivators for us. We see how we can align ourselves with our Higher Self by giving up the need of the ego to know, by giving up the mind's need to understand.

We have laid our ego's insecurity and fear to rest for good, as we begin to be able to see the holistic version of reality that belongs to the Higher Self. Thus we begin to re-experience the unity that once belonged to us when we were a part of the Garden of Eden.

When You get This Card in a Reading

Use your imagination to create a world of your choice.

Meditation

Your mind experiences your imaginary thoughts as real. A gymnast who uses her imagination to envision a successful pass, is actually executing the event in the perception of her mind. We can create a new reality by allowing ourselves to imagine it.

Related to

The Star/THE REVELATION (Key #17)

8—WANDS

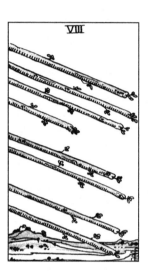

S = SYMBOLS

LANDSCAPE = material existence

WANDS = energy-to-matter conversion

E = ENERGY

Strong DIAGONAL movement.

E = EMOTIONS

Flow. Alignment. Speed.

R = NUMBER

This card shows the beginning of the Eight's powerful energy, flowing towards an ultimate manifestation.

Rider Waite Smith Tarot

Eight wands fly through the sky. This image is very simple and enigmatic. Notice that the wands in this picture are all going in the same direction—this indicates the meaning of the image: the words *flow*, *fast*, and *aligned* come to mind.

KEYWORDS
flow/alignment
speed/rush/fast
resolution/culmination
message/announcement
attracting abundance
success/manifestation

When You get This Card in a Reading

If you get this card in a reading be prepared for things to move fast.

Meditation

What you started is now about to finally manifest, don't be confused by the sudden rush of energy.

8—FIRE

FLOW • RESOLVE

Tarot of Creativity

The Tarot of Creativity card contains two words: *flow* and *resolve*. The flow of energy must be maintained through personal resolve in order to manifest or build your dreams.

When You get This Card in a Reading

The number Eight is about building power, and the Wands/FIRE suit is the beginning of the energy of this number, meaning that the beginning of the end of the manifestation process is happening now. To use the beautiful flow of this energy, resolve to hold the original intent of your idea.

Meditation

Allow yourself to flow with events/a test of your resolve.

8—SWORDS

S = SYMBOLS

BLINDFOLD = not able to see the future
BINDINGS = bondage of old beliefs
CASTLE = difficulties, old goals
MOUNTAIN = high, goals, unassailable
PALISADE of swords = initiation
SWORDS = thoughts, judgment, beliefs
WATER = subconscious, emotions

E = ENERGY

The VERTICAL lines of swords in this image resemble a palisade or defensive barrier. The woman's blindfold and binding form a spiral, "unraveling" shape that is continued by the flowing lines of the water.

E = EMOTIONS

Blockage. Emotional despair. Not able to see the future. Having to feel our way forward blindly.

R = NUMBER

The Eight of Swords shows the difficulty the mind has with progress if the belief system and emotional attachments to the past form a barrier to the forward movement forecast in the Eight of Wands.

KEYWORDS
restricted/restrained
blocked/limited
victimization
persecution/obstacles
confusion/frustration
lack of direction
blind/unconscious
powerless/inactive
cautious/insecure
shamanic initiation

Rider Waite Smith Tarot

A blindfolded and bound woman is stepping carefully through a barricade of swords. The Querent must walk through a gauntlet of societal conditioning and discard old thoughts before she can fully release old goals and the past.

As she walks past the barriers of swords she is "unraveling" her old beliefs and limitations, leaving the unattainable old paradigm behind (the castle on the mountain). In the distance a castle perches on the summit of a craggy mountain with no apparent access route. Despite the emotions in this card, the figure on this card is on her way, as she experiences an initiation into a new world that she cannot yet see. She must endure the blindness of this initiation as she casts off all that she knew, if she is to truly build a new future.

When You get This Card in a Reading
The blindness indicated by the image in the card is only temporary. It indicates an initiation into a different awareness; a blindfold renders other senses more acute.

Meditation
Shamanic/spiritual initiation, a test of inner vision and resolve.

8—AIR

UNIFY • INTEGRATE

Tarot of Creativity
The Eight is made up of the marriage of two Fours; visualize the Four as a square and stack those squares on top of each other to make a squared figure eight.

Eight is the number of karma, which is simply the law of cause and effect. The Eight of Air in *The Tarot of Creativity* contains two words, *unify/integrate*: in order to integrate the diverse elements of your life, you have to understand what it means to truly accept them and welcome them into the totality of you. Once you do, you can go forward and build a new future. The wise Querent learns that she should not suppress or judge her old thoughts or beliefs but she should no longer give them energy. Otherwise she will recreate a future that she doesn't want.

When You get This Card in a Reading
To build or go forward, you must learn how to unify and integrate.

Meditation
Focus your attention on unification and integration.

8—CUPS

S = SYMBOLS

MOON = subconscious, dreams, emotions
MOUNTAINS = lofty goals, wisdom
NIGHT = leaving the past, contemplation
STAFF = mastery, walking aid; going forward
STREAM = flowing emotions

E = ENERGY

The RED cloak of the figure and the bright YELLOW moon call our attention as a bright accent in an otherwise monochromatic image. The ACTIVE diagonal line of the retreating man directs our attention to the distant mountains. There is a non-equilateral triangle composition formed by the figure, the moon and the eight cups in the foreground.

E = EMOTIONS

Cutting one's losses. Going into the unknown. Leaving for higher ground.

R = NUMBER

The lesson of the number eight in the Suit of Cups has to do with the need to release the emotional bondage that keeps us from going forward.

KEYWORDS
surrender/let go
gain perspective
take a vacation
resolution/end
hopeless/burned out
spiritual realization
emotional detachment
cut your losses

Rider Waite Smith Tarot

A man walks away from all his cups on a moonlit night. As a card in the Cups suit, this card refers to your emotional reality, not to your mental reality. Many esoteric practices talk about attaining the state of detachment. But they are not talking about attachment to things, or even attachment to thoughts; they are referring to *emotional* attachment. The whole manifestation process depends upon emotions. Emotions are the catalyst that takes a lifeless thought and gives it life.

The figure in this image is taking a journey under the cover of night toward a far-distant mountain—he is leaving all that he has known. This leave-taking might be a temporary retreat; perhaps he goes to the mountain for a respite from the pressures of his life, or he may be choosing to contemplate on top of the mountain like a hermit in order to gain a new, higher perspective on his life.

When he comes down, he may decide that the cups (emotional reality) he left behind no longer serve him. Or he may be leaving for good. There is a kind of sadness in this image. Perhaps it is a regret that he faced already, but that somehow still clings to him, a sadness or nostalgia for that which can never be again.

When You get This Card in a Reading
As an Eight, the energy of emotions is emphasized as the building mechanism that it is.

Meditation
Walking away may be the best solution at this time; leave no attachments and have no regrets.

8—WATER

RECEIVE • RELEASE

Tarot of Creativity
Consider that you are on a journey, a long walk to the mountains in the distance. There is no goal; you know that you will be on this journey your whole life. Do you need any of the baggage that is weighing you down?

The Eight of Water in the TOC comforts us with the thought that the process of releasing emotions to release the past is a natural preliminary to manifesting the new reality promised by the Eight. The *receive/release* pattern traces the natural flow of the infinity sign, which is the figure 8 on its side. In order to obtain the aabundant life promised by the number eight, you have to experience both sides of the flow of life.

The infinite line of the lemniscate teaches us that in order to experience abundance, we have to be able to give as well as receive. And a person who is not able to *receive* or *release* is stopping the natural flow of life, which expresses itself as change and abundance.

When You get This Card in a Reading

If you get this card in a reading think of what you are holding on to, and how your life would change if you decided to release it. Alternatively, you may find yourself on the other side of the figure eight sign, you might have done a great job of releasing all that doesn't serve you on your journey; now is the time to allow yourself to open up to receive.

Meditation

Learn to let go in order to experience the flow of abundance in your life.

8—PENTACLES

S = SYMBOLS
CITY = social approbation/acceptance
HAMMER = hammering out the details
WORKBENCH = hard work, labor

E = ENERGY
The VERTICAL line of six Pentacles on a wall dominates this image. The leg of the man and the hammer leads the eye to his face. The gaze of the man directs our attention to what he is making.

E = EMOTIONS
Hard work. Labor. Attention to detail. Contentment. Being in the moment. Creating. Realizing one's dreams.

R = NUMBER
The energy of the number Eight that started in the Eight of Wands manifests into physical form when it arrives at the suit of Pentacles.

KEYWORDS
attention to detail
diligent/consistent
hard work/production
skill/craftsmanship
dedication/steadfast
learning new skill
research/fact finding
detective work
painstaking/careful
methodical disciplined

Rider Waite Smith Tarot
A craftsman seems to be engraving or making pentacles on a work bench. The suit of Pentacles refers to very physical issues such as health and wealth. The figure in the RWS card seems to be literally making money. Or perhaps he is working hard to regain his health.

The artisan is engraving the magical symbol of the five-pointed star—the pentagram—into the pentacle. He is using the magic of this talisman to build a manifest reality through his energy, will, and hard work. The pentacle is an ancient mystical symbol. The five-pointed star represents man, and the circle represents Spirit; together they mean "man in Spirit," or the spiritual man. The esoteric meaning of this card is that the figure is building his perfected Self by understanding and working with the divine materials or tools at his hand, matter and spirit. He is building a new world with his enhanced spiritual understanding.

189

When You get This Card in a Reading

Time to make money, pay attention to detail; demonstrate your workmanship, perseverance, and hard work. If you get this card in a reading, know that it is time to go forward with your project, and hammer out the details.

Meditation

"The details are not the details. They make the design." ~ Charles Eames

8—EARTH

CONFIGURE • BUILD

Tarot of Creativity

The Eight is the number of *manifestation*. You can trace the creative process of manifestation through the suits of the Tarot. The path starts as pure energy in the Eight of FIRE/Wands; the intent is filtered through the belief system in the Eight of AIR/Swords; the Eight of WATER/Cups washes away emotions and karma. Finally the energy that started out as intent in the suit of Fire manifests in the Eight of EARTH/Pentacles as a physical form.

When You get This Card in a Reading

There are two parts to the final stage of manifesting eight energy indicated by the Suit of Earth: the first stage—configure—prepares the ground for the next stage—build.

Meditation

Spend time properly configuring your design/build according to your plans.

8

wisdom/knowledge
silence/reflection
solitude/spiritual path
inner search
deep understanding
retreat/philosophical

S = SYMBOLS

BEARD = wisdom gained through time
CLOAK = material existence, the body
GRAY = the balance of duality, wisdom
HERMIT = pilgrim, master, teacher
LANTERN = container for consciousness
LIGHT = Christ consciousness
MOUNTAINS = spiritual attainment
NIGHT = ignorance, unconsciousness
SNOW = purity, wisdom, time
STAFF = magical support

E = ENERGY

The DIAGONAL LINE of The Hermit's staff directs attention to the Hermit's forehead.

E = EMOTIONS

Age. Wisdom. Hard-won arcane knowledge.

R = NUMBER

THE NINE SERVES—nine is the final number in the sequence; it signifies completion, attainment or mastery.

THE HERMIT

ARCHETYPE

Rider Waite Smith Tarot

THE HERMIT.

The DIAGONAL LINE of The Hermit's staff directs the viewer's attention to the Hermit's forehead, the position of the third eye, or pineal gland—the spiritual vision of the Hermit. He gazes with affection towards the light in his lantern. The YELLOW of the light is echoed in the color of the STAFF which brings the attention back down in an oblique circle to the bottom of the staff resting on the mountain.

Key #9 THE HERMIT shows an old man who has attained spiritual enlightenment. In his youth, he climbed the mountain, and spent many years alone in a cave on the heights. He was determined to gain spiritual wisdom, so he persevered though all the challenges and loneliness of his solitary path, but he didn't realize at the beginning of his journey that it would take him his entire life, or that he would have to sacrifice everything that he valued to achieve his goal.

The Hermit as an archetype brings to mind the ancient techniques practiced by all spiritual aspirants: meditation, silence, solitude. He has taken a lifelong vision quest on the MOUNTAIN and now comes back down into the valley—back into the world—to teach what he knows. He is the Magician at a higher level; he combines the Strength/I-MAGE of the Eight with the ATTENTION of the Magician.

The Hermit enjoys a long tradition in mythology. One example in Western tradition is the legend of the mage Merlin. Merlin was the wise advisor of King Arthur, the ruler who desired to recreate a heaven on Earth, which Arthur called "Avalon." The numerology of the name, Avalon is: 1 + 4 + 1 + 3 + 6 + 5 = 20 = 2—the number of balance and harmony. This mythical Eden of all spiritual seekers may come under other names, but it always represents the same principle of balance and wholeness: the goal of the spiritual seeker is not to escape duality for oneness, but to be aware of oneness *while experiencing duality.*

The Hermit has learned that the point of spiritual awareness is not to deny the flesh and leave the earth for heaven, but to bring a higher consciousness back down into the collective. As an enlightened man, he wants to bring Heaven to Earth. The Hermit descends the mountain of his ATTAINMENT and seeks to share his LIGHT with others in the Valley of Darkness that is below. He started out as a young FOOL fresh and new to life, and now he is an old man. He has long forgotten what it is to live among people, but he desires now to share his light with others. So he journeys down the mountain. His STAFF, which is a longer version of the WAND he wielded as a young man in The Magician, helps him maintain his footing on the slopes, signifying that his MAGIC sustains him now.

The Hermit has attained personal power, but knows that power is only attained after a lifetime of personal discipline. Power is never used against another, since the nature of true power is solely a personal affair.

He carries the light of his wisdom in a LANTERN in his right hand, holding it aloft to share his LIGHT with others, and light their path. This light is a six-pointed STAR symbolizing Christ consciousness—unity consciousness. The six-pointed STAR is the perfect divine balance and unification of the male and female principles of duality. The knowledge of the unity that underlies all appearances is the gift of wisdom that he wants to share with the people of the valley—those that he left behind in his youth when he started up the mountain in search of truth.

Will the people in the valley listen? Probably not. The Hermit doesn't preach, and after years of solitude he has either lost his power of speech, or more likely, lost his desire to speak. Talking cannot convey what he knows. But all The Hermit has to do is shine the light of higher awareness, and it will change all those who see it.

When You get This Card in a Reading
It is time to come down from the mountain and share your knowledge.

Meditation
Learning cannot lead to wisdom: wisdom is not learned, it can only be remembered or discovered, since it is always within you.

THE HERMIT

EMERGENCE
THE HERMIT

EMERGENCE

Tarot of Creativity

The title of Key #9 is EMERGENCE. The Hermit represents the perfected man, a man who has realized his spiritual nature while in physical form; the disciple of consciousness is transformed into the teacher.

The Seeker's life as an ordinary man and a seeker is over. Like a butterfly, he was completely changed by his long incubation period in the chrysalis (his cave on the mountain); now he emerges into a new life, which has transformed to meet him.

The number Nine is the number of individual attainment: the seeker that started out his descent into matter as The Fool is now on the other side of his life as an old man; he has journeyed through the previous numbers to reach the number Nine, and now his search is done. His long spiritual apprenticeship is over; no longer does he seek anything outside of himself, as he knows that all that he ever sought has always been buried inside of him, buried under the conditioning of the holographic projection of daily life. While on the mountain in the isolation of hermitage, his life became a vision quest. Finally, the wisdom of wholeness settled upon him, comforted him, and revealed its secrets to him. He carries this vision with him as he emerges from the cave—the womb of incubation—on the mountaintop and descends back down to join the human collective.

Most mystics seek the same thing: the release from the limitations of our social condition and to be able to see beyond the illusion of duality. They seek to become "clairvoyant"—a word that simply means "clear-seeing." The ability to "see clearly" is gained by those who purify and activate what is referred to as the "third eye"—the activation of the pineal gland. The mystics and spiritual adepts who have been able to do this are called "seers" in Native American traditions. The Hermit has become a seer who now returns down the mountain to help his fellow man.

What did The Hermit find on the mountain? He sought the snow-covered heights in search of the truth behind appearances. He instinctively knew that what others took for truth was just the illusion of duality—the lie of separation. It took him much time—his whole earthly existence, in fact—but he attained the wisdom he sought when he finally merges completely with his Higher Self: this is what the ancients call "faith."

When You Get This Card in a Reading
Time to emerge from the cocoon.

Meditation
The butterfly emerges from the cocoon fully formed, but few suspect what the lowly caterpillar had to experience first before it could fly.

Related to
The Moon/DREAMING (Key #18)

9—WANDS

S = SYMBOLS
BANDAGE on head = survival of difficulties
PALISADE = difficulties overcome, initiation
WANDS = spiritual, intent, energy

E = ENERGY
UPRIGHT lines of eight wands form a STATIC structure or background behind the figure. The only active line in the picture is the staff in the man's hands which is at a very slight angle off the vertical. Overall, this is an INACTIVE composition.

E = EMOTIONS
Initiation passed. Rest. A hard-won fight. Difficulties in the past. Personal mastery. Victory.

R = NUMBER
The number Nine is the second spiritual number: the number of personal attainment.

KEYWORDS
defense/protection
achievement
hard-won success
wariness/suspicion
perseverance
wounded warrior
willpower/integrity

9

Rider Waite Smith Tarot
A man with a bandage on his head leans against a staff, and looks over his shoulder at the other eight wands behind him. There are eight wands forming a palisade, wall, or matrix behind the figure. This implies that the man has built something, or that some expenditure of energy is behind him, in the past, and now he is resting upon his staff, the ninth wand. It looks like he needs that rest; the bandage on his head indicates that he has fought for the attainment that is the meaning of the number Nine. Notice that the figure is alone; the Nine is about personal mastery—individual attainment.

When You get This Card in a Reading
If you receive this card in a reading, remember that just because you have worked hard to get to this point, you don't necessarily have to defend your gains, but you can take a moment for reflecting on how you got here.

Meditation

Courage in the face of adversity, able to take all comers and handle any situation.

9—FIRE

INDEPENDENT • RESPONSIVE

Tarot of Creativity

The Nine of Fire is the beginning of the energy of the number Nine, which is the last spiritual number in the progression from 1-9 in the number sequence.

The person who attains the wisdom of this number understands that he is on his own, that he must attain personal mastery. He understands that at this point he must think and act independently of his social conditioning and respond to inner guidance, rather than to his ego's needs and concerns.

The Nine of Fire shows that the Querent has achieved success after a difficult rite of passage or initiation; this is the first stage of the energy of the Nine: the level of intent.

When You get This Card in a Reading

Use the power of intent to define your independence and be responsive to the direction of the will of your Higher Self.

Meditation

Think and act independently of your social conditioning/respond to inner guidance.

9—SWORDS

S = SYMBOLS
BED = rest, dreams, nightmare, the Earth
HEAD in hands = worry, distress
ROSES on quilt = physical needs, desires
SWORDS = mental, thought, fears, beliefs
ZODIAC on quilt = 12 states of consciousness

E = ENERGY
Strong HORIZONTAL lines dominate this picture. Horizontal lines are lines of CALM and rest, but the figure's UPRIGHT figure interrupts this calm by intersecting or INTERRUPTING them. The figure has his head in his hands, and this small circle of attention is the main focal point of the image.

E = EMOTIONS
Distress. Worry. Nightmare. Disturbed rest.

KEYWORDS
anxiety/fear
worry/doubt
guilt/regret
despair/depression
dark night of the soul
sleeplessness/unwell

R = NUMBER
The number Nine is the last number in the sequence of numerology; it means attainment, completion. In the suit of Swords, it shows what happens when the mind tries to be in charge, overthinking or over-planning.

Rider Waite Smith Tarot
A woman sits up in bed, head in hands, nine swords above her bed. The ego identifies with thinking; it defines itself with thoughts, preferences, and beliefs. Many times these thoughts and beliefs are inherited and arbitrary, but this is how the ego tries to establish its identity and uniqueness. The incessant chattering of the unenlightened mind is what the Buddhists call the "monkey mind." Although the ego thinks that what it is chattering about is important, it is only mindless chatter.

The egoic mind associates change with death; it thinks any change equals the death of the ego; and in its megalomania, the ego thinks that when it dies so does the whole person. When the ego feels threatened, it will fight tooth and nail to preserve the comfortable and relatively safe status quo. Even if you have nothing to worry about, an unhealthy ego will invent something to worry about.

The brain/ego is always trying to figure things out; it needs to know everything and to control everything. But this is the reverse of the proper order. The Higher Self is supposed to be the director of the whole Self, not the other way around.

Nine is the number of individual attainment; in this case, since it is in the Suit of Swords/AIR, this card is about thinking. If you think too much, or take the mental path too far without disciplining your mind, you can find yourself worrying about the future or regretting the past. In either case, your mind's incessant chatter is not allowing you to be present.

This card shows the misuse of the power of the mind represented by the Suit of Swords. Mental mastery does not mean that the Self engages in worry or negative fantasies; instead, the ego must surrender control to Spirit. Otherwise, the mind persists in useless mental confabulation; it misuses the power of imagination to worry about the future or regret the past instead of being present.

Is your mind going around in circles like a dog chasing its own tail? Try to build silence into your life at regular intervals. Pay extreme attention to details and really feel the world through your senses; this shuts off the mind for short periods of time.

When You get This Card in a Reading
If you get this card in a reading, think about what is worrying you or uppermost in your mind.

Meditation
Does worry ever solve anything? Does anxiety ever produce a positive result?

9—AIR

WISDOM • LUCIDITY

Tarot of Creativity

The number Nine signifies personal attainment of the path represented by the suit, in this case, mental mastery. Since the Nine is the number of personal power and individual mastery, the card in the Air suit shows how this mastery might be carried out in the mental body as wisdom, which gives us the lucidity of a mind that is calm and rested.

A calm mind provides the perfect blank canvas for the Higher Self to write upon. If action is required she will know what to do because it will come as an inspiration in her mind. Until then, she can let her mind rest in security, confident in the guidance of Spirit.

Meditation is not contemplation or focusing, rather the purpose of meditation is to arrive at the state of no-thought. In that state, we receive all kinds of "silent knowledge" and are guided in every detail of our lives. We have merged our lower self with our Higher Self in a more integrated way.

When You get This Card in a Reading

When you have accrued enough "inner silence" you start to see the reality underlying the chatter of the mind, the energy that supports and charges everything with life.

Meditation

Clearing your mind of old thought patterns is the goal of mindfulness: this is called "wisdom." Mindfulness isn't thinking—it is the absence of thought. Paradoxically, this state of non-thought is a state of utter lucidity.

9—CUPS

S = SYMBOLS
CUP = emotions, abundance, offering
LEMNISCATE = the reciprocal nature of life
MAN = innkeeper, landowner

E = ENERGY
The UPRIGHT lines of the curtain, sitting man, and cups indicate a strong foundation.

E = EMOTIONS
Satisfaction.   Fulfillment.   Harmony.
Self-satisfaction. Smugness. Self-confidence.

R = NUMBER
As a Nine in the Suit of Cups, it expresses personal mastery in the area of emotions.

Rider Waite Smith Tarot

A man sits satisfied and sated before a row of cups poised on a wall behind him. The folded arms of the innkeeper are drawn in the shape of a LEMNISCATE, indicating a reciprocity of emotions (Cups suit); the giving and receiving of love, affection, wellbeing, and the establishment of a mood of harmony and good-feeling. This card is often called the "wish fulfillment" card. And while it speaks of personal fulfillment, its deeper meaning is that of reciprocity: as Shakespeare said that the more love you give, the more you have, for "both are infinite." (Romeo & Juliet, II,ii).

The Nine of Cups is about the mastery of emotions. The enlightened individual pours love out into the universe, and the universe returns (or reflects) that love three-fold. The Three of creativity multiplied by itself equals the Nine of personal mastery, and foreshadows the next number: the Ten of harmony and social awareness.

When You get This Card in a Reading
Even if your wishes are fulfilled today, they may not be fulfilled tomorrow. You can't be at the top of the Wheel of Fortune all the time.

KEYWORDS
success/smugness
fulfillment/satisfaction
indulgence/pride
contentment/hedonism
sensuality/savoring
enjoyment/appreciation

Meditation

What will you do when your wishes are finally fulfilled?

9—WATER

SOBRIETY • INTEGRITY

Tarot of Creativity

The Nines are about personal mastery and about solitude, contemplation, and independent effort. In *The Tarot of Creativity*, the Nine of Water indicates a mastery of emotional awareness, *sobriety*. To master your emotions doesn't mean to suppress, deny, or destroy them but to consciously choose them.

Emotions are the main tool of creation on the earth plane. We are creating our reality with the energy of our emotions all the time. This is called karma, which in the plane of duality is simply a function of the binary system of cause and effect. All of duality is a mathematical equation; it seeks balance. If you drop a ball from the top of a building, it will certainly fall. The law of gravity seeks a 100 percent conclusion to the equation or relationship of time and space.

The decision to become a conscious creator carries with it the responsibility to use the tools of creation wisely. We can continue to be ignorant of our power, and continue to be a victim of the results of our unconscious behavior; or we can choose to take responsibility for the creative power of our thoughts and emotions.

When You get This Card in a Reading

Emotions are a tool in the hands of a master, but in the hands of the average person they are like a runaway bulldozer. A master uses his emotions to build his world.

Meditation

Emotional sobriety: the prerequisite of wisdom and the forerunner of integrity.

9—PENTACLES

S = SYMBOLS

FALCON = clear vision; (hooded) domesticated
GARDEN = life, bounty, abundance, harvest
GRAPEVINE = fertility, abundance

E = ENERGY

The VERTICAL lines of the woman direct our gaze to the hooded falcon that is resting on her arm. This is a STATIC picture that indicates domesticity and an established foundation or achievement.

E = EMOTIONS

Wellbeing. Luxury. Comfort. Sensuality. Hedonism. Attainment. Dominion.

R = NUMBER

The path of the Nines end with the Nine of Pentacles: this card shows how the Querent benefits from the manifestation of the energy invested in all the preceding cards.

KEYWORDS
independent
self-sufficient
self-disciplined
refined tastes
comfortable/leisure
luxurious/artful
gracious/diplomatic
success/achievement
patron of the arts
support/abundance

Rider Waite Smith Tarot

A woman in a garden surrounded by a harvest of nine pentacles holds a hooded falcon. The Pentacles are about material existence: health, wealth; well-being. This figure enjoys her success as a personal Garden of Eden. For now, she is content to enjoy the luxury and the sense of rest for which she has worked so hard.

The woman in the garden is alone; she might have sacrificed her freedom for the comfort of material possessions, as the hood on the falcon indicates. The falcon will not attempt to fly while the hood of domesticity is on his head, and the woman may have sacrificed her higher goals for personal comfort. Perhaps she chose to marry for money, rather than go for success of her own.

Or perhaps the reverse is true; in vying for independence and self-sufficiency—laudable goals in themselves—she refused help that would have brought her friends and a social circle. But this may be a good experience; aloneness is not the same as loneliness.

When You get This Card in a Reading
If you get this card in a reading, look at the current period as a way of taking stock of your life. Something feels complete. Put yourself on a mini vacation of the senses; enjoy the fruits of your labor. You have achieved something on your own.

Meditation
Relax and enjoy all that life has to offer.

9—EARTH

COMPLETION • KNOWING

Tarot of Creativity
The Nines complete the numbers in the system of numerology. There is a sense of completion in your life as you look back and see your path and see how all the energy that you have invested up until now has manifested. You are content and confident in your inner knowing.

When You get This Card in a Reading
Allow yourself to enjoy the feelings of security, confidence and protection that comes from the knowledge that your Higher Self is participating in your life.

Meditation
Something is finally complete. Trust your inner wisdom, the silent knowledge that is the voice of your Soul.

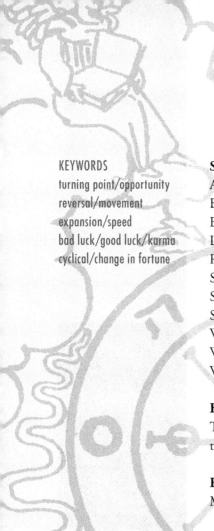

S = SYMBOLS

ANGEL = Aquarius
BULL = Taurus
EAGLE = Scorpio
LION = Leo
RED FIGURE = Egyptian god Anubis
SNAKE = Kundalini, life
SPHINX = the riddle of life
SYMBOLS = elements
WHEEL = the symbol of the goddess Fortuna
WRITING 1 = TAROT
WRITING 2 = YHWH

E = ENERGY

The CIRCULAR LINE of the wheel dominates this image.

E = EMOTIONS

Mysterious, hints at arcane knowledge.

R = NUMBER

THE TEN IS HOLISTIC—the TEN is a combination of the One of The Magician and the Zero of Spirit. The ancient Greeks claimed that the Ten was the number of perfection. The Ten expresses wholeness, completion, and social harmony.

WHEEL OF FORTUNE

ARCHETYPE

Rider Waite Smith Tarot

Key #10, The Wheel of Fortune, features the four fixed astrological signs in the corners, pinning down the edges of the Earthly plane—the meaning of the number Four.

The word TAROT is spelled out in the hub of the wheel. The letters T-A-R-O (clockwise) or T-O-R-A (counter clockwise) can be found aligned against four of the spokes. These four characters can be reorganized into three different words:

1. TARO, which refers to TAROT; ROTA, Latin for "wheel" or the act of turning

2. ORAT, which is Latin for "spoken or speech"

3. ATOR, which is possibly another spelling for the ancient Egyptian goddess, Hathor. One of the hieroglyphs for Hathor's name means "house of Horus," the god who symbolized the rising Sun.

The Wheel of Fortune admonishes us to remember that any turn of fate—whether we see it as good or bad—has a deeper message and lesson for us. We should not be blinded by the temporal, because the veil of forgetfulness prevents us from seeing the deeper pattern in our lives. The inner spokes of the wheel are inscribed with alchemical symbols representing the four elements: Earth, Air, Fire and Water, which symbolize the four fixed astrological signs.

These emblems also represent the four suits of the Tarot and symbolize the four paths of knowledge available to us on the earth plane. These symbols are prominently displayed by The Magician to The Fool at the beginning of his journey through the Tarot. The fixed astrological signs are shown as the four animals at each corner of this image. Astrological signs "rule" the

10

Earth, her progression through the solar system; they govern our feelings and regulate evolution.

The symbology of this card references the number of the Earth, Four, in four different ways. Thus the meaning is clear: this card is about the Earth, and physical existence. When you multiply four times four, you end up with the square of four: sixteen, one of the hidden numbers of this card; Key #16 is The Tower/THE AWAKENING in suit of the Major Arcana.

The wheel represents a cycle or circle. This wheel turns and always comes back to the beginning; it repeats the same passage. The Wheel of Fortune represents the average person's experience of a "karmic loop." If taken to the level of reincarnation (which is really multiple versions of oneself existing simultaneously), the cycle resembles the Old Testament adage of "an eye for an eye, a tooth for a tooth." In a karmic loop, someone who victimized others might have to come back in the next life as a victim. This system allows the pure Spirit symbolized by the FOOL to experience all sides of duality, or physical experience. And this is OK for one or several revolutions of the Wheel of Fortune; however a Karmic loop repeated endlessly means that there is nothing more to be gained or learned—the Soul is not evolving.

All esoteric practices are trying to get their aspirants off the Wheel of karma by evolving their consciousness. The key to getting off the Wheel of karma lies in the number of this card: ten. The Ten is the combination of the One of The Magician—ATTENTION—and the Zero of Spirit. The mage uses his power of attention or focus as a tool that allows him to access the power of the infinite void: he knows how to consciously choose from all possibilities before him. Like a scout who carefully chooses the right path through the forest, the mage uses his attention or focus to choose his thoughts and emotions. If he does this with consistency and determination he can leave the realm or the "playpen" of duality for a paradigm with a higher frequency. The way to travel to other dimensions is by matching your frequency with the reality you desire.

The Wheel of Fortune is like a pottery wheel; it turns and turns, going fast or slow, but not actually going anywhere. But the clay on the wheel becomes a shape if held consistently in that shape: emotions are the hands that shape the clay of matter on the Wheel of Fortune. So the Wheel of Fortune could actually be called the Wheel of Karmic Manifestation, as it creates form out of circular motion just like the pottery wheel.

The natural shape of evolution is a spiral, not a circle. The energy of a circle or karmic loop cannot shape an object in any other way than it has been shaped before. Every time the wheel revolves, it returns to the exact same location: location is defined by frequency, not space. The infinite source of creation, if so directed, will keep on recreating the shape of the past as it comes around once again on the circular path of the karmic loop. It repeats and repeats itself until something bounces it out. The only thing that can do this is an evolved self-conscious that exercises its right to make a *conscious* choice in order to have a different experience. The choice is not a material choice, but a choice of frequency. The Tarot teaches us that power lies in our intent—our frequency choice shown in the Wands/FIRE suit— not in the final product of the manifestation process, matter (the Pentacles/ EARTH suit).

When a pendulum swings, the two apexes of the pendulum's journey must equal each other. This is physics: the principle of equilibrium at the heart of duality. The Wheel of Fortune represents a path bound by the limits of a materialistic perspective. The system of duality requires opposition and poles of equal value. The poles seem to be against each other, and in fact, this is how things manifest: through the tension of opposites. Thus, just like a piece of a fractal image faithfully reflects the whole fractal, the experience and beliefs of an unconscious individual who resides inside this system reflect the polarized nature of the system: good vs. bad, up vs. down, male vs. female, etc. It can seem to be a battle between the opposites that requires your participation, but this is the view from the perspective *inside* duality.

As the ego on its path of development had to separate from its progenitor in the card Strength/I-MAGE, so the purpose of duality may be to introduce the concept of valuation to the growing Soul. After all, when one is ONE with all, there is no distinction between one thing or another. There is no end to you, or the universe: you don't know what is in the foreground and what is in the background; what is important and what is not.

Without valuation, the Soul cannot distinguish between individual expressions of the underlying implicate field, but more importantly, the Soul is not capable of defining itself. One way it learns to define itself, or grow its individuality, is through personal preference. And just as you would give simple choices to a small child, the system of duality presents us with very simple choices of polarized opposites. It is teaching us how to *choose*; choice is the main power of a being with free will. A field of choice is the prerequisite to knowing that you have the power to direct your ATTENTION, as the Magician taught us in Key #1. The power to focus attention consciously is the main attribute of an evolved being.

In such a polarized system of greater and lesser than, better and worse, wealth or poverty, one is either up on the top of the wheel or on the bottom. While it may seem better to be on the top—and one may rejoice to be there finally after years of poverty, struggle, and hardship—in a system that is constantly seeking balance, what comes up must go down. When the Wheel of Fortune goes down, the ego takes quite a blow; not surprisingly, the gravity of the blow that must equal the intensity of the joy felt at the top of the Wheel.

As long as one is on the Wheel of Fortune, you cannot access greater understanding or knowledge: you are confined to the limits of the swing of Fortune's pendulum, which shows us the karmic loop of cyclical consciousness: the Punch and Judy binary system of cause and effect. The Wheel of Fortune is a test: are you going to exit the loop of causality or choose another path, the higher road of directed consciousness?

When You get This Card in a Reading
The natural form of evolution is a spiral, not a circle. The way to get off the Wheel of Fortune and out of the karmic loop is to stop repetitive behavior, and choose a new frequency by deliberately choosing new thoughts and emotions.

Meditation
Know that everything that happens to you is in your highest and best interest, no matter how it looks on the surface.

WHEEL OF FORTUNE

ACCELERATION

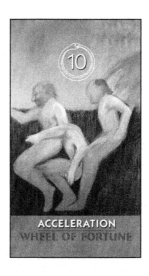

ACCELERATION
WHEEL OF FORTUNE

Tarot of Creativity

This card is about the neutrality of a law, a law of duality: equilibrium. Duality is a binary system that always seeks balance and equilibrium. The principle of equilibrium is the mechanism underlying both the wheel of karma and the cycle of evolution/incarnation. The system of duality works like a mathematical equation. If you swing the pendulum of duality in one direction, the law must balance the swing with a counter-swing of equal, opposite force. Like algebra where each side of an equation must equal the other side, the system of duality must balance out or cease to exist.

The attribute of The Wheel of Fortune is ACCELERATION—the word is emotionally neutral. Like the law of gravity, what comes up must go down. And when you get to this card, the fall or rise is sudden, like a fast elevator.

From the viewpoint of an inhabitant of a 2D world, a spiral would seem to be a circle in motion, just as the apparently circular systems of karma and reincarnation seem to an individual looking at them from a lower state of consciousness. In order to see the figure as a spiral, the seer would have to achieve a higher dimensional vision provided by a third point of view. They have to *accelerate* in frequency in order to obtain this higher vantage point.

If you accelerate a wheel it produces centrifugal force that throws off anything that isn't attached to it Metaphorically, this could mean that if you succeed in detaching yourself sufficiently from the things that hold you to the Wheel of Fate, then you are naturally thrown off that wheel when you force the wheel to accelerate.

The question is: do you want to go where fate—the fruit of your karma—is leading you? Can you escape or manipulate your fate, and thereby change your destination? This card shows you the answer: to get off the Wheel of karma, which could be called the Loop of Repeating Time, you must know how to consciously choose your thoughts and emotions. When you do this consistently, you accelerate your frequency and escape the loop of karma;

you exit the circle of duality, on the spiral of evolution. Otherwise, you have to complete the circuit once again.

The Wheel of Fortune cannot deliver good luck without balancing it with bad luck. Stop believing that anything outside can affect you, for good or bad. Realize that you are the one who is generating your "luck" or "fate" by the thoughts that you think and the emotions that you allow. The only way out of the karmic loop is to stop judging things; judgment serves to keep you in polarity—on one side or the other of a polarized reality.

The pendulum can be slowed and nearly stilled when you reach the neutrality of a higher viewpoint. Physicality relies upon duality, so things won't disappear, however, the world will feel more balanced, peaceful, and secure. The balance-point of neutrality is just another term for unconditional love.

When You get This Card in a Reading

If you want to get off the wheel of karma and drama, take responsibility for your life and everything in it. When you do so, you accelerate your process and throw yourself off the Wheel of Fortune.

Meditation

To get off the wheel of unconscious behavior, you have to accelerate past your own perceived limits.

Related to

The Magician/ATTENTION (Key #1)
The Sun/CREATIVITY (Key #19)

10—WANDS

S = SYMBOLS
PLAIN = distance, effort
VILLAGE = civilization, group effort, harmony
WAND = intent, energy, magic

E = ENERGY
A strong "X" is formed by the wands being carried by the figure.

E = EMOTIONS
Burdened. Responsibility. Duty. Heaviness. Blinded.

R = NUMBER
Ten is the number of social awareness, while the suit of Wands/FIRE is about energy or intent, therefore, this card is about energy or intent applied to the social sphere.

Rider Waite Smith Tarot
A man carries ten huge wands towards a village. The figure in the foreground of this image seems to be burdened down by the ten wands he is carrying. He is unable to see where he is going or how long it will take him to get there.

KEYWORDS
burdened/overworked
over-extended/overtime
overloaded/responsible
debt/struggle duty
labor/taxed/accountable
guilty/hard work
uphill battle/resistance
against the current
blind to facts
can't stop for a minute
social awareness
social activist/leader

He will never get where he is going because new burdens keep on coming to add on to existing ones. Perhaps, like Zeno's famous paradox, he can never reach the far off destination because he can never get even halfway there. To those people who present you with the duties and obligations that weigh you down, there is no halfway point: you are either dedicated to them wholeheartedly or you are nothing to them.

In Western civilization, an X is often used to denote "no" or "not." The "X" formed by the ten wands seems to imply that all his effort is not working, probably because his heart is not in his task; instead it is something that he feels that he has to do.

The Suit of Wands represents energy; the Ten represents social consciousness. In this card, the Querent is taking his responsibilities very seriously; he feels burdened by what he perceives as his duty or responsibility to others in his family, work, or community. Furthermore, the man is blinded by the wands he is carrying; his energy is so spent by the end of the day that he is so tired that he can't see straight.

When You get This Card in a Reading
Think about where you are expending your energy in social situations.

Meditation
The burden that you are carrying is not yours. Slay the dragon of "thou shalt."

10—FIRE

INCLUSIVE • UNITY

Tarot of Creativity
The Ten is the number of social awareness; the number of community. It combines the One of individuality with the Zero of Spirit, and brings an awareness of both into play.

The Ten of Fire is about taking the energy of your creative desires out into the community. This card advises us to include others in your plans, and work to achieve unity in all our social interactions.

When You get This Card in a Reading
Focus on that which brings a feeling of unity and inclusion in all your relationships.

Meditation
A sense of unity and communion naturally results from a policy of inclusion.

10—SWORDS

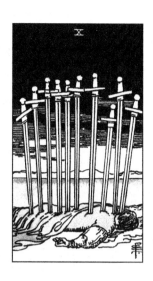

S = SYMBOLS
DARK CLOUDS = depression, ominous
LAKE = emotions
RED cloak = material existence
YELLOW sky = ego, identity, control issues

E = ENERGY
UPRIGHT lines of ten swords dominate picture, all embedded in the man's back.

E = EMOTIONS
Betrayal. Injury. Victimization. Loss.

R = NUMBER
The Ten is the number of social awareness; the suit of Swords/AIR is the energy of the Ten on the mental level.

KEYWORDS
victim/self-pity
powerlessness
betrayal/martyrdom
self-pity/defenseless
sacrifice/surrender/loss
forgiveness

Rider Waite Smith Tarot
A man lies on the ground with ten swords in his back, night is falling. To understand why this terrible thing may have happened, look at the preceding card in the Tens: the Ten of Wands was about personal duty taken to a social level; the sense of social duty whether for your family or nation, or community was starting to become a burden: you weren't doing it for the sheer joy of it, but because, for some reason, you felt you had to. Now, you feel betrayed, but how did your expectations color your experience? If you had not taken on these tasks would anyone have noticed? Did anyone ask you? Did you think it out before you took them on?

Swords are about thought; the Swords tend to be the most "negative" suit in the whole deck. This is because the ego is often involved whenever we are thinking; language is the function of the left brain, and that is where we do most of our egoic thinking. But remember that the brain can only receive thoughts that fit its programming. Everything that is not in the belief system is shut out.

The egoic mind has set itself up as the gatekeeper. It will only allow ideas and thoughts that fit into your belief systems. So, if you believe that you can be injured by someone else, you can. If you believe that you are a victim, you are going to experience everything that happens in this light. You cannot experience that which is outside your belief of what is possible.

The only way to change your experience is to change how you view everything, and that results from a change in your basic mood, or signature vibration. When you have a frequency of love and welcome all experiences equally, you can have the kind of experiences that resonate with your higher frequency.

When You get This Card in a Reading

Remember that you always have the power to choose where to focus your thoughts and emotional energy.

Meditation

It is always darkest before dawn. Despite the apparent endings and betrayals, take the higher ground, see the bigger picture.

10—AIR

CHANGE • PERSPECTIVE

Tarot of Creativity

The Tarot of Creativity reminds you that your beliefs, thoughts, and emotional reality are reflected in the world around you. In order to change the world, you have to change yourself. That means that even though change is coming, you can *change your perspective first*. See change—whatever it is—as something that takes you closer to your dreams. The power lies always within you.

The belief in suffering, betrayal, and injury depend upon a base "kernel" belief that the world is a cruel place where some people triumph over others. If you no longer give emotional energy to these thought forms, they simply wither and die. Then you have more energy to give to beliefs that support a more empowered reality, one that reflects the frequency of your choice. The lesson of the Ten of Air is to learn how to surrender the beliefs that keep you out of the "Kingdom of Heaven" and thus enter the paradise of the divine moment that belongs to your ascended soul.

When You get This Card in a Reading
As you focus your attention, you form the world, creating like The Magician, seemingly out of thin air. If you think of thoughts as geographical locations, then you literally change your location when you choose a different thought.

Meditation
Change your perspective and the whole world changes to suit..

10—CUPS

S = SYMBOLS
CHILDREN = innocence, joy, love
HOUSE = home, family, shelter, wellbeing
LANDSCAPE = bounty, health, happiness
MAN & WOMAN = marriage, family
RAINBOW = joy, happiness, good omen
STREAM = emotions, abundance

E = ENERGY
The couple's arms direct the gaze towards the RAINBOW of cups above them.

E = EMOTIONS
Celebration. Richness. Joy. Coming home.

R = NUMBER
The Cups suit is about emotions, and at their highest expression, they are about LOVE. The Ten as a "perfect number" shows us the wholeness of family love, love that goes to the "10th generation."

KEYWORDS
joy/happiness
celebration
good fortune/success
inclusion/family
love/harmony
truce/peace
connection/bonding
marriage/family

Rider Waite Smith Tarot

A couple raises their arms at a rainbow of cups above them while their children dance. Love expresses itself in many ways. Here it is shown as affection, joy, and partnership as the couple in the foreground raise their arms to a new day. Their children are dancing in the background.

The little girl is the inner child of the woman, and the little boy is the inner child of the man; notice that they are even dressed the same as their adult counterparts. The inner child rejoices at discovering love, once again. Love was forgotten in the experience of incarnation: we forgot that no matter how dark the path, or severe the circumstances, that love and only love can sustain us.

There is harmony as the man accepts the woman, and the woman accepts the man. This is the experience of accepting the duality inside oneself—the wholeness of the parts—what Carl Jung called the *anima* inside the man, and the *animus* inside the woman. Like the mysterious yin-yang symbol, there is always a small part of the divine Other inside the wholeness of you. To deny it is to deny life and to deny yourself. This is why the children are celebrating, because the harmony produced by a marriage of opposites brings freedom to all.

When You get This Card in a Reading

Your "cup runneth over" with the joy of being alive.

Meditation

A rainbow is a prism; all the colors of light are there. Celebrate your achievements.

10—WATER

CLARITY • FULFILLMENT

Tarot of Creativity

The card from *The Tarot of Creativity* expresses a similar idea as the corresponding card from the RWS deck, except it focuses on the mastery of the Suit of Water—emotions. The Querent has achieved (or needs to achieve) clarity in their emotions. This happens only when you no longer believe that you are a powerless victim. The Law of Free Will is often misunderstood; free will merely grants us the right to choose our emotional reactions to established beliefs. We cannot rid ourselves of old beliefs until we detach from the emotions that energize and enliven them.

The Water suit refers to the emotional body. Many people don't know that they have the power to choose their emotions; if you don't choose your emotions you are subject to them, a victim to the frequency that you are unconsciously projecting.

When You get This Card in a Reading

This card reminds you to be the master of your emotions—not by suppressing them or denying them—but by consciously choosing your thoughts. Only when you achieve clarity can you feel fulfilled.

Meditation

The state of fulfillment does not depend on outside conditions; it is an internal state brought about by emotional clarity.

10—PENTACLES

S = SYMBOLS
ANCESTRAL HOME = gnerational
CHILD = the future generation
DOGS = loyalty, love, respect
GRAPE (robe) = abundance, harvest
COUPLE = harmony, partnership, present generation
OLD MAN = ancestral line

E = ENERGY
The composition of the picture is a large CIRCLE in the lower half of the image formed by the direction of the gazes and attention of the people and animals in the image. The man looks to the woman. The woman looks to the man. The child holding his mother's hand pets the dog with his other hand. The dogs look to the old man, who gazes towards the man, thus completing the circle.

E = EMOTIONS
Satisfaction. Harmony. Honor. Love. Respect.

R = NUMBER
The number Ten in the Tarot is about mastery in the path indicated by the suit—in this case, the Ten shows us the results of mastering your emotional awareness: good relations.

KEYWORDS
good fortune
financial security
good health/good genes
an inheritance
help from the family
success/abundance,
family/tradition
conventional/conservative
family inheritance
family fortune
family matters
past lives/ancestors
planning/investments
social awareness

Rider Waite Smith Tarot
A family of three generations is gathered in one home. Here we see respect for the elder, harmony in the couple, and love for the child. Everyone in this picture honors the past, but looks to building a solid future on the abundant present. The love in this picture is not a passionate blaze but the solid feeling of affection and inclusion that is the foundation for the best relationships.

Your primary relationship is first with yourself, and then with others. You will accept others to the degree that you can accept and love yourself.

When You get This Card in a Reading
No social laws are needed except the Golden Rule—"Do unto others as you would have them do unto you."

Meditation
"From one grain, ten thousand grains." ~ George Ohsawa

10—EARTH

GENEROSITY • ABUNDANCE

Tarot of Creativity
The Ten of Earth in *The Tarot of Creativity* follows the number's meaning of social awareness. In the Earth suit the energy of this number translates as *generosity*. But in order to be truly generous, you have to feel that you have enough yourself.

Generosity is not a value exchange—that is what the phrase "a gift with strings attached" means. Love isn't an investment—if you feel that you are investing in someone, then you are "selling your soul" in order to buy theirs. To truly give means to give back to Spirit, because that is the nature of abundance—the flow of love that isn't stopped anywhere along the line, and naturally circulates back to you.

When You get This Card in a Reading
The natural flow of abundance and love always circle back. Reflect on how others support you and on how abundance appears in your life.

Meditation
Which comes first: generosity or abundance?

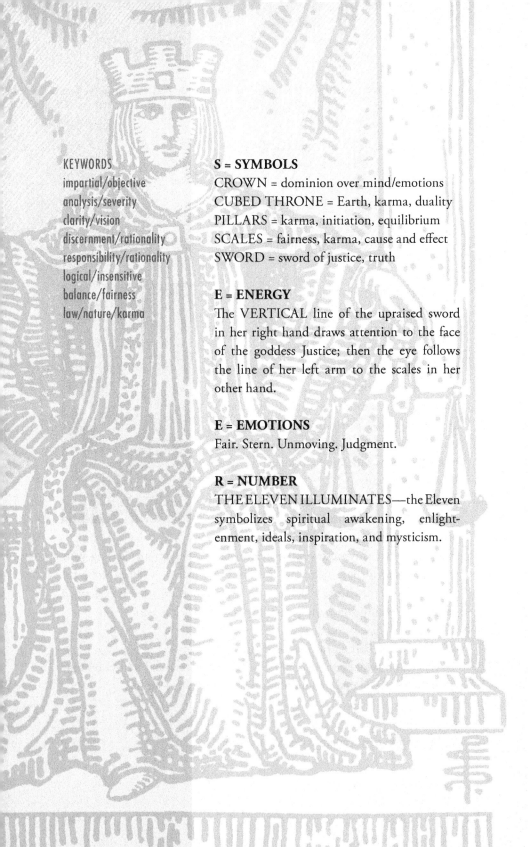

S = SYMBOLS
CROWN = dominion over mind/emotions
CUBED THRONE = Earth, karma, duality
PILLARS = karma, initiation, equilibrium
SCALES = fairness, karma, cause and effect
SWORD = sword of justice, truth

E = ENERGY
The VERTICAL line of the upraised sword in her right hand draws attention to the face of the goddess Justice; then the eye follows the line of her left arm to the scales in her other hand.

E = EMOTIONS
Fair. Stern. Unmoving. Judgment.

R = NUMBER
THE ELEVEN ILLUMINATES—the Eleven symbolizes spiritual awakening, enlightenment, ideals, inspiration, and mysticism.

JUSTICE

ARCHETYPE

Rider Waite Smith Tarot

The Eleven is the first Master number; it means "illumination." It also means "the teacher," or "the messenger," which relates it to the angels. The title of this card refers to the Greek Goddess, Astraea, who later became the Roman goddess Justice:

> Astraea or Astrea (English translation: "star-maiden") was the virgin goddess of innocence and purity and is always associated with the Greek goddess of justice. Astraea, the celestial virgin, was the last of the immortals to live with humans during the Golden Age, one of the old Greek religion's five deteriorating Ages of Man. According to Ovid, Astraea abandoned the earth during the Iron Age. Fleeing from the new wickedness of humanity, she ascended to heaven to become the constellation Virgo. Justice can thus be considered related to the figure of Astraea on historical iconographic grounds.
>
> According to legend, Astraea will one day come back to Earth, bringing with her the return of the utopian Golden Age of which she was the ambassador.[1]

Notice that the image of the Goddess Justice is not wearing a blindfold; the blindfold was added in the 15th century to denote objectivity. The earliest Roman coins depicted Justitia with the sword in one hand and the scale in the other, but with her eyes uncovered. In the original Greek version, it was the innocence and purity of her virginal state that allowed her to judge fairly.

The principle or concept behind this card is best represented by the ancient Egyptian Goddess Maat, who weighed the heart of the recently deceased against a feather. If the heart was heavier than the feather, the Soul would have to return to physical life, and not pass on. This is a test

1   en.wikipedia.org/wiki/Astraea_(mythology)

of emotions and beliefs. The Soul cannot not pass if it is weighed down by heavy negative beliefs, petty thoughts, and unconscious emotions; it has to be "light-hearted," not burdened with guilt, hatred, victimhood, or other unresolved experiences.

> Maat represents the ethical and moral principle that every Egyptian citizen was expected to follow throughout their daily lives. They were expected to act with honor and truth in manners that involve family, the community, the nation, the environment, and god.[1]

To pass by the PILLARS of JUSTICE, you have to become NEUTRAL to all unconscious thought forms and emotional baggage. Otherwise, you are in for another round of karmic lessons. The figure of JUSTICE looks severe because she is the representative for the LAWS of the universe, which are the same as the laws of Nature.

If you see her sword of truth and are dismayed by her severity, it may be because you do not want to experience the austerity of personal discipline that is required to ascend to the next level of consciousness. The sword that Justice carries represents the "ruthlessness" you have to have toward unconscious behavior; you have to be able to persistently chop off limiting thoughts and eliminate emotional debris if you are to succeed. This process requires discipline, consistency, awareness, and persistence. If you cannot pass the TEST of inner discipline represented by JUSTICE, you are still attached to something that binds you to the lower state of consciousness, which acts like gravity on the heart of your Soul.

When You get This Card in a Reading

The message of this card is not about vengeance or redress, it is about releasing illusions. Your reality is based upon the thoughts and emotions that you are projecting; if you are projecting these unconsciously, you cannot pass by the pillars of Justice.

Meditation

Justice seeks to balance the scales of duality.

---

1   en.wikipedia.org/wiki/Maat

JUSTICE

ILLUMINATION

Tarot of Creativity

Your reality is based upon the thoughts and emotions that you are projecting. If you cannot pass the test of inner discipline, you are still emotionally attached to something. The Goddess Justice will not let you pass.

This card stands for Nature and the way she works. Justice/ILLUMINATION tells us that what we experience is the result of what we are imagining (as outlined in Key #8/

ILLUMINATION

Strength/I-MAGE); this is a law of nature: the Law of Cause and Effect, which is one of the ways that duality achieves Equilibrium. If you ignore the laws of the universe, you are ignorant of your own power to imagine new realities and incapable of manifesting your desires.

Nature in the system of duality works through the principle of *equilibrium*. The ignorant man chooses to ignore this law and attempts to control Nature, to impose his desires upon it. The wise man learns to work with the laws of Nature by learning to work with his own nature first.

The power to choose is the essence of mastery. The master knows how to express the Law of Equilibrium: he demonstrates ease, poise, and emotional balance in his daily life. This card shows how once the man decides to be fully conscious, the subconscious responds by changing his body and outer reality to vibrationally match the positive images that he projects.

In the TOC, this card shows darkness where there should be light, but there is a balance contained inside the paradoxical nature of the image. The inner Spirit understands what seems to the mind to be a paradox. Just as a Buddhist master would present a koan[1] to help his student, the resolution of the apparent paradox cannot be solved from the logical left brain. The left brain tends to get stuck when it tries to make sense out of a paradox, like a computer in a loop of logic. Without the benefit of intuition, the logical left brain stands outside the realm of magic and possibility. When the student uses his intuition to "understand" the koan, he can resolve the paradox

---

1   Koan: a paradoxical anecdote or riddle, used in Zen Buddhism to demonstrate the inadequacy of logical reasoning and to provoke enlightenment.

from a higher level of understanding; this is the meaning of spiritual illumination. To pass the test of this card, you are capable of understanding not just the way that Nature works, but how the workings of duality express a variable truth that hints at a greater truth underneath: namely that everything is good and perfect even in its imperfection.

The TOC title of the Justice card is ILLUMINATION—the meaning of the number of this card. The Master number Eleven is a gateway or a portal to the next level of consciousness. To deal justice, one must see clearly, and without bias, which is why Justice is not blindfolded in the RWS card.

There is nothing more fair than Nature; Nature is not sentimental, she is not swayed by beliefs, wishes, or prayers, no matter how heart-felt or well-intentioned. Only those who seek to dominate and control others have anything to fear from Mother Nature, as they are at war with her and with themselves. Nature is at your command only if you have mastered your four bodies: mental, emotional, physical, and creative. When you have reached this state of mastery, the illumination of your being heals all that was formerly hidden in the shadows of your subconscious.

The enlightened master is aligned with his true nature and with Nature herself. The shadow and darkness that seemed to plague your life were just clever disguises, as old beliefs and limitations suddenly open up like flowers to reveal themselves as true gifts of Spirit.

When You get This Card in a Reading

In order to experience the illumination of higher awareness, you have to fearlessly face everything, and stop judging it as good or bad.

Meditation

A shadow defines the light, just as light defines a shadow.

Related to

The High Priestess/MEMORY (Key #2)
Judgment/THE EPIPHANY (Key #20)

PAGE OF WANDS

S = SYMBOLS

FEATHER in cap = spiritual
MOUNTAINS = Higher Self
SALAMANDERS in tunic = FIRE element
YELLOW robe = the mind or self-conscious

E = ENERGY

The gaze of the Page of Wands directs the eye towards the sprouting staff in his hands.

E = EMOTIONS

A message from on high. A gift of Spirit.

PAGE of WANDS.

R = NUMBER

The Eleven as the first Master number is an appropriate number for the Pages in the Tarot, as the meaning of the number is "message." In the Wands/FIRE suit, this refers to a divine message.

KEYWORDS
a message/sign/omen
an announcement
new direction/inspiration
enthusiasm/optimism
beginning/new venture
passion/excitement
an offer/a date

Rider Waite Smith Tarot

A young man with a feather in his cap gazes at the staff that he holds, against a sunlit landscape of barren hills. All the Pages are about a message of some sort, but the Page of Wands is especially attuned to the voice of Spirit, because the Suit of Wands is the suit of intent, the suit that expresses the pure energy of the Higher Self. This is the card of the psychic, the channeler, and the healer.

When You get This Card in a Reading

If you get this card in a reading, pay attention to your intuition.

Meditation

Look for a new direction, pay attention to the clues all around you left by your Higher Self.

PAGE OF FIRE

THE ICONOCLAST

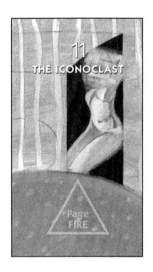

Tarot of Creativity

In *The Tarot of Creativity*, the court cards represent mastery in the path symbolized by the suit, in this case, the Fire suit. This card signifies that a message of illumination is coming through the primal, fiery energy of this suit.

The word "iconoclast" means a person who criticizes or opposes beliefs and practices that are widely accepted. Just as the sword of Justice in the Major Arcana cuts through falsehoods, so the iconoclast breaks down thought patterns and erroneous belief systems, and illuminates the darkness of unconsciousness. At the beginning stage of this path, the iconoclast focuses her attention on social matters; she considers it her job to point out what is wrong with the world; she wants to break down what she sees that doesn't work so the system can be replaced with a better one. But once she becomes enlightened through the process of illumination, the iconoclast knows that what is "out there" is only a mirror for what is inside. She knows that the way to change the world is by changing her attitude towards it. So she focuses not on what others are doing "wrong" but on what elements she wants to include in her world.

She has gone from being *exclusive* to being *inclusive*, from supporting the state of separation in her soul to supporting the energy of inclusion. The path of creative manifestation starts in the Fire suit of intent. The Iconoclast stops the loss of creative energy by tracking down and eliminating all thoughts and emotions that are not consciously chosen. When she smashes the idols of her beliefs, and melts down the emotional blocks of lack and limitation, she rediscovers the gold of her creative power.

When You get This Card in a Reading

Your Higher Self is knocking on your door. Will you open it?

Meditation

Drop outmoded beliefs and unconscious habits.

PAGE OF SWORDS

S = SYMBOLS
CLOUDS & WIND = confused turbulent
LANDSCAPE = changing Earth plane
SWORD = thoughts, beliefs

E = ENERGY
A strong line goes from the Page's right leg up through his sword. The clouds eddy around the figure.

E = EMOTIONS
Fighting the wind.

R = NUMBER
As an Eleven, the card refers to an inspiration.

Rider Waite Smith Tarot
A young man waves a sword in front of turbulent clouds. The ego can present formidable opposition to information that may not jibe with its established thought patterns or beliefs. The Page here may be fighting those beliefs, or he may be simply trying to fight the winds of change with his reason—not the most effective use of anyone's mental energy.

PAGE of SWORDS.

KEYWORDS
message/sign/omen
a challenge/difficulty
diligence/impartiality
justice/equality/fairness
editing/ruthlessness
resolve/self-discipline

As the Page cuts through the clouds of confusion, more light can come through—we become enlightened as everything around us is bathed in light. The Page's left leg represents his intuition; this leg is supporting his weight, while his right leg—his reason—is not solidly planted. The Page is learning to use the Sword of Clarity to cut through the clouds of irrational beliefs and emotional baggage.

When You get This Card in a Reading
Use the sword of your mind to eliminate all beliefs that do not serve you.

Meditation
Just as you cannot fight clouds, you will always lose a battle with your mind.

PAGE OF AIR

ENVISION

Tarot of Creativity

The Page of Air in the TOC is about using your mental powers to envision something new—to dare to see what isn't in material form yet. The power to ENVISION is the mark of any great thinker. If no one tried to imagine a different reality than the one that presents itself to us, we would never evolve. There is a misunderstanding of the process of illumination or enlightenment that comes from our tendency to emphasize only our left-brain capabilities. The left brain lives in a world of words, categories, and data; it thinks that more data or information equals enlightenment. But there is no freedom in this kind of information.

The Page of Air shows you how to edit out thoughts and beliefs that do not serve you. This gives us enough space so we can envision something different. You don't have to spend hours meditating, you can do this as a practice during your normal day. Attaining a state of bliss, or being in the NOW, is a matter of accrual—bit by bit, you can add to your inner silence by being present for small moments during the day. Once you have accrued even a small measure of inner silence, your creative abilities simply open up.

When You get This Card in a Reading

Cut through the confusion and be present in the Now.

Meditation

Dare to envision a new future.

PAGE OF CUPS

PAGE of CUPS.

S = SYMBOLS

CUP = emotions, subconscious, offering
FISH = unexpected, imagination
FLOWERS on tunic = abundance, purity, love
WATER = emotions

E = ENERGY

The Page gazes at the fish in his tankard, and the fish looks at him.

E = EMOTIONS

Romantic. Playful. An offering. A surprise.

R = NUMBER

One of the meanings of the number Eleven is "message." Since this is a card in the Suit of Cups, the message is coming through your intuition, or emotional body.

Rider Waite Smith Tarot

A royal page with a flowered tunic is puzzled to find a fish in his cup. In this card, we have one of the most playful images in the Tarot. The fish in the cup looks like an unexpected surprise; like a delivery of a musical telegram that declares the love the sender has for the recipient.

When you are entertained by a film, you accept the vision of the director, and you use your own imagination in order to interpret the emotions of the actors and understand the plot. From an early age we are admonished to be realists, to be grounded in what is thought to be reality. Children are told that they shouldn't daydream in school; instead they are taught to focus only on the accepted "facts" of the day, but this strips them of what it means to be human—our creativity. We are creators by nature; we use our imagination to build the world. Imagination is a great gift; only by using the power of imagination can we envision a better world. All the great advances in the world were achieved because someone dared to dream.

KEYWORDS
opportunity/opportunist
an offering of love
friendship/romance
surprising turn of events
magic/delightful
sharing/playfulness
an affair of the heart
passion/compassion
forgiveness/relationship

Notice the gently waving lines of the ocean behind the page, and the position of his left hand on his hip. The waves represent the flow of the dreamlike state of emotional awareness; like a compass, they allow us to gain information about where we are energetically.

Emotions are the gateway to intuition.[1]

This card is about imagination and the delightful and surprising ways that creative inspiration and intuition can suddenly pop up in your life. The fish of imagination emerges from your emotions (water) to play with you.

When You get This Card in a Reading
Allow your imagination free rein.

Meditation
Can you see the gift—the opportunity—in this moment?

---

1 *Parallel Mind, The Art of Creativity*, by Aliyah Marr

PAGE OF WATER

THE CURRENT

Tarot of Creativity

The Higher Self communicates with us in two ways: through emotions—our reaction to "reality"—and through our intuition. This card shows us how this communication can be a delightful game if we allow it. But first we must provide a clear space in our minds and hearts by clearing out stale beliefs and emotions. We cannot have access to the new currents of Spirit while mired in the mud of the old.

This is the "brainstorm" card, and the "inner voice" card. Psychic ability and creativity are twins that come from the same womb of imagination. Imagination is a power that we use all the time, unconsciously by default, but consciously when we become masters of awareness. This card shows us how we can learn to use our emotions as a compass and our intuition to guide us.

The Page of Water tells you that the CURRENT of imagination is there all the time, running alongside your life, but you must use the rudder of your will or intent in order to master the direction of your vessel. Getting this card in a reading is like a playful invitation from Spirit as the fish of intuition suddenly leaps into your boat.

When You get This Card in a Reading

Let your mind play with possibilities.

Meditation

What would happen if you just allowed yourself to go with the flow this time?

PAGE OF PENTACLES

PAGE of PENTACLES

S = SYMBOLS
LANDSCAPE = material existence/Earth
MOUNTAIN = success, wisdom, attainment
PENTACLE = talent, wealth, skills, magic

E = ENERGY
The gaze of the Page directs the eye towards the Pentacle in his hands.

E = EMOTIONS
Awe. Welcome. Delight.

R = NUMBER
The Page of Pentacles shows us how to take the energy of the magical Eleven to the material plane, by treating Matter with the same respect as we treat Spirit; as both are essentially the same energy.

KEYWORDS
message/sign/omen
new direction
inspiration/new idea
enthusiasm/optimism
belief/confidence
beginning/new venture
passion/excitement

Rider Waite Smith Tarot
A page seems to admire a pentacle that he holds aloft. A wave collapses into a particle when we look at it, and back into a wave when don't; this is the magic of creation—the magic of the quantum field, which shows us the sleight of hand directed by consciousness itself. The Page looks at the Pentacle with awe and wonder, approving and welcoming it as a magical gift that has suddenly appeared.

When You get This Card in a Reading
The symbol of the Pentacle could be considered a magic talisman. When you get this card in a reading, allow yourself to see the magic in the world around you. Something appears out of nowhere.

Meditation
New things are starting to manifest.

PAGE OF EARTH

DESIRE

Tarot of Creativity

DESIRE is the title of the Page of Earth card. The message represented by the number Eleven is the Divine Intent that emanates from the Higher Self. Intent at the higher level of Spirit translates as *desire* when it hits the self-conscious. The master naturally follows the path of his desire, but the master's desire is not that of an unrefined or ignorant ego. He has refined his emotions and thoughts until his desire is perfectly aligned with the direction of his Higher Self— direction that appears before him in the moment as a flash of inspiration.

Both the adept of creativity and the spiritual aspirant know that nothing is more important than following the path of the heart; desire is the light that illuminates the way. This is the same light that was in the lantern of The Hermit; it is the light that comes from the Higher Self or the Super Conscious. The Higher Self uses the gift of desire to lead the Self towards empowerment, fulfillment, and full consciousness. It is by following the light of desire that the Self comes back home to the fuller consciousness in a marriage with the Higher Self.

Have you ever tried to see the back of your head by using two mirrors? You had to jockey yourself and each of the mirrors to just the right position. When you peered into the reflection, wasn't it a bit of a surprise? The goal of the Self is to know itself by seeing its reflection in the mirror of duality.

> The object of one's desire becomes more attainable once desire is aligned with one's thoughts, and activated with emotions. The energy of desire draws us toward the object of attraction. When we attain that object, it transforms into something else, because in attainment or consummation of the desire, the object of desire is no longer attractive.
>
> We move onto the next desire, the next attraction. This might be disappointing until one realizes that the real energetic function of desire and attraction is movement, or to bring it

full circle—the real function of desire is manifestation, the secondary attribute of sexual power.

When the Buddhists say that the cause of all suffering is desire, this is what they mean: the unconscious cycle of desire and consummation that is life for most of us. Until we learn how to use desire skillfully, we can never be happy for long, because there is always another thing to avoid or desire.

Like a horse that perennially circles on the track because of the carrot in front of its nose, we are not happy in the cycle of desire and consummation, because once attained, the object of desire simply changes into something farther off. The real trick is to learn how to use the generative force of desire without becoming stuck in the cycle of desire and consummation.

…The trick to using desire in any creative act is to retain the feeling (or tension) of desire, while losing the idea of attainment, possession or consummation; ultimately to the point of not even of having an object of desire. It is this energy of desire that creates, not the desire or the inspiration itself[1]

The creative master learns how to move it from the *emotion* of desire (perception of lack) to the *feeling* of desire (intent). This is what is meant by the purification of desire: you graduate from an emotion of *lack*, to the feeling of *wholeness*, from the separation induced by the time-space field, to the unification in the moment of now—outside all temporal forms. Desire spurs the impulse, the movement of creation.

When You get This Card in a Reading
Allow the energy of desire to move you towards the life of your dreams.

Meditation
Desire is the light that illuminates the path to your dreams.

---

1   *Parallel Mind, The Art of Creativity*, Aliyah Marr

KEYWORDS
meditation/deep meaning
sacrifice/surrender
acceptance/contemplation
new point of view/
renunciation
patience/inner peace
wisdom/non-conformity

S = SYMBOLS
HALO = Christ Consciousness
POSITION of legs = 4/the Earth
RIGHT FOOT = conscious descent into life
TREE = Tree of Life/cross of incarnation
T-SHAPE = Tau cross/the dying/rising god

E = ENERGY
The UPRIGHT LINE of the Tau cross formed
by the shape of the tree is crossed by both arms
and by the left leg of the hanging figure.

E = EMOTIONS
Illumination. Revelation. Reversal.

R = NUMBER
THE TWELVE is the combination of the
One of the individuated consciousness: the
attention of The Magician, paired with the
Two of The High Priestess: the power of the
universal Source.

THE HANGED MAN

ARCHETYPE

Rider Waite Smith Tarot

The Hanged Man symbolizes the resurrection of the light of awareness in physical form. He is shown hanging on the Tree of Life. The crossed legs of the Hanged Man resembles the number Four, which is the number of the Earth/physical existence, the number of suits in the Tarot, and the number of elements in the physical plane. The Hanged Man is actually The Magician, who is descending head-first (consciously) into life. He is becoming the master of his consciousness while on Earth. The term "monkey mind" is used by Buddhists to describe the agitated, easily distracted, and incessantly moving behavior of normal daily human awareness.

> Just as a monkey swinging through the trees grabs one branch and lets it go only to seize another, so too, that which is called thought, mind or consciousness arises and disappears continually both day and night.[1]

The Hanged Man could be said to have suspended the busy, monkey mind of daily consciousness. He has transformed his mind through meditation into a mind that is clear and untroubled.

The head of the Hanged Man is surrounded by a NIMBUS or HALO—the energy/light that represents higher consciousness. The nimbus symbolizes the Sun's light—spiritual awareness—inserted into matter, which is why the man is upside-down. The halo is a graphical way to show enlightenment; in this picture it is a symbol for the rising or setting sun.

The Hanged Man hangs from the same tree that forms the border of the image in The Magician card. The tree symbolizes the "cross of incarnation:" he has been "sacrificed" upon the cross of "time and space." The man's Higher Self was "crucified" on the cross of incarnation when it descended consciously into physical existence. He is subject to the same vicissitudes of

1 Siddhartha Gautama, known as the Buddha

matter, duality, and the lower, negative, reactive emotions of all unevolved beings. Even as a more evolved being, he must obey the rules of physicality and embodiment. It is the *social structure of mankind*—the collective conscious—*that has crucified him*, not nature or even his own physicality. Christ was crucified by the people because his higher consciousness didn't fit the social structure of the times: he was seen as a threat by the powers that ruled the land.

But the figure on this card is shown upside-down, which means that he has transcended the illusions of duality and brought a higher consciousness—symbolized by the nimbus or halo around his head—into his physical incarnation or reality.

The Hanged Man is often associated with Odin, the primary god in Norse mythology. Odin hung upside down from the world-tree, Yggdrasil, for nine days to attain wisdom. With the knowledge he obtained, he was able to retrieve the runes from the Well of Wyrd, which in Norse cosmology is regarded as the source of all sacred mystery and knowledge. The moment he glimpsed the runes, he died, but the knowledge of them was so powerful that he immediately returned to life. Odin is associated with the universal attributes of wisdom, shamanism, magic, poetry, and prophecy.

The tree upon which he is suspended is the TAU CROSS, a very important symbol of regeneration and enlightenment. It is an ancient pre-Christian symbol, dating from ancient Egypt and perhaps beyond.

The upper bar of the Tau Cross symbolizes the rising or setting of the Sun; the "resurrection" of the Sun god, which represented spiritual "enlightenment." This meaning is particularly significant when you associate it with the number of this card: Twelve, the number of the month of the winter solstice. The Tau cross is a variation of the Ankh, the ancient Egyptian symbol for life. The rounded top of the Ankh is feminine; it symbolizes the womb, while the staff is the phallus or the birth canal. It is a very balanced symbol, representing both the male and female polarities. Together, the two pieces of the symbol signify a spiritual "birth" or renewal.

Ancient people knew of their connection and reliance on the Earth's seasons: they saw the Sun as the source of life, the source of sustenance and light. They looked for the Sun's yearly resurrection at the winter solstice, and they were governed by its death and renewal each and every day. The Tau Cross is an archetype: it universally symbolizes rejuvenation, freedom from physical suffering, hope, immortality, and divine unity. The ancient peoples of the Americas also used a symbol of a "sacred tree" like the Tau Cross in the same way:

> A transcendental synthesis of human religious experience is inherent in the word "The Sacred Tree," which emerged from the words" teol" and "teotl:" the names of God the Creator in Mayan and Nahuatl. These most revered and sacred words of the ancient people, symbolized by the Sacred Tree, were represented in the Mayan hieroglyphs as the symbol "T." Additionally, this symbol represented the air, the wind, the divine breath of God.[1]

In his book The Pictorial Key to the Tarot, A. E. Waite, one of the designers of the Rider-Waite Tarot deck, wrote:

> The gallows from which he is suspended forms a Tau cross, while the figure—from the position of the legs—forms a fylfot cross. There is a nimbus about the head of the seeming martyr. It should be noted that the tree of sacrifice is living wood, with leaves thereon; that the face expresses deep entrancement, not suffering; that the figure, as a whole, suggests life in suspension, but life and not death...It has been called falsely a card of martyrdom, a card of prudence, a card of the Great Work, a card of duty... I will say very simply on my own part that it expresses the relation, in one of its aspects, between the Divine and the Universe.
>
> He who can understand that the story of his higher nature is imbedded in this symbolism will receive intimations concerning a great awakening that is possible, and will know that after the sacred Mystery of Death there is a glorious Mystery of Resurrection.[2]

The Hanged Man is often is said to represent the concept of sacrifice. Sacrifice is the ability to give up the *lesser desire* for the *greater good*. It doesn't mean that you must sacrifice your good for the good of others, it means that you have to learn to give up your lessor egoic concerns of selfishness,

12

---

1   Hunbatz Men, Mayan daykeeper, artist, and historian
2   The Pictorial Key to the Tarot, A. E. Waite

pettiness, and separation—for the greater consciousness, the realization of Love.

The Hanged Man, as Spirit, has taken a brave step into physicality (the legs of the figure in the shape of the Earth number, "4") when he consciously descended into the density and darkness of the material plane. He willingly sacrificed a "normal" human life of materialistic impulses for the higher path of spiritual aspirations. As he brings the light of Christ Consciousness into the physical plane he causes the automatic rise in the frequency of all that surrounds him.

The moment shown here is the moment when his Spirit makes the choice to descend; choice is what alights this man's consciousness. *Choice* implies that The Hanged Man has *earned the power to choose*: he has mastered all the cards that preceded this one. The universe opened up to him because he has achieved the emotional/mental neutrality necessary to pass the test/gate offered by the last card, Key #11, Justice/ILLUMINATION.

When You get This Card in a Reading

It probably isn't a permanent thing, this moment of insight into the inner workings of the world provided by the reversal you are experiencing. In the next moment, you may rejoin the hectic pace of daily life, or you may form a new belief, a new reality system, just as unconscious as the old one, where the Foolish are Foolish and the Wise are Wise, and the only people hanging legitimately upside-down have bats in their belfry.

Meditation

The common wisdom states that we live in a world where some things are absolutely true. But a Wise Fool knows that truth is relative, and the truths that are true when you are standing upright are false when you are upside-down.

Related to

The Empress/IMAGINATION (Key #3)
The World/TRANSCEND (Key #21)

THE HANGING MAN

REVERSAL

Tarot of Creativity

In numerology, the number Twelve reduces to the number Three, which in the Major Arcana of the Tarot is The Empress/IMAGINATION card; the "hidden" or secret meaning of this card. Only an individual with creative imagination can see the new perspective afforded by a sudden REVERSAL or change in fortune.

After the ILLUMINATION of the last Key #11 Justice, the Fool tumbles from the heights, as anyone who has striven for enlightenment has to do at one time or another. The REVERSAL that the Fool experiences is not a bad thing in itself. In fact, the Fool is enjoying the new point of view, which makes it clear to everyone why he is called the Fool.

The world's consensus opinion is that the effort to strive for spiritual illumination is foolish. "What good is that?" they all say, as they see the Fool's tattered rags and see that his search has placed him on a path that seems to eschew worldly goods. Those who look at the *world* from the limited standpoint of materialism cannot know what drives the Fool. But from his upside-down position, he sees that it is as he suspected all along; from his standpoint, it is the world that is foolish. And he begins to see that if he compares himself to them in any way he reverts back to their kind of foolishness. So he never claims that he is wise; he just maintains that he has a different point of view.

The Hanged Man realizes that his system of thinking is just one way to think—just one possible reality—in a multitude of potential realities or viewpoints. One is not better than another, they are all equal. The concept of *equal but different* has been revealed to him in three previous cards: in The High Priestess/MEMORY, in The Lovers/LOVE, and in the Justice/ILLUMINATION cards. Now he understands that all systems are equally valid; he realizes they are all formed from our thoughts and emotions.

A system of beliefs is like wearing dark glasses; you filter what you see by the lens of your beliefs. So those who see the Hanged Man as "foolish" are right, according to their belief system. The Fool who foolishly hangs by one foot simply sees life with a different set of glasses.

But when you turn those beliefs upside-down, you reverse reality and see how the collective belief system makes up what everyone seems to think is "reality." When you reverse your ideas you find that you suddenly are graced with a new point of view, a broader perspective.

Suddenly, you come to realize that the "normal" world is upside-down and you are the only one actually standing right-side up. For a moment you see that you are in charge of your beliefs, and you can choose a different thought any time you want. This reversal reveals the undergarments of reality; you look under the curtain of the Wizard of OZ and see the legs of a man.

When You get This Card in a Reading
Allow yourself to enjoy the new perspective of your reversal.

Meditation
An artist learns to turn his canvas upside-down in order to see the composition of the artwork from a new point of view. If you find your world turned upside-down, check out the new vista before you try to turn it back; you may find that there are valuable ideas to be found in your new point of view.

Related to
The Empress/IMAGINATION (Key #3)
The World/TRANSCEND (Key #21)

KNIGHT OF WANDS

S = SYMBOLS
FEATHERS = element of FIRE
SALAMANDERS in tunic = FIRE/Wands
YELLOW landscape = ego, self-conscious
YELLOW robe = self-conscious/third chakra

E = ENERGY
SWIRLING energy in the forelegs and neck of the horse focus attention on the man's hands on the reins.

E = EMOTIONS
Raw desire. Power barely restrained.

R = NUMBER
The Twelve reduces to a Three in the art of numerology.

Rider Waite Smith Tarot
A young knight and a rearing horse on a deserted yellow plane. The Knights are the doers and shakers of the court cards. The Knight of Wands kicks off the mastery of the suit by showing us how raw desire can be channeled into a direction of conscious choice.

Although this card is full of energy, force and enthusiasm, the Knight of Wands keeps his eager steed on a tight rein. The horse, as a symbol of the emotional body, wants to charge ahead, but the master takes a moment to consciously choose his direction, and align himself with intent. This card symbolizes the moment of decision: it is the point of taking off, the horses about to charge out of the starting gate. The Knight of Wands represents "desire in action."

If he is the more evolved version of this energy, he knows how to channel the raw energy of the Wands. He knows how to choose his focus and direction; he restrains his horse—the symbol of his physical body, emotions, and subconscious—and looks before he leaps.

KEYWORDS
passionate/energetic
restless/adventurous
daring/cocky/hotshot
confident/headstrong
likes novelty/superficial
frustrated/angered
self-righteous/bragger
charming/attractive
sexy/exciting
heroic/foolhardy
fiery/hotheaded
irrepressible/charismatic
social activist

12

How you are focusing and deploying your energy?

Meditation
Intent is the rein that directs the raw power of the creative subconscious.

KNIGHT OF FIRE

THE SHAMAN

Tarot of Creativity
The Shaman works in the etheric realms, having learned through a long and difficult apprenticeship how to walk "between the worlds" and work with the lines of energy directly. He is unafraid of what he sees in the vast, incontrovertible, and often inconceivable worlds that he explores. He knows that he cannot indulge in unconscious thoughts or emotions as he faces the unknown, stares down the corridors of time and space, or in the face of the unknowable.

The Shaman expresses his impeccability in every moment. He is a model of emotional sobriety; he maintains a balance even as he teeters precariously on the razor edge between worlds. He is impassive in the face of major change, at once immovable and in constant movement.

As a court card in the Fire suit this card indicates a mastery of INTENT and will. The Knights are the active members of the royal court, but in this suit, it doesn't signify action in the outer world, rather it means the beginning of action, the point in which you decide your direction and focus your intent.

When You get This Card in a Reading
A shaman works with the lines of infinite potential—energy in its purest form—desire and intent.

Meditation
"The world is a feeling." ~ Don Juan Matus

KNIGHT of SWORDS

KNIGHT of SWORDS.

S = SYMBOLS
CLOUDS = element of AIR/Suit of Swords
FEATHER in helmet = AIR/Suit of Swords
YELLOW LANDSCAPE = power, ego, self-conscious

E = ENERGY
Poorly planned, rash, hasty action.

E = EMOTIONS
Righteous. Headlong. Unthinking.

R = NUMBER
The Twelve in the Suit of Swords/AIR is creativity in action: the swift and efficacious execution of an idea.

KEYWORDS
blunt/direct
confident/self-assured
in a hurry/action-oriented
opinionated/quick witted
argumentative
intellectual/critical
logical/analytical
quick to judge
dispassionate
sarcastic/witty
charismatic leader

12

Rider Waite Smith Tarot
A knight and his steed charge heedlessly forward.
The Suit of Swords is, by and large, the most negative suit in most traditional tarot decks. This is because the Swords represent the mental body and the ego, both of which tend to be unhealthy due to our social conditioning.

The Dalai Lama says, "Suffering is optional." The Tarot tells us that only the ego (mental body) can suffer or be harmed. Whether the ego-driven soul is on the top of the Ferris Wheel of karma and drama—otherwise called The Wheel of Fortune—the egotistical personality will eventually take a fall off his high horse. This is what happens when you try to direct life with your mind. An unhealthy ego will always take the path that brings about its own downfall. Even though it seems the ego would rather not fall, the Soul needs the lessons that it will learn by falling or failing. Through the collaboration of the Higher Self and the Soul, a difficult lesson may be in the works: the ego must learn the difference between control and self-discipline; between personal power and power over others; between allowing and controlling; between following inner guidance and being led by the lower desires/needs of the ego. The more controlling and needy the ego, the harder the lesson that it has to learn. The ego must surrender its needs and lower desires to the Higher Self and follow its dictates—shown in the Hanged Man/REVERSAL card—or it will end up in a hell of its own making, illustrated so beautifully in The Devil/THE SHADOW card.

The Knight of Swords charges ahead; notice that he charges from right to left—contrary to the normal Western way of reading. This direction gives a subconscious message: the Knight of Swords chooses to "go against the grain" instead of "going with the flow." The Knight of Swords chooses a path that is deliberately contrary to the status quo: he could a social activist or a rebel, with or without a cause. He has so much self-confidence that he appears egotistical and self-righteous to the people who scatter before the thundering hooves of his horse and his missionary zeal. He is can't see things in shades of gray; he truly believes that he is always right, and because he is right, everyone else must be wrong. He is out to correct their delusions, even if it means he must chop off a lot of heads in order to prove his point. He never seems to be able to put all those "wrong" people in their place, and as he shouts what he thinks must be the absolute truth, the wind drowns out his words.

The Knight of Swords charges ahead, sure of himself and his mission. The clarity he finally achieved in his long apprenticeship struck him like a bolt of lightning, and the truth of his vision intoxicates him into heedless action. His thoughts circulate through his body like the ragged clouds that swirl around him. Clarity has become an enemy on the path of his enlightenment because it has given him tunnel vision: he thinks that the truth he has worked so hard to achieve is the only possible truth there is. For the Knight of Swords the world is black and white, with clearly defined, absolute truths that he defines, and which he champions against the ultimately insurmountable tide of global ignorance. He fights what he thinks is "the good fight." He cuts with satire and slices ruthlessly with the sharp edge of logic. And while his ego is certainly inflated by his "wins," he can never truly succeed, as all judgments that the Knight of Swords renders on the world outside ultimately go against him.

In the path of enlightenment, the adage, "Offense is the best defense" simply doesn't apply. It doesn't matter whether anyone knows that you are a master, or more importantly, whether anyone ever understands you or your truth. The only question that you should ever try to answer is, do you understand it, or rather, are you putting your truth into action?

When You get This Card in a Reading
Consider what points you are defending, what truths you champion. Why do you need other people to believe as you do, to agree with you?

Meditation
Clarity lets you to see through shades of grey and prime you to make decisions. Be careful that that clarity you have worked so hard to achieve doesn't blind you to a world of color and to subtle shades of meaning.

KNIGHT OF AIR

ENGAGE

Tarot of Creativity
The TOC follows the creative process through the suits. Each suit represents a path of mastery; every number builds upon the number before. In *The Tarot of Creativity* the Knight of Air is the master of thought-in-action.

The court cards are the masters of the suit; they show how to creatively manifest using the toolkit of the suit, in this case mental skills and self-discipline. The Page of Wands started to envision a new future/creation that the Knight of AIR, as the card of action, is now prepared to carry out, as he actively engages in life.

When You get This Card in a Reading
Time to fully engage with your idea, and implement what you have planned.

Meditation
The time to sit on the sidelines is over.

KNIGHT OF CUPS

S = SYMBOLS
FEATHERS = freedom, spirituality
RED FISH on cloak = suit of Cups/WATER
STREAM = the subconscious/emotions
YELLOW LANDSCAPE = power, ego,
self-conscious

E = ENERGY
A largely STATIC image with slow movement
that flows from left to right.

E = EMOTIONS
Calmness. Steady affection. Loyalty.

R = NUMBER
The Twelve reduces to the number of creativity,
the Three; in the suit of Cups, this symbolizes
creativity in the realm of emotions.

Rider Waite Smith Tarot
*A calm and steady knight with wings on his
helmet and on his spurs holds a cup out in front
of him.* Whereas the Knight of Swords charges
ahead, the Knight of Cups seems calm and
collected, sure of himself. This Knight is the
one of legend, "the knight in white shining armor" who rescues fair maidens
in emotional distress. The suit of Cups is about emotional awareness.
Emotions are the primary tool of creation on the manifest plane of physical
reality. A thought cannot create, it can only stand for something; it represents an archetype, a symbol, a direction, or a concept. Only when you
attach an emotion to a thought does it become a belief; when you apply the
emotion in a consistent way, your thought manifests in the physical. This
happens whether you are conscious of the process or not. The lesson that
the Tarot wants to impart is that you can use your thoughts and emotions
to create consciously.

KEYWORDS
sentimental/romantic
devoted/secure
appreciates beauty
sensitive/imaginative
prone to self-delusion
loves magic/visionary
refined tastes/subtle
a rich inner life
introverted/shy
slow/careful
thoughtful/empathetic

The Twelve reduces to a Three. Nature is the creative Three that you see in the Major Arcana card, The Empress/IMAGINATION. Nature is the machine of creation; it is the womb that the implicate field uses to generate form. Nature is your physical body, your personal subconscious, and the global agreement (collective subconscious) all at the same time. As your subconscious is directed by your thoughts and your emotional frequency, it creates automatically. Your body reflects the thoughts and beliefs hidden in your subconscious. Mother Nature takes your thoughts and emotions for commands, thus creating what you see before you, in the *smoky mirror* of manifest "reality."

The horse in this card is the body of the knight, representing his subconscious, emotions, and physical body at the same time. The horse marches steadily on, in loyal partnership with the knight on his back. Your physical body is the faithful vehicle for your emotions; like the horse in this picture, it carries and stores each emotion in a physical location in your body. Just as the mental body is expressed and put in motion (e-motion) by the physical brain, so the horse of the body carries the emotions forward, enabling emotions to act, or express themselves, in the outer physical world. As the horse is guided by the reins of the rider, so emotions follow the state of your consciousness. Emotions are given an outlet and way to express through the body. If you rush about like the Knight of Wands, or crash ahead heedlessly through life like the Knight of Swords, your body will take the brunt of the unconscious thoughts and emotions that lie buried in your subconscious.

The Knight of Cups displays a calm demeanor. He is aligned with his horse; he is a rider who doesn't need spurs to compel the horse forward, he just needs to touch its sides gently and guide it with his knees. The only spurs that this knight has are the spiritual wings attached to his feet.

The horse is a willing partner and companion because the knight has gentled his horse (his subconscious/physical body) with love, instead of breaking its spirit with control and domination. The knight offers the cup of his emotions without pushing himself on anyone. He is not in a hurry to gain anything; he has nothing to prove. Instead, he uses his emotions to align himself with what he desires. Emotional mastery means that you have learned how to carry and nurture the emotional vibration that matches the frequency of what you desire. This is how the Law of Resonance works; it is a law that works mechanically, like gravity.

12

Resonance occurs when two or more interconnected
objects share the same vibrational frequency.[1]

When You get This Card in a Reading

You are about to receive a gift, an offering, or maybe even a proposal. The emotions around the event are the determining factors in how, or whether, you should accept the offer; if you sense that the source of the offer is ungrounded or emotionally turbulent, you may be in for a rough ride. Alternatively, you may find that this card signifies the beginning or the end of a quest of the heart.

Meditation

A clear offering; will you accept or pass it by?

KNIGHT OF WATER

THE QUEST

Tarot of Creativity

The Knight of Water surrenders to the current of emotions without suppressing or becoming attached to them. He knows that emotions are meant to flow and not be contained; like a karate master, he simply doesn't resist the energy that surrounds him.

As a rock in the stream allows water to flow and swirl around it, so the knight is aware of the flow of his emotions, but doesn't allow himself to become identified with them. At the same time he recognizes the wisdom of the water as it slowly erodes and dissolves the stones that block it. Now that he understands what it means to choose and channel his emotions, he can use emotions as a tool. The Knight of Water is ready to finally take action, and go on a hero's quest.

What is the goal of his quest? None other than the Holy Grail—the cup, the womb of life. The Grail represents the hidden Divine Feminine, symbol of the female principle, the *anima* lost in the masculine paradigm

1   ascensionglossary.com/index.php/Law_of_Resonance

that sought to exclude or exploit it. Like most seekers, the knight may be mistakenly searching in the outer world for what is hidden deep in his Soul. His Higher Self wants him to attain the wholeness represented by finding the partner of his self-conscious—he seeks to find (rediscover/remember) his feminine subconscious, represented by the CUP of the Holy Grail.

This will balance the masculine active, outer nature of the knight. Finding the Grail of his Soul—the Divine Feminine principle—will quench his thirst for wholeness and completion. In the legend of Percival, the knight goes on a quest for the Holy Grail, and finds the Fisher King who represents himself at a later stage of life (King as opposed to Knight), wounded in the "groin" and rendered impotent. His injury is the Wound of Incarnation that became an affliction when he denied the totality of himself, when he denied the greater part of himself, his Divine nature and the creative feminine side of himself (the Jungian "anima").

> In Chrétien de Troyes' *Percival, the Story of the Grail*, Percival, meets the crippled Fisher King and sees a grail, not yet identified as "holy," but he fails to ask a question that would have healed the injured king.[1]

In seeking healing through his quest for wholeness, he learns to love, and to love all parts of himself. He achieves atonement—"at-one-ment," or "of one mind"—when he stops striving to force completion by dominating Mother Nature; instead he has learned to listen and be still in the presence of Divinity, which suddenly isn't on the horizon of his quest, but surrounds him with the balm and wholeness of love.

When You get This Card in a Reading
Quench your desire in action.

Meditation
Go forth on a quest of the heart.

---

1   en.wikipedia.org/wiki/Percival

KNIGHT OF PENTACLES

KNIGHT of PENTACLES

S = SYMBOLS

OAK LEAVES = strength, permanence, life, stability
RED bridle & tunic = earthly desires
YELLOW sky = personal power , ego, self-conscious
PLOWED FIELDS = planting desires (seeds)

E = ENERGY

The Knight of Pentacles is stable and unmoving.

E = EMOTIONS

Stability. Solidness. Patience. Trust.

R = NUMBER

This suit is closest to both the meaning and the result of the Twelve's reductive number, Three as represented by the Major Arcana card #3, The Empress/IMAGINATION—the card that represents Mother Nature/Earth.

Rider Waite Smith Tarot

A standing knight on a heavy destrier offers a pentacle. In the Knight of Pentacles/EARTH, the number Twelve reaches the final point in the creative process: material manifestation. The Knight of Pentacles in the Rider Waite Smith deck shows a very solid knight mounted on a large horse. The horse in this card is different from all the other horses in the knight cards: it seems to be a destrier—a war horse that was bred to carry knights in war. But this horse is calm, collected: a stolid mount. It seems to be a draft horse, meant for pulling a plow or large vehicle—a work horse. The human rider and his horse form a perfect partnership. The fields that this team planted and plowed are in the background of this picture.

In the early days of the Roman empire, the generals were drafted from farmers, and after the war, they humbly returned to their farms to continue cultivating their fields. The Knight of Pentacles is just such a man. Perhaps

KEYWORDS
unimaginative/stolid
hard worker/persistent
attention to details
loyal/stubborn
one-dimensional
pragmatic/industrious
uncompromising/ethical
perfectionist
resists change
prudent/careful

unimaginative and stolid, he is nonetheless the man you want to call upon to do the work you need done. With his help you can build a house, a business, a family, or a whole new paradigm. He is the laborer and the contractor all rolled into one.

He doesn't envision the project nor does he have lofty visions of new worlds. He is content to build according to someone else's direction or plans. He is dependable and doesn't shirk at work. He knows that what we are collectively building takes patience and understanding—he knows that there is a time to plow, a time to nurture, and a time to harvest the crop.

This knight is worthy of your trust and you would do well to cultivate him for a friend. He will be there when you need him. He is the tree in the forest that shelters all the other trees under his foliage. He is the man who nurtures and provides for others because that is his nature. He asks nothing from you that he is not willing to give: loyalty, love, solidity, friendship.

He wears oak leaves in his helmet and the same symbol adorns the head of his steed. Oak is a symbol in all Western cultures of steadiness, solidity, patience, and time. It takes a lot of time for an acorn to turn into a robust oak tree. But the result, like a well-constructed house, is worth it. When you want to manifest something that lasts, call upon the Knight of Pentacles; you will be glad that you did.

When You get This Card in a Reading

A solid offer is before you. Consider it from all standpoints before you commit yourself.

Meditation

Abundance is natural; it is the true reality underlying all human artifice. .

KNIGHT OF EARTH

CONCEIVE

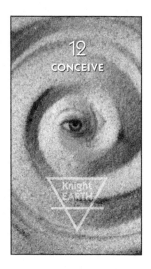

Tarot of Creativity

In *The Tarot of Creativity*, the title of the Knight of Earth is entitled CONCEIVE. We might consider a knight to be masculine energy, but the TOC does not have gender bias; instead it promotes the concepts of inclusion and wholeness. A woman can be a warrior, and a man can birth a child.

To understand this card in the TOC it is necessary to look at the preceding card in the suit: the Page of Earth, which is inscribed with the title, Desire. The Suit of Pentacles/EARTH is the last stage in the creative process, where the energy of intent (Fire) is coalesced into matter (Earth). As stated previously, the court cards are the masters of their suit. Here is the process shown in the Earth suit:

Page of Earth: Desire
Knight of Earth: Conceive
Queen of Earth: Incubate
King of Earth: Create (birth)

Following the path of Earth through the court cards, you would proceed from the intent of Desire to merge with your intended (intent), which inspires Conception. Next, you Incubate your creative idea, eventually resulting in the act of Creation, when you succeed in birthing your desire into form.

When You get This Card in a Reading

This is the moment you have been working toward for a long time. Now is the time to focus on practical considerations.

Meditation

The Higher Self *conceives*; the mind *perceives*.

S = SYMBOLS

CHILD/FLOWERS = life in the face of death
DEAD KING = death of the ego
SKELETON = death of form
POPE = belief is no defense against change
RISING SUN = awakened pineal gland
WHITE HORSE = Spirit
WHITE ROSE = the purification of desire
WOMAN = surrender to change

E = ENERGY

The main directive line is the horse that is proceeding from left to right; from Spirit to matter.

E = EMOTIONS

The inevitability of death and change.

R = NUMBER

THIRTEEN is the number of the Divine Feminine; it is the natural number of months in the year, based upon the lunar calendar. Thirteen reduces to FOUR, the number of the Earth—the number of the Divine Mother, or "mater" (matter/mother) in Latin.

DEATH

ARCHETYPE

Rider Waite Smith Tarot

Many people are afraid of this card because they have been taught that Death means the end of life but this card really signifies *change*; it says that the deeper meaning of death is simply a change of form. Energy—like consciousness—cannot be created or destroyed, it can only transform. Key #13 signifies that change is a principle of creation, and it comes to all of us, whether we wish it or not.

The white horse of Death marches from left to right, as if it is going to ride over the figures in its path. Each figure in the picture deals with the apparition of Death in a different way: the ecclesiastic tries to importune the rider, the woman swoons, while the child offers a nosegay of flowers under the very hooves of the massive steed. Of the three upright figures, only the child is answering the change represented by Death with welcome, the only empowered attitude to impending change. The child represents the innocent inner child of Spirit. Spirit has the capability to understand the greater perspective; it sees change from a higher standpoint.

The dead king on the ground represents the ego that was dethroned when the old king, representing materialism, lost his reign. The horse of Death has crushed the crown of the king under its hooves when it rode over the king. In the Tarot, a crown symbolizes the crown chakra, the mind, or ego. The ego seeks to rule the material world, but the real ruler of the material world is the principle of change that Death symbolizes. Change is simply the transformation of one form into another. Death, or change, will always triumph.

The ego seeks to impose an unnatural stability on the world it knows. The ego resists the things that it cannot control because it is afraid of change, even when the change is for its eventual good. The ego is short-sighted because it lives in the left brain of reason and linear logic. It can only see what it has already experienced, because the left brain lacks the imagination to see a different future.

Notice the discrepancy in the size of the three figures on the right side of the image versus the size of the horse and rider. In the art of the Dark Ages, importance and power were conveyed by the relative size of the figures: important and powerful figures were portrayed larger, while unimportant, powerless figures were depicted proportionately smaller. This is the opposite of the art from the next period, the Renaissance. Italian perspective sought to represent an "objective" reality, rather than a subjective one.

The overwhelmingly large size of Death demonstrates the inevitability, importance, and power of death. The WHITE ROSE on the black flag represents the purification of desire, not by diminishing or eliminating it, but by purifying it.

The rose on the flag is the same one that was carried in the hand of the Fool when he descended to Earth. Man's destiny is to eventually become the Angel, or Perfected Man. This card shows how this transformation is done, by burning away the carbon of old, materialistic desires. As man creates his world whether he is conscious of creating or not, the death of old desires represents a new level of consciousness, that of the evolved man, or Angel. He becomes the Angel through the purification of the basis of his desire—no longer based upon need and lack, but instead upon truth and surrender to desires (the intent) of the Higher Self.

When You get This Card in a Reading

The caterpillar has to die in order to fly as a butterfly. When it enters the cocoon, its body entirely liquefies.

Meditation

A flower cannot bloom without dying first as a seed.

DEATH

METAMORPHOSIS

Tarot of Creativity

The Thirteen is the combination of the One of The Magician and the Three of The Empress. This combination shows how the principle of intent (The Magician) results in change when applied in the field of Nature.

Death is METAMORPHOSIS in the TOC. Since death is change, and change is one of the primary, immutable laws of the universe, it is not to be feared. Metamorphosis hints at the continuance of life. Energy cannot be created or destroyed in the universe; it can only be transformed.

The metamorphosis represented in this card is the man's ability to recognize the impulse of Spirit under the appearance of the material form. The evolved man has learned to purify his desires from the temporal and materialistic to what he really desires, which is beyond all temporal forms. Eventually he learns that the higher truth is not to eschew all temporal desires, but to find the Divinity inside the Desire.

Many of our material desires are simply stand-in desires for something else: for instance, we desire food because it is a symbol of the nourishment that we all subconsciously know we need. The only reason we need nourishment is because the illusion of separation tells us the lie that we are not deserving of love. The lie of separation tells us that we have needs and that these needs can remain unfulfilled unless we go out and supply them ourselves. Need is the opposite of faith.

Faith is not built on belief or on proof, it just *is*. Faith is the result of the ego's surrender; the ego has to learn to "die" in order to be transformed from a petty energy form filled with incessant needs and desires, into an effective tool of the Higher Self and a partner for the Self.

The figure on the TOC card dances like the Hindu goddess, Kali.

> Kāli is the Hindu goddess associated with empowerment, called Shakti. Shiva is called Kāla, which means "the eternal time," and the name of Kālī, his consort, also means "Time" or

"Death" (as in "time has come"). Hence, Kāli is the Goddess of Time and Change.[1]

Thirteen is the magical number of the divine feminine. Like the Hindu goddess Kali, the divine feminine force demonstrates the ultimate mystery of death in life and life in death. The cells of the body accept death as a part of life and growth. The individual cells cooperate for the good of the whole; they sacrifice their life on the anvil of Life. Evolution depends on change; life depends on change. Without individual cell death, we have cancer, which could be said to symbolically represent a denial of the necessity of death in life.

Each cell of your body is constantly recreating itself; it is up to you to supply the images that direct it to build a better cell every time it reproduces. If, through the power of the Magician, you use your magical powers for good (life) rather than for evil (the opposite of life) then the power of Nature will see to it that each new cell is a better one. Nature is at your command. It is up to you to discipline your thoughts and emotions by removing those that do not serve you. Then Nature will execute your higher, conscious desires instead of your lower unconscious ones.

The death of the ego is really the death of the small desire for the larger one. Or, you might say that the death of the ego is really the death of the idea of separation as the basis of reality. We exchange the concept of separation for a new (actually ancient) idea of inclusion and love as the basis of all that is.

When You get This Card in a Reading
Have faith that change is always for the ultimate good.

Meditation
The caterpillar cannot imagine the life of the butterfly.

Related to
The Emperor/INSIGHT (Key #4)

---

1 en.wikipedia.org/wiki/Kali

QUEEN OF WANDS

S = SYMBOLS
CAT = magic, assistance
LION symbols = sign of Leo, fixed sign of Fire
SUNFLOWERS = symbol of life, the Sun, Wands
YELLOW mountains = attainment of personal power
YELLOW robe = personal power, mastery of ego

E = ENERGY
The Queen of Wands is a static figure. She is surrounded by an equally static environment. Nothing is moving or stirring.

E = EMOTIONS
Calm. Collected. Self-assured.

R = NUMBER
The Wands/FIRE suit is the beginning of the path of creativity or process of manifestation; the number Thirteen is the number of the Divine Feminine, therefore in the suit of Wands/FIRE, the mastery indicated is that of intent, expressed as a feminine form.

QUEEN of WANDS.

KEYWORDS
calm/collected
enthusiastic/sincere
open/helpful
helps others gain
self-confidence
energetic/athletic
healthy/vital
optimistic/confident
psychic/compassionate
a good manager
quiet/self-assured

13

Rider Waite Smith Tarot
A queen sits on a throne of lions holding a staff as a scepter and a sunflower; a black cat sits alertly at her feet. When you reduce the number Thirteen, you get the number Four, which is the number of the Earth and the number of the heart chakra. The heart chakra stands in the middle of the seven chakras of the physical body like a bridge between the lower and higher ones. When its original function is restored, the unconditional Love emanating from the heart chakra flows out to bridge the physical world and the spiritual world.

This card refers to the archetype of the wisdom of love, the principle of the wise mother, the Holy Spirit, or divine Sophia, that resides in the heart of all of us.

All goddesses are representations of the principle and energy of love that underlies all form. The Goddess Sophia represents a universal principle or archetype; symbolizing the nurturing, unconditionally loving aspect of the Holy Spirit that is buried deep within our psyche.

Who can thrive without the love and care of their mother? How long would we live if the planet Earth did not sustain us? The energy of the wisdom of love infuses all matter, it is a wave that undulates below all material existence. Love is the energy that supports the cornucopia of matter,* the ever-flowing breast of the Divine Mother that feeds all life. The archetype of the Goddess Sophia represents the understanding that love is the energy that supports everything in the physical. We can use this archetype to induce love to flow in our life by allowing the principle of love to move freely through us, using us as a channel on the physical plane.

Like a shaman, the Queen of Wands/FIRE is an expert at "seeing" the energetic reality underlying the world of appearances. She is an expert in the unseen world of energy. A black Cat sits watchfully at her feet. Cats are known to be psychically aware. They walk in other worlds and see things that we cannot. The Queen of Wands is allied with her small feline friend. Like her Cat, she is not afraid to walk between worlds.

The purr has been scientifically proven to promote healing. The cat will purr to heal itself or its human friends. In the same way, the Queen of Wands uses frequency to heal or manifest what she desires. She works with the lines of intent and energy to restore wholeness in the broken and disconnected world that she finds around her. The magic of the Queen of Wands is natural magic; it is the magic of the alignment of personal intent with the general Source of Love. We are all capable of such magic; it is part of our natural human inheritance.

The Queen of Wands doesn't advertise her skills or proclaim her mastery. She doesn't need the adulation of others. Her needs are few, she has learned that setting her intent to align with that of Spirit is all she has to do; this has to be a constant practice, as all masters know. In this way, the perfect next thing in her life simply comes to her without effort or worry. When it is time, it simply manifests before her: do you choose me? And she can choose or not.

Her emblem is the sunflower, in French this flower is called the "tournesol," which means "to follow the Sun"—this definition sheds light on the meaning of this symbol in the card. The Queen of Wands has mastered the pure energy (intent) of the suit, or path, of Wands by "following the light" of the Sun, which dispenses life and awareness on Earth. The Sun is a symbol for the state or process of enlightenment; in the case of the Queen of Wands, she, like the sunflower, absorbs or ingests light. Light is synonymous with knowledge, not the knowledge of dry, rational facts, but the light of inner knowing; the Queen of Wands expresses the light inside her.

When You get This Card in a Reading

When you get this card in a reading, pay attention to the energy of passion in your life. What excites you? Desire is the energy trail that your Higher Self is laying down for you.

Meditation

The Queen of Wands banks the fire of her passion for a long slow burn.

QUEEN OF FIRE

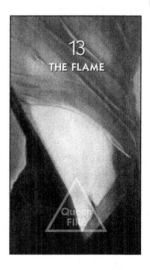

THE FLAME

Tarot of Creativity

In *The Tarot of Creativity*, the Queen of Fire is THE FLAME of pure intent and desire. The mastery of intent and desire requires a strong individual who has erased the lower, unconscious emotions from her life, and purified her desire in the flame of her original, innate being.

The Queen of Fire is a female Merlin with the ability to walk between worlds. A master of the energetic reality that underlies all form, she knows that to effect true change and manifest a new reality, one has to employ focused intent and work with the lines of pure energy. At an intuitive level, she uses the nature of quantum reality to make a particle shift into a wave and back into a particle again.

The preceding card in the Suit of Fire is the Knight of Fire, THE SHAMAN, who is a master of the energy of desire and intent. The Shaman was preceded by the Page of Fire, THE ICONOCLAST, who serves the path of intent by smashing the false idols of beliefs. In doing so, he has prepared the way for the Queen of Fire, who lives light, without the baggage of unprocessed emotions.

Desire, when it has been purified of heavy unprocessed emotions, is a powerful force. This is why only a master of creativity can handle the force of desire, and the power of the Flame of Pure Desire is withheld from the grasp of the ego-driven man. It is only possible to handle this force when you are no longer driven to succeed in the outer world or want to obtain power at the expense of others.

The Queen of Fire reflects the principle of true mastery in her demeanor: alignment with her inner nature and with the intent of her Higher Self. Like a flame, she is a fluid being who needs nothing except energy; she channels energy to produce what she desires—or rather what her Higher Self desires—into a fluid experience that flowers naturally into perfect form, and then, in its time, dies down to reform again: the particle collapsing back into its waveform counterpart.

The Queen of Fire is in perfect, balanced alignment with her Higher Self. As the material version of her Higher Self, she executes the intent of her Spirit, and she achieves her desires as if by magic, or truth be told, by magic indeed.

When You get This Card in a Reading

The Queen of Fire represents the mastery of the primal force of creation. But mastery isn't domination, it is a feeling of alignment, a partnership of your lower self with your Higher Self. The Fire that bridges your material experience with the intent of your Spirit is the FLAME of passion.

Meditation

A flame can heat a house or burn it down.

QUEEN OF SWORDS

QUEEN ⚔ SWORDS.

S = SYMBOLS
BUTTERFLIES = transmutation, magic
CHERUB on throne = angel
CLOUDS = symbol of Air suit (Swords)

E = ENERGY
The Queen of Swords is static against a background of movement: the turbulent lines of the clouds. This indicates that she is able to maintain her inner balance even when surrounded by unrest and change.

E = EMOTIONS
Discerning. Fair. Swift.

R = NUMBER
The number Thirteen is expressed through The Queen of Swords/AIR as the creative combination of two masculine or active numbers—the One and the Three—which combine to make the number of the Earth, the four.

KEYWORDS
discerning/honest
impartial/clear-seeing
blunt/fair/calm/wise
intelligent/guileless
astute judge of character
non-judgmental/realistic
straightforward
sees through illusions
neutral cool/self-assured

13

Rider Waite Smith Tarot
A queen sits on a throne embellished with angels and butterflies. The queen pictured here is a fair but stern ruler. As the Queen of Swords she is a master of her mental body and her ego. She has learned to use the sword of clarity and justice to cut through all the smoke around her: through the falsehoods and false beliefs that most people use as armor to protect them from the onslaught of life. She is clear-seeing; she could be a clairvoyant or a judge or a seer.

No matter which role she fills, her lack of personal beliefs allows her to catch a vision of a future and see through lies, emotional confusion, wishful thinking, and illusions. The feminine form of mastery indicated by the number of this card is tempered by the suit, so it symbolizes the mastery of thought. This card could be said to symbolize the Goddess Athena, who represented high principles of fairness, equality, discernment and emotional sobriety:

> ...the poet [Homer], assert that he meant by Athena "mind" [nous] and "intelligence" [dianoia], and the maker of names appears to have had a singular notion about her; and indeed calls her by a still higher title, "divine intelligence," as though he would say: "This is she who has the mind of God." Perhaps, however, the name Theonoe may mean "she who knows divine things" (ta theia noousa) better than others. Nor shall we be far wrong in supposing that the author of it wished to identify this Goddess with moral intelligence (en ethei noesin), and therefore gave her the name Etheonoe; which, however, either he or his successors have altered into what they thought a nicer form, and called her Athena.[1]

Though Athena is a goddess of war strategy, she disliked fighting without purpose. Athena emphasizes that we should use intuitive wisdom, rather than anger or violence, to resolve disputes.

The Queen of Swords uses her sword as an editing tool, as such, she could be the goddess or muse for the literary arts; she represents the left-brain skill of editing and ruthless analysis that all artists must learn. She doesn't allow sentiment or emotions to guide her decisions. She knows how to cut out what is superfluous and unnecessary in order to reveal the pure truth at the core. Like the sculptor Michelangelo, she confidently cuts away everything that is not germane to the subject, releasing the figure inside the stone.

Her attitude may seem ruthless, and on one level it is: she doesn't put up with fools, but her most stern ruthlessness is reserved for herself. As a master of the Swords suit, she has shed most, if not all, of her limiting beliefs and egoic manipulations. But she doesn't allow herself the illusion of the outer forms of power. She maintains her own ego under a tight leash. She knows that any thought of "power-over" others is a dip into unconscious behavior; the chief ploy of an unhealthy ego that is trying to wrest control away from the larger Self.

She is not in a battle with her ego, but she hasn't yet learned to make it a friend either. One could say that she is a master of impeccability and

---

1   Plato, Cratylus, 407b

sobriety. Not succumbing to old beliefs, she exhibits a razor-sharp intellect and vision that gives her an air of impeccable fairness. You can trust the Queen of Swords to be true to her own ideals first, and while she can see your heart and mind in a swift glance, she doesn't judge you. Rather she registers what she sees without emotional inflection. This makes her a sober ally and friend. But don't expect sugar-coating or romantic embellishments for the sake of agreement or friendship.

The Queen of Swords is blunt, honest, just and fair. She is a being in constant battle with herself, and thus she maintains a kind of tense equilibrium, while she presents a poised demeanor to the outside world that others take for a rather unearthly calm, and sometimes mistake for a cold demeanor, or a judgmental nature. She doesn't look to battle with you, but she won't lie to you either, or allow you to deceive yourself.

The process of creation proceeds from the pure implicate (Fire) to the explicate or material form (Earth); from wave to particle, and from particle to wave. Like the goddess Athena who emerged fully formed from the head of her father Zeus, the magic of inspiration when combined with the energy of passion and the potency of intent produces a child of the Mind, perfectly formed.

13

When You get This Card in a Reading

Allow yourself to use discernment and judgment in order to choose wisely. Cut out whatever is superfluous in your life.

Meditation

Form follows function.

QUEEN OF AIR

REMEMBER

Tarot of Creativity

The Queen of Air in *The Tarot of Creativity* shows a parent and small child walking hand in hand down a path. The child has no shadow. The card is entitled REMEMBER. This refers to the ability of the mind to access memories past the current incarnation or lifetime: what people refer to as the Akashic records.

This kind of memory is an innate function of the higher mind. While the Queen of Swords in the RWS deck shows a stern warrior who has learned to discipline her mind in order to achieve mastery, the equivalent card in *The Tarot of Creativity* focuses on what happens when you go a step further, beyond mental discipline, and learn how to use the mind as a clear channel for your Higher Self. Just as in the movie, *The Matrix*, Trinity could download the ability to fly a helicopter in the instant before she had to fly it, so we can download any ability from the incredible resources hidden in the quantum implicate, by tapping into the hidden resources of our universal mind.

While the quantum implicate symbolized by The High Priestess/ MEMORY contains all there is, plus all that could be, it is frozen, locked into stasis because time does not exist in the implicate. Existence in material form requires time, while the implicate is locked into non-existence and hovers outside form in an unexpressed state; it "exists" only as pure potential.

The implicate field is a box that is bigger on the inside than it appears on the outside; inside the apparently finite box is an infinite space that exists outside time. The treasure house of potential in the implicate field is waiting for the right key to unlock it: the conscious direction of the self-conscious, represented by the principle of ATTENTION in the Magician card. When you insert the One of ATTENTION from the Magician into the Three of IMAGINATION, the power of your directed consciousness releases the power of the implicate field. The key that unlocks this box of virtually limitless content is clear intent, but like her RWS counterpart the Queen of Swords, the Queen of Air can only access intent by living a life of emotional sobriety and mental discipline.

When the Fool finally reaches the mastery of this card she finds that she now remembers her original pre–incarnate Self. And when she inserts her personal key of intent into the locked memory box of the quantum Akash, she accesses the incalculable riches of her Soul, releasing the frozen resources of the quantum implicate into her life and onto the field of time and space.

When You get This Card in a Reading

Mental clarity is the key that unlocks the treasures of the real, unfettered, original mind that is our inheritance.

Meditation

What is natural to you? The Queen of Air asks you to remember.

QUEEN OF CUPS

S = SYMBOLS

CUP = a ciborium, a sacred container
CHERUBS = innocent subconscious
WATER = flow of the subconscious
ROBE with water pattern = subconscious

E = ENERGY

The Queen of Cups sits on a throne that is surrounded by flowing water. The swirls and eddies express a fluidity of motion that contrasts with the Queen's still pose. Her gaze directs the viewer's attention to the cup that she holds.

E = EMOTIONS

Sweet. Nurturing. Understanding. Compassionate.

R = NUMBER

The number Thirteen in the Suit of Cups/ WATER is almost a redundancy, as the feminine principle is often credited with intuitive skills. The Queen of Cups as a feminine master of the Suit of Water certainly knows how to use her emotions as the intuitive tool they were meant to be.

KEYWORDS
nurturing/empathetic
unconditionally loving
Earth-loving/spiritual
psychic/telepathic
emotionally wise
patient/accepting
kind/understanding
heart-centered person
emotional healing

Rider Waite Smith Tarot

A queen sits on a throne surrounded by flowing water and looks at a lidded cup. The Queen of Cups represents unconditional love which is at the heart of what is called "Christ Consciousness." As the mistress of her suit, the Queen of Cups allows herself to flow with the energy of her subconscious. She knows that the real power in creative activity is emotional awareness. Regardless of the state of one's consciousness, emotions create our reality. Once we realize that we are projecting what we feel onto the screen of holographic reality, we can step back and learn to master the tool of emotional awareness.

This doesn't mean that you should try to control or suppress your emotions. As a wise master, the Queen of Cups allows her emotions to swirl and eddy around her. And even though she is surrounded by water, the symbol of emotions, she remains in balance, detached yet nonetheless engaged. She sits in the flow of the water of her emotions (subconscious) as it swirls around her, loving and conscious, patient, like a rock in a stream. She knows the wisdom of patience, the guidance of intuition, and the healing power of love.

"There but for the grace of God go I" would be her philosophy if she chose to state it, which she never does, because she knows that to teach someone what she innately knows would be a violation of the universal law of Free Will. She knows that everyone has a unique path, and the joy of every path lies in the act of self-discovery.

This queen is nurturing, patient, kind, and loving. She is a steady and balanced lover, mother or loyal friend, ready to listen even when you are at your most vulnerable. When you are at rock bottom she is there, the steady rock in the stream of your emotions.

When You get This Card in a Reading

When you get this card in a reading, remember that any creative project requires nurturing in order to grow; let the energy flow naturally like the water under the feet of the Queen.

Meditation

Unconditional love is the Holy Grail of material existence; the energy of love transcends time and space.

QUEEN OF WATER

IMMERSION

Tarot of Creativity

All emotions create. Starting with a thought or belief, emotions energize mere concepts into life. Then these creations—our brain children—start to have a life of their own. We are constantly either feeding our beliefs with our emotional energy, or manifesting new forms from our mental/emotional state. The master of the magical tool of emotions realizes this, and starts to choose her emotions. This is what it means to create consciously.

The Queen of Water is the mistress of emotions, which are simply a vibratory state. Our emotions range from the low frequency of depression to the high frequency of joy, with a range of nuances in between. Emotions may stem from us, but they are also inherited from our family, our ancestral line, or our friends. And then there is the collective conscious that creates the agreed reality/hologram with our beliefs and emotions. We live in a sea of emotions that are emitted from every human being on the planet.

The queen knows how to swim like a mermaid in that sea; is her natural habitat. She fearlessly IMMERSES herself in the stream of emotional awareness, never drowning, nor losing her way. She not only knows how to how to deal with emotions that are flowing around her, but she also knows how to use her vibrational state—her emotions—as a creative tool.

Our thoughts are given form with our vibrational state on the material plane: this is our emotional state. These thought forms are imbued with life in direct proportion to the amount of emotions that have been input in them. The longer amount of time that the beliefs and emotions that support them are held, the more "solid" the form that evolves out of the belief. A collectively created thought form such as an archetype or societal pattern has more life than a personally held belief, while the personal belief has more reality to the person who holds it than to someone who doesn't agree with it. These thought forms are our creations: they are literally the children of our minds.

Emotions are the gateway to intuition.[1]

Like a good mother, the Queen of Water doesn't deny the children of her imagination. She knows that any emotion contains a seed of information behind the energy: this information is received in the right brain as intuition. The mistress of Water listens to her emotions attentively, responding to their message rather than succumbing to their emotional turbulence. A good parent doesn't criticize or punish a child, but learns to redirect or channel their energy, not denying the child's emotions but not indulging their tantrums either.

Thought forms are the emotional creations of our personal pasts, as well as the creations of the collective conscious. And these children of our minds—our creations—each desire the energy that only we can provide. We must choose what emotional reality and concepts we want to support in our lives. If we feed a thought form with our emotions it will continue: negative thought forms require unconscious, negative emotions while empowering thought forms require conscious thoughts accompanied by positive emotions.

If you are ever in doubt as to whether a belief is true for you or not, pay attention to the emotions surrounding it; a true thought will feel good—you feel empowered, as if you have limitless possibilities. A false belief will feel bad—you feel as if you are blocked or trapped within the emotions that it engenders within you.

If we choose to not feed a thought form with our emotional energy, it dissolves and discharges its energy back into the neutral energy of the implicate (represented in the Tarot as The High Priestess/MEMORY).

When You get This Card in a Reading
The Queen of Water shows us how to deal with emotions by allowing ourselves to immerse fully and fearlessly in them. She tells us to listen and translate the messages they have to give us. Only then can we transmute the energy back into a more neutral form through our unconditional love and acceptance.

Meditation
Immerse yourself in your art, in your creativity, in life itself.

---

1   *Parallel Mind, The Art of Creativity*, Aliyah Marr

QUEEN OF PENTACLES

S = SYMBOLS

ANGEL head = spiritual, Aquarius
CRAB = emotions, shelter, Cancer
GARDEN = abundance, Mother Earth
MOUNTAINS = spiritual attainment
RABBIT = fertility, sexuality, abundance
RAMS head = potency, virility, animus, Aries
RED ROBE = earthly existence, desire
ROSES = material desire, sensuality
THRONE = the lap of power and abundance

E = ENERGY

The Queen of Pentacles gazes fondly and fixedly at the Pentacle in her lap.

E = EMOTIONS

Fulfilled. Sated. Supported. Comfortable.

R = NUMBER

The Queen of Pentacles/EARTH completes the path of creativity through the number Thirteen, as she shows how Nature can work in fruitful cooperation with us.

KEYWORDS
loving/down-to-earth
nurturing/healing
wise-woman
loves children & animals
generous/unselfish
practical/direct
sensual/imaginative
loyal/steadfast
good with plants
honest/sincere
home/hearth

Rider Waite Smith Tarot

A queen sits in a garden and holds a pentacle on her lap. This card shows a woman who knows how to birth new worlds, like her counterpart in the Major Arcana, the Empress/IMAGINATION. She cradles a pentacle like a newborn baby in her lap. The lap of a woman is a visual metaphor for the womb. It symbolizes the abundance and creative power of Mother Nature. In the TOC, this card's title is INCUBATE. This is what the Queen is doing in the RWS deck. The womb is the incubation chamber for physical life. As the second chakra, it is also is the incubation chamber for creative projects. The sacred chamber in the "sacral" chakra (men and women both have a "womb of creation") is integral to how we manifest physical reality on Earth. This card represents the ancient symbol for the archetype of the

Divine Feminine, the Goddess Gaia, who was none other than the divine representation of Mother Earth.

> In Greek mythology, Gaia, from Ancient Greek, Ge, "land" or "earth" was the personification of the Earth, and one of the Greek primordial deities. Gaia was the great mother of all: the primal Greek Mother Goddess; creator and giver of birth to the Earth and all the Universe; the heavenly gods, the Titans, and the Giants were born to her. The gods reigning over their classical pantheon were born from her union with Uranus (the sky), while the sea-gods were born from her union with Pontus (the sea). Her equivalent in the Roman pantheon was Terra.[1]

The Pentacle featured here is an ancient mystical symbol of great import. The pentacle merges two ancient symbols into one: a five-pointed star, which represents man, housed and encompassed by the circle of Spirit. The circle is the glyph for the concept of the sphere, which symbolizes Spirit/God/the Infinite as the universal principle of Wholeness and completion. Spirit is described as the circle "whose center is everywhere and the circumference is nowhere." Thus, the pentacle symbolizes the enlightened man, he who lives in full consciousness of his spiritual nature.

The Queen of Pentacles is the mistress of Nature, which is at once material existence, Mother Nature, and her own physical body. Because this is a feminine form of mastery, she attracts what she desires instead of trying to pursue it. She sits in a Garden of Eden which is the manifestation of her conscious intent. The queen as a master of consciousness uses all the available tools for material manifestation. The result of the proper use of these tools is the final symbol that this Mistress of Manifestation holds in her lap: the Pentacle.

When You get This Card in a Reading
A woman knows how to incubate new life in her belly; the wise Queen of Pentacles tells us that we need to be patient while things are developing.

Meditation
Love is the power behind all creation.

---

1 en.wikipedia.org/wiki/Gaia_(mythology)

QUEEN OF EARTH

INCUBATE

Tarot of Creativity

This card shows us how the Thirteen when reduced to Four produces "matter" as a result of the integration of the information in the previous cards. Material manifestation on Earth is a natural result of the input of the energy of desire (Wands/FIRE), inspiration (Swords/AIR), and passion (Cups/WATER). The result of this alchemical union of the Divine Masculine and the Divine Feminine principles is the birth of a new form of matter.

In the TOC the Queen of Pentacles/EARTH is INCUBATING the energy of the previous suits. The Earth suit is the final stage of the creative process—manifestation. This card shows us that the form is already here, even as it is hidden in the magical cauldron: the Womb of the Infinite, as yet unexpressed in the implicate field.

When You get This Card in a Reading

The creative process requires a period to incubate in order to manifest.

Meditation

Time to incubate and nurture your creative ideas.

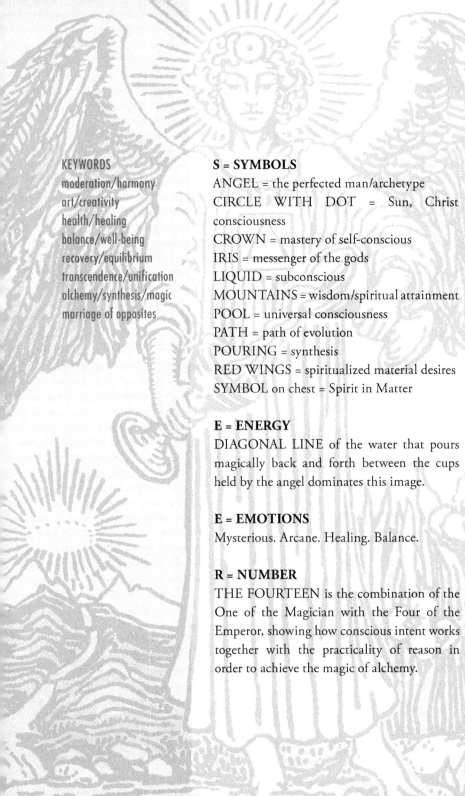

KEYWORDS
moderation/harmony
art/creativity
health/healing
balance/well-being
recovery/equilibrium
transcendence/unification
alchemy/synthesis/magic
marriage of opposites

S = SYMBOLS
ANGEL = the perfected man/archetype
CIRCLE WITH DOT = Sun, Christ consciousness
CROWN = mastery of self-conscious
IRIS = messenger of the gods
LIQUID = subconscious
MOUNTAINS = wisdom/spiritual attainment
POOL = universal consciousness
PATH = path of evolution
POURING = synthesis
RED WINGS = spiritualized material desires
SYMBOL on chest = Spirit in Matter

E = ENERGY
DIAGONAL LINE of the water that pours magically back and forth between the cups held by the angel dominates this image.

E = EMOTIONS
Mysterious. Arcane. Healing. Balance.

R = NUMBER
THE FOURTEEN is the combination of the One of the Magician with the Four of the Emperor, showing how conscious intent works together with the practicality of reason in order to achieve the magic of alchemy.

TEMPERANCE

ARCHETYPE

Rider Waite Smith Tarot

Temperance shows an angel with red wings mixing and blending a liquid by pouring it from one cup into another. This card is only another aspect of The Hierophant, as the number of this card, fourteen, reduces to the number Five.

Thus, like The Hierophant, Temperance is a teaching card; the angel is showing us how to artfully blend opposites in order to achieve a new substance, hinting at universal principles of balance and reciprocity. The insignia on the chest of the angel represents the figure of the pyramid in diagram, like an architectural plan: the square floor shown flat with the triangular side laid on top, just as you might collapse the pieces of a model upon one another. The triangle is inside the square, which signifies that Spirit is now inside matter. Seven is the esoteric number of the pyramid: Four is the square base (grounded/built on Earth) and Three is the number of the triangular side: the side that ascends into space to provide the higher perspective of enlightenment.

Temperance has two meanings: it means moderation—not going to extremes—and a technique to strengthen metal. Tempering is a heat treatment designed to achieve greater toughness by decreasing the hardness of the alloy, reducing its brittleness while increasing its flexibility and strength.

> While there are many criteria for evaluating a sword, generally the four key criteria are hardness, strength, flexibility and balance.[1]

The same criteria are applicable to the evolution of consciousness, the tempering of a man to become an Angel, or Perfected Man. The angel represents your Higher Self. The task of the Higher Self is to subject you to tests to determine if you are now a perfected vessel ready for more light, the light

1 en.wikipedia.org/wiki/Sword_making

of higher consciousness. This card asks: are you ready to pass to the next level of mastery? Or will you fail and have to repeat the lesson through another cycle of karma?

In the Tarot Tableau, this card falls directly under the last card in the first row: number Seven, The Chariot. This is significant for several reasons. Both cards are the summation of their respective row; they embody all the qualities of the preceding six cards.

Both cards have to do with preparing the body for more light, for the descent of the Higher Self into the physical form. Not a total descent, because our physical form could not take all this light at once—it would burn out our cells and fry our nervous systems. These two cards are necessary testing points, and represent gates to the next level.

In the TEMPERANCE card, the Angel mixes the opposites—the male and female aspects of the Self. He/she judiciously mixes these two opposites in equal measure in his/her own body, as the Angel is an androgynous being by nature.

Like a scientist in a lab, the Angel must have fine judgment: if the individual parts of the mixture are not first "tempered" or prepared properly before mixing, he/she may not succeed. In fact, if these substances are too raw, they may explode or otherwise ruin the experiment. The Angel seeks to mix these two substances in a way that produces a new substance that is more refined and wholly different than its parts.

When You get This Card in a Reading

This card asks: are you ready to pass to the next level of mastery? Or will you fail and have to repeat the lesson through another cycle of karma?

Meditation

Duality is a game of balance. The goal isn't to exit the game but to learn how to work within it.

14—TEMPERANCE

ALCHEMY

Tarot of Creativity

Alchemy is the study of the principles of the universe as related to the physical plane. The images in the Tarot suggest that the principles of alchemy were actually part of the reason for the cards, especially for the cards of the Major Arcana.

In the eyes of a variety of esoteric and Hermetic practitioners, the heart of alchemy is spiritual. Transmutation of lead into gold is presented as an analogy for personal transmutation, purification, and perfection. This approach is often termed 'spiritual,' 'esoteric,' or 'internal' alchemy.[1]

Spirit has always been inside matter but through the alchemy of evolution the amount of Spiritual awareness has been changed; as the density of the old consciousness is penetrated by the Higher Self, matter itself transforms and lightens; rising like steam from a boiling pot, or like steam from a sword plunged into a vat of water. The cosmic mind, Atman, or Higher Self worked with the ego of the adept to temper the mental/egoic body and the emotional/subconscious. The result is a new, more rarified blend of the divine triad—the renewed divine partnership of the Super Conscious, subconscious, and the self-conscious; a new partnership of Spirit, Heart, and Mind. This card shows the results of the magical synthesis of the three parts of the Self, which demonstrates the true purpose of ALCHEMY.

The true magic of alchemy can be observed in the world around us; the drive of opposites to experience synthesis or blending, as in the union of male and the female principles, the little bit of YIN inside the YANG and visa versa, the Animus inside the female and the Anima inside the male. At a higher level it shows the spiritual drive to experience unity with Spirit while in a physical body.

---

1   en.wikipedia.org/wiki/Alchemy

More than any other card in the Tarot, Temperance/ALCHEMY shows the magic of creativity in action. One of the prime functions of creativity is synthesis; the paradoxical nature of the attraction and marriage of opposites. Alchemy's main interest is the transmutation of energy and, ultimately, the transmutation of the self. Creative activity is the ultimate alchemy, transforming any experience, no matter how extreme or traumatic, into art.

In science, sublimation means that a substance has gone from one state to another state, without going through an intermediary state—such as going from a solid to a gaseous state, without becoming a liquid. An artist who releases and expresses his emotions through his work may find that his process carries him smoothly from one state—for example, depression or longing—into a state of happiness and attainment.

The artist's emotional expression can be transformative on not just the artist, but on the viewer as well. Artwork of this kind is a window on the human experience, revealing things that may otherwise remain in the dark for an entire lifetime.[1]

When You get This Card in a Reading
Only in duality can we have the experience of seeing creation in action.

Meditation
The whole is greater than the sum of the parts.

Related to
The Hierophant/INTUITION (Key #5)

---

1   *Parallel Mind, The Art of Creativity*, Aliyah Marr

14—KING OF WANDS

S = SYMBOLS

LION heraldry = Fire suit, LEO sign
OUROBORUS = eternity, cyclical, infinity
RED robe and hair = Fire (Wands) suit
SALAMANDER = the Fire element
YELLOW crown & robe = the self-conscious

E = ENERGY

The King of Wands gazes intently towards the left side of the card, drawing the viewer's attention to the left. Although there is one strong diagonal produced by the gray platform upon which his throne rests, there is no real movement in the composition of this image.

E = EMOTIONS

Confident. Capable. Ready to act.

R = NUMBER

The Kings express the number FOURTEEN; the One of action (masculinity) combined with the Four, the number of the Earth. Modified by the suit of Wands, the Fourteen conveys the masculine mastery of the power of intent.

KING of WANDS

KEYWORDS
creative/expressive
brilliant strategist
natural leader
authoritative
charismatic/enthusiastic
sexual/attractive
passionate/daring
confident/self-assured
projects aura of mastery
not self-conscious
courageous/bold

14

Rider Waite Smith Tarot

A red king sits on a throne emblazoned with symbols of fire. The kings and the queens are masters of their respective suits or paths of mastery in the Tarot. The difference between a king and a queen is in the *kind* of mastery, not the level of mastery. The Fourteen when reduced becomes a Five, the number of man, of freedom, and of change; thus the number Fourteen produces change when it employs the base energy of the Five. The kings are the masters of the path represented by their suit; they represent the male form of mastery, as a counterbalance for the queens.

The King of Wands gazes off-stage towards the left side of the card. As the normal direction for reading in English and most Western languages is from left to right, this indicates that his attention is focused not upon the results of his actions, but upon the source of his power.

The King of Wands is the master of the element of Fire as shown in his heraldry: the lions for the astrological sign of Leo and the salamander on the floor. The ancients believed that salamanders lived in fire, thus the salamander became a symbol for the element of Fire. The salamanders on the back of the king's throne is a variation of a very significant symbol:

OUROBORUS = eternity, cyclical, infinity, the human psyche (see Circle, Lemniscate Wreath, Sun) The Ouroborus or Ouroborus, from the Greek meaning tail-devouring snake, is an ancient symbol depicting a serpent or dragon eating its own tail.

The Ouroborus often symbolizes self-reflexivity or cyclicality, especially in the sense of something constantly re-creating itself, the eternal return, and other things such as the phoenix which operate in cycles that begin anew as soon as they end. It can also represent the idea of primordial unity related to something existing in or persisting from the beginning with such force or qualities it cannot be extinguished.[1]

The Ouroborus indicates the kind of power that the King of Wands possesses. The King of Wands is a master of the element of Fire; he stands at the beginning of the path of material manifestation. As the master of intent, the energy of focused will, the King of Wands knows how to trigger and direct the power of the implicate to begin the process from pure potential to eventual manifestation.

In pre-Christian times, the king was often held responsible for the health of the land. The original meaning of "husband" was a "tiller of the soil," which also seemed to mean a (good) manager of the land. Blood was considered to be the basis of life in earth-based cultures. In this, perhaps the ancients were correct, as the DNA in the blood (white blood cells) is the actual building block of all life. Women contributed their menstrual blood to the Earth every month in their childbearing years to help the land be fertile; this was their sacrifice. The borders of their tribe's lands were thus

---

1 en.wikipedia.org/wiki/Ouroborus

claimed by the women. Blood was considered a powerful magic and bond among all peoples worldwide.

The king was considered the temporal husband of the Earth or Gaia as a representation of the Divine Feminine. As he was symbolically responsible for tilling the land, he planted the seeds that would later be harvested to feed his people. The position of the king was not intended to be all-powerful; his position symbolized the relationship, the connection, and the responsibility of the people to the land that they respected as sacred. The king was response-able to both the blood (life/wellbeing) of the people and to the land which nourished them. Another meaning for husband means to "conserve resources"—which would, of course mean the responsible conservation of the Earth. The king was responsible for the harvest and for maintaining justice and fairness among his people.

Blood was considered the real agent in reproduction and thus women were revered for their ability to increase the bounty of the land and increase the number of the tribe. If the harvest did badly, a king in ancient history was called upon to make the ultimate sacrifice: they killed him and spread his blood over the land; this was to fertilize the land and allow it to bear fruit.

In a culture that respects all life and sees its children as its future, it would not be a good idea to kill women who could bear more children. The women gave their menstrual blood to help fertilize the land and their actual blood in giving birth, so the king as a representative of his sex was allowed to show his care for the Earth by the sacrifice of his life. It was considered not only his duty, but an honor.

The ancient practice of killing the king as a temporal sacrifice is referenced in the story of Christ; he was a king that made the ultimate sacrifice that others might live. The blood sacrifice of Christ not only echoes the sacrifice of ancient kings, it is linked to the archetype of the Holy Grail. In French, the Holy Grail is called the *Sangreal:*

> In Old French, san graal or san gréal means "Holy Grail" and the French phrase "sang real" means "royal blood;" later writers played on this pun.[1]

The mastery represented in this card tells you how to create new worlds: align your Soul's will with the intent of Spirit, surrender to the current

---

1 en.wikipedia.org/wiki/Holy_Grail

of the greater will, and allow yourself to flow into the future. The King of Wands gazes left, fearlessly, powerfully focused on the Zero Point of creation—he gazes straight into the face of oncoming time.

When You get This Card in a Reading
Intent is how you align with the forces of the universe, with all aspects of yourself, and with the Earth itself. Are you aligned with your intent? Or are you "putting the cart before the horse?" Before you start planning or constructing anything, first consider whether your idea/project is something that is worth the investment of your passion, energy, resources, and time.

Meditation
Before you act, you must know your direction. Feel your direction by aligning with your Soul's intent.

KING OF FIRE

ACTION

Tarot of Creativity
Fire is one of the most masculine elements in astrology: this element includes the signs of Leo, Sagittarius, and Aries. In the TOC, the King of Fire takes Action; but what kind of action does the King of Fire take? The clue is in the suit's position in the four-part process of creative manifestation: intent is the spiritual action that one takes before even planning how it might manifest (Swords/AIR), before investing any emotional passion in the idea (Cups/WATER), and certainly before you start to build the project or amass your resources (Pentacles/ EARTH).

The King of Fire is a sovereign being who understands how things work in the underlying reality of the quantum, as well as in the binary system of duality. He has learned not to put his attention on the *effects* of the causality loop, but instead places his focus on the *cause*; which is where his point of power resides. He understands that form does not engender energy, instead, energy engenders form. And as the master of the suit of energy—Fire—he has learned how to work with the creative energy behind it all—intent.

The court cards in the Fire suit are masters of the raw creative energy of intent; they understand why this powerful force should be put first, and why it should be respected for the power it represents. With the power of intent, you tap into the wealth of the infinite implicate, the massive machine of creation: the wonder of material existence, which rests upon the directed will of the conscious creator.

When You get This Card in a Reading

When you get this card in a reading, consider where your energy is going. Ask yourself what is in your highest interest. Ask your Higher Self to reveal the path to you and align yourself with it; the only path worth following is the path with heart.

Meditation

Now is time to act upon your dreams.

14

KING OF SWORDS

S = SYMBOLS
ANGEL = Higher Self, guidance
BUTTERFLIES = transformation
CLOUDS = mental clarity

E = ENERGY
The King of Swords stares directly but non-aggressively at you. The clouds behind his throne are few and float peacefully in the clear air.

E = EMOTIONS
Detached. Self-assured. Fair.

R = NUMBER
As a number Fourteen in the suit of Swords/ AIR, the King symbolizes mental mastery, combining the One of individuality with the Four of the practical builder.

Rider Waite Smith Tarot
A stern king faces us with a raised sword in his right hand. The King of Swords shows that mental mastery is achieved after a lifetime of discipline. He is a master of detachment, rationality, and logic. But he is not harsh or aggressive like he was when he was the Knight of Swords; the King of Swords shows the maturity of a disciplined ruler who has overcome the pettiness of his ego, and achieved emotional maturity.

KEYWORDS
rational/logical
intellectual/analytical
clear communicator
good writer
incisive mind
discerning/fair
sees the big picture
learns quickly
impeccable character
just/objective
high values/moral
socially conscious
fights against injustice
a quiet super hero

In the court cards of the Tarot, power always means personal power, not power over others. Where the Knight of Swords, in his flight of passion, might be tempted to use his "might" to convince others of his "right," the King of Swords has tempered his thoughts with experience and tolerance, and now possesses the maturity of wisdom. Unlike the Knight of Swords, he isn't rushing anywhere, he doesn't have any points to defend, and he doesn't have to convince anyone of anything. He knows that he is the master of his mind.

While the King of Swords now appears calm and collected, he has spent his life in battle. When he was young he was the knight who battled against the system, against intolerance, inequality, and slavery. Then, as he gained more wisdom on his path, he learned that the true battle was against his own self-importance: in order to become king he had to dethrone his own ego.

As he integrates his feminine side, he understands the wisdom of balance, symbolized in the East as the Tao. There is no longer any battle, either inside or outside, there is only flow. He uses his sword only to cut into the air of confusion and to slash through mental blocks. He has come to realize that his wise old sword master was right—the sword should flow through the air as if it were made of air. Mental mastery does not mean suppression or control, instead it means that you choose to think thoughts that flow rather than thoughts that block. And finally, when you become a master, you enter the state of no-thought, where freedom exists.

When You get This Card in a Reading
Use the finely honed sword of your mind to cut through unnecessary thoughts and beliefs.

Meditation
See the deeper truth underneath murky beliefs and emotions.

KING OF AIR

THE VISIONARY

Tarot of Creativity

Wisdom is the realm of this king, wisdom that respects the rights of others, and obeys universal laws: Free Will, Equality, and Abundance for All. He enforces this ethic in himself, but he will not enforce it in others—that would be a violation of their free will. He serves as an example to others; they can see the harmony that results from the mastery of the mind and the ego.

The King of Air in *The Tarot of Creativity* has learned to hone his consciousness into a sharp tool. He shed all his limiting beliefs and no longer engages in mind chatter; his mind is now clear. With a clear mind, he is receptive to the visions coming from his greater mind, and can tap into the power of the quantum implicate.

This king builds new worlds with thought. But while his castles in the air are not illusions, they are not yet built; they are concepts, plans, or blueprints for the final structure. The Suit of Air is the second step in the four steps in the creative manifestation process, coming after the Fire of intent and before the Water of passion, which flows to nurture life on Earth.

When you remember who you really are, you can become anything because you have faced being *nothing*. You have removed all your "shields" and shed the unconscious thoughts that bound you to the collective; you have faced the dragon of "thou shalt." When you have examined every thought, every nuance of feeling, and every emotion for authenticity and originality, you have entered the Void, the cave of the dragon.

The Void is the Zero Point of creation. When the Querent first enters the Void, it feels like a sensory deprivation chamber: there are no desires, no direction, no thoughts, and no emotions. Eventually he enters into a point of stillness, the same still point that precedes the birth of a universe. The Querent feels he is dying, and he is—to his old self. He can no longer react to anything, he no longer can feel anything; and so he finally surrenders to his fate. He incubates his next self, as he surrenders to the experience of nothingness in the Creative Void. The Void is the womb, the incubation chamber; it is like the cocoon of a butterfly. The butterflies on the throne behind the King of Swords in the RWS deck are a clear indication of the King's power of self-metamorphosis. The body of the caterpillar must completely liquefy in order to transform into a creature with wings. In order to become something new, he had to first become nothing.

A creator is nothing; he is a box that contains nothing but the Void of infinite potential. He has no points to defend, and no points to make, no opinions to offer, or arguments to wage.

The process of ascension requires that you empty yourself of all material concerns, insecurities, and fears. In becoming what you really are, you get rid of everything that is superfluous; you become the Void. With nothing inside, you are everything and nothing at once. You become freedom personified, in a moment's notice you shift into a clear breeze, a soft wind, or a tornado of action; whatever suits the moment and the direction of your Soul.

When You get This Card in a Reading

Empty yourself of thought, and you will never have to plan anything ever again. With a mind empty of the past, empty of mindless data, and empty of beliefs, you will simply *know* what to do in every moment. Life becomes play: inspiration blows through your mind like a gentle breeze.

Meditation

A wise man sees a whole forest when he looks at a single tree.

KING OF CUPS

S = SYMBOLS
FISH = flow, ease
SHIP = mastery of suit, direction
WAVES = emotional turbulence

E = ENERGY
The figure of the king on his throne is a STABLE center in a background of moving lines. The water heaves; the ship in the distance rides turbulent waves.

E = EMOTIONS
Measured passion.

R = NUMBER
As a number Fourteen, the King of Cups/WATER is a master of emotions, combining the active male number of the One with the feminine Four, the number of the Earth.

Rider Waite Smith Tarot
A king sits on a throne placed like an island in a sea of turbulent water The Suit of Cups is about emotion; the king and queen of each suit are the accomplished masters of their path. The King of Cups sits on his throne in the middle of the sea. The lines of the water that surround him are heaving and turbulent, but he remains calm. Many people couldn't weather this turbulence, but the King has chosen to place his throne right in the middle of it. He is the "eye in the storm"—the quiet center around which everything else seems to revolve.

The King of Cups could be said to represent the Fisher King, who in Arthurian legend was the last in line of kings who was chosen to live in the Grail Castle; his responsibility was to protect the Holy Grail.

In Arthurian legend the Fisher King, or the Wounded King, is the latest in a long line charged with keeping the

KEYWORDS
unflappable/calm
caring/compassionate
diplomatic/peacemaker
psychic/heart-based
open/loves diversity
patient/a good teacher
healer/therapist
high personal values
social awareness
a good leader
social architect

KING of CUPS.

Holy Grail. Versions of his story vary widely, but he is always wounded in the legs or groin and incapable of moving on his own. In the Fisher King legends, he becomes impotent and unable to perform his task himself, and he also becomes unable to father or support a next generation to carry on after his death.

His kingdom suffers as he does, his impotence affecting the fertility of the land and reducing it to a barren wasteland. All he is able to do is fish in the river near his castle, Corbenic, and wait for someone who might be able to heal him. Healing involves the expectation of the use of magic. Knights travel from many lands to heal the Fisher King, but only the chosen can accomplish the feat. This is Percival in earlier stories; in later versions, he is joined by Galahad and Bors.

Chrétien's Perceval (1180) is the first piece of work that mentions the Fisher King. In this work, Percival encounters a man and his servant fishing on a lake. These two individuals have a short conversation with Percival, which ends with them directing Percival to the Grail Castle. Upon entry, Percival sees a beautiful castle and is surprised when he discovers that the Fisher King is the one to welcome him in. After entering, Percival is given a sword by the Fisher King and then celebrates Percival's arrival with a huge feast. During the feast, at the beginning of every course, a procession containing a candelabra, a bleeding lance, and a grail are all brought through the dining hall. Percival watches the objects go by and fails to ask the Fisher King about each procession. After the feast ends, Percival retires to his room, and once awake from slumber, discovers that the castle is in ruin and everyone gone. Over time Percival discovers that the failure to ask about the procession causes the Fisher King's wound to remain unhealed. Unfortunately the story ends here, since Chrétien dies before the story's completion.[1]

In the story above, the three objects brought into the hall represent three of the four elements or suits in the Tarot: the candelabra is a symbol for *fire*, the bleeding lance is the symbol for *air*, while the grail represents *water*.

1   en.wikipedia.org/wiki/Fisher_King

The "wounded" lance (Sword/AIR suit) symbolizes the wounded mind of the king, as he denies the power and respect due to the Divine Feminine; the power that supports his physical existence and his very kingdom. The element/suit that is missing in the story is *earth*; the universal archetype for the Divine Feminine.

The root of the word "matter" is the same root as the word for "mother" in Latin, *mater*. The question that Percival must ask in order to heal the king concerns the element of Earth, "mater-mother," the recognition of the Divine Feminine that would restore the king to wholeness. The Fisher King was wounded in a way that affects his power on the *material* plane, rendering him impotent: this wound comes from the personal and global denial of the Divine Feminine within, expressed as the exploitation of women and attitude of disrespect for Mother Earth.

The knight Percival is the only one who can restore the king to wholeness. Percival is actually the Fisher King at a younger stage (see Knight of Cups). The idealism of the knight reminds the Fisher King of the pure wisdom of his younger self. The magic of healing restores the king to his original ideals. Healing is a task of remembering wholeness; once the king remembers the wholeness of himself, he is restored.

When the Fisher King retrieves the lost portion of himself represented as the Divine Feminine, he is restored to potency; he becomes a complete, powerful male—the balanced, mature ruler you see in the King of Cups. He recognizes that he has the duty to nurture the land, to respect the Earth, honor women, and to support the community. He has become the representation of the Divine Male in earthly form; he is a true King once again.

When You get This Card in a Reading

Pay attention to your emotions. Emotions are your psychic awareness; they can give you invaluable information about everyone and everything in your life.

Meditation

Be the eye in the storm. A master of emotions can allow emotions to swirl and eddy around him without drowning in them.

KING OF WATER

THE WAVE

Tarot of Creativity

The King of Water in *The Tarot of Creativity* is entitled THE WAVE. Nothing can survive in the ocean if it resists the power of the waves and the pressure of the water. The wisdom of every fish or animal in the sea is to flow with the water instead of resisting it.

The King of Water learned early on that life is ruled by our emotions, so he learned how to master them; not as in control or suppress them, but how to use them properly. The King doesn't resist his emotions; he utilizes them as tools. He uses his intuition in order to gain access to his higher mind. He employs his emotions as a compass, adjusting his path as he goes. If he feels bad when he considers something, he doesn't go that way; if he feels good, he goes in that direction. He doesn't try to suppress or control his emotions; he knows that like water, they will just flow somewhere else.

He knows that emotions don't just happen; they are a result of either conscious choice or conditioning. If you are not a master of your emotions, then you are a victim of them. Emotions are our inheritance as human beings. We can use them consciously as tools for creation or we can allow others to manipulate us through our emotions. It is always our choice.

Emotions are the final tool in the creative process. You can intend to do something, you can have a great inspiration, but without the passion—the emotional energy—to carry it through, nothing happens. Most great ideas are stillborn because the mind cannot infuse them with passion. Only the heart can deliver the energy needed to bring a creative project through time into fruition.

Creative projects are like plants—they have to be watered; but too much water kills them. Passion, like water, can be poison if not properly handled. A beginner might be enthused about their work, but their uncontrolled passion can be like a flash flood in a garden; it drowns the new shoots and leaves their roots exposed to bake in the sun. A master artist learns to respect his emotions as a creative tool, and knows how to use his passion over time as the energy for producing his work. Desire is how passion first shows itself: desire is how we create in duality. If we didn't have desire we would be totally static, because desire is what causes us to want to create. And desire, like a drip irrigation system, can be measured out with just the right amount of passion over time to nurture a creative project into full bloom.

Passion, in this sense, isn't unrepressed desire. The artist feels the lines of his desire lengthen and stretch out into the future, as he envisions, and then completes what he set out to do. The King of Water will always find enough passion to fuel his creative life, because he knows that the measure of his desire will always be equal to the size of the final created form. This is the Law of Equilibrium; the equation that regulates the flow of energy to matter and matter back to energy. And in this certainty and knowledge the King of Cups/WATER knows himself, as he flows with the tide of his desire and his life is nourished with his passion.

As master of the emotional realm, the King of Water knows how to thrive in a sea that would drown even the most accomplished surfer. What is his secret? He doesn't resist the WAVES; he swims with them. He knows that the rhythm of the tides of the ocean match the rhythm of his heart. Everything comes in its time. And so he flows with the current.

This king might show up in your life as a passionate lover, a wise counselor, or a person with whom you can share your innermost secrets. The King of Water is in touch with his feminine side. If he is a true master of emotions, he can keep your secrets and is not afraid to divulge his own. But still waters run deep, and remember that this is not a superficial person; this King feels deeply. He is in love with life. You are here to help him explore the depths of that love.

When You get This Card in a Reading

The chief wisdom of the King of Water is *allowance*. Go with the flow. If anything obstructs you, remember the wisdom of the WAVE that finds a rock on the shore: flow around it.

Meditation

You can fight the wave or use it to carry you.

KING OF PENTACLES

S = SYMBOLS
BULL HEADS = sign of Taurus
CASTLE = material success, attainment
FRUIT = final stage of growth
GLOBE = achievement, mastery
GRAPEVINES = abundance, fruition
WALL = defense, "behind" him

E = ENERGY
The king on this card is a very STATIC figure sitting in a garden of riches, but the upright lines of the wall, the throne, and the castle all emphasize the stability of the central figure. A stable triangle is formed by the head of the King, the Pentacle in one hand, and the globe in the other.

E = EMOTIONS
Success. Satisfaction. Achievement.

R = NUMBER
The King of Pentacles/EARTH expresses the last stage of the number Fourteen as it works through the suits of the Tarot: the masculine energy of the One combined with the practical skills of the Four.

KING ᴏ PENTACLES

KEYWORDS
successful/opportunist
dependable/trustworthy
responsible/supportive
CEO/entrepreneur
philanthropist/generous
angel fund/sponsor
authoritative/sovereign
emotionally stable/wise
meticulous/careful
promotes steady growth
nurtures creative ideas

Rider Waite Smith Tarot
A king surrounded by symbols of abundance, fertility, and power. The King of Pentacles/EARTH shows you a man in a veritable Garden of Eden. He is the King Arthur of legend. King Arthur embodied the archetype of an enlightened leader who dreamed of establishing a just kingdom. The archetype of Eden is recorded in many cultures as a "heaven on Earth," in the Arthurian legend this place is a real island called Avalon.

The island of apples which men call "The Fortunate Isle"

(Insula Pomorum quae Fortunata uocatur) gets its name from the fact that it produces all things of itself; the fields there have no need of the ploughs of the farmers and all cultivation is lacking except what nature provides. Of its own accord it produces grain and grapes, and apple trees grow in its woods from the close-clipped grass. The ground of its own accord produces everything instead of merely grass, and people live there a hundred years or more. There nine sisters rule by a pleasing set of laws those who come to them from our country.[1]

The name of the Isles of the Fortunate signifies that they bear all good things, as if happy and blessed in the abundance of their fruits. Serviceable by nature, they bring forth fruits of valuable forests (Sua enim aptae natura pretiosarum poma silvarum parturiunt); their hilltops are clothed with vines growing by chance; in place of grasses, there is commonly vegetable and grain. Pagan error and the songs of the secular poets have held that these islands to be Paradise because of the fecundity of the soil. Situated in the Ocean to the left of Mauretania, very near the west, they are separated by the sea flowing between them.[2]

There is strong evidence that every variety of the name "Avalon" was derived from a word that meant "apple." In the Middle Ages, apples were a sign of the goodness and bounty of nature. When you cut an apple in half vertically, a five-pointed star shape is revealed in the design of the seeds at the core. The apple is a deciduous tree in the rose family. The rose, a flower with five petals, was a significant symbol in many esoteric philosophies and religions; it figures prominently in many cards in the Tarot.

Five is the ancient number signifying "man," most probably the enlightened man. Man has five senses and five limbs (arms, legs, and head). The number Fourteen reduces to a Five, so this card of the King of Pentacles is the "enlightened man" of the Tarot; as a court card he is the "enlightened ruler" that Plato foresaw as the ruler of Utopia; the "philosopher king" who had to study for fifty years in order to gain the wisdom necessary to rule.

[Plato's Republic] proposes a categorization of citizens

---

1   The Vita Merlini, Geoffrey of Monmouth, translated by John Jay Parry
2   Isidore of Seville's Etymologies, Priscilla Throop

into a rigid class structure of "golden," "silver," "bronze" and "iron" socioeconomic classes. The golden citizens are trained in a rigorous 50-year-long educational program to be benign oligarchs, the "philosopher-kings." The wisdom of these rulers will supposedly eliminate poverty and deprivation through fairly distributed resources...

The educational program for the rulers is the central notion of the proposal. It has few laws, no lawyers and rarely sends its citizens to war, but hires mercenaries from among its war-prone neighbors (these mercenaries were deliberately sent into dangerous situations in the hope that the more warlike populations of all surrounding countries will be weeded out, leaving peaceful peoples).[1]

The Suit of Pentacles is about achievement and material success. As a royal card, the King is the masculine ruler of the suit. While his partner, the Queen of Pentacles, actively nurtures and births form, he protects the material realm and shelters her. In fact, these two are great partners, very alike in their attitudes. As an expression of the energy of Taurus, he is sensual and enjoys life.

He has worked hard to get where he is. As a page, he yearned for the Pentacle that he holds in his hand. As a knight, he was the workhorse that tilled the Earth and brought in the harvest that he now enjoys. As a youth he led an austere life, believing the adage that hard work is necessary to obtain riches.

This king is not here to exploit the land or the people that he rules. He knows that he loves what he has created, and he loves the little details of his home. He can be a bit of a hedonist, but never does he indulge himself to excess. This is because at the base of philosophy is an enduring respect for the land and for those he protects.

When You get This Card in a Reading
Everything you have ever desired is there, with you—now. But can you see it? Seeing in this case means, "can you appreciate what is in front of you?" In order to achieve the future of your dreams, you have to love *what is*.

---

1   en.wikipedia.org/wiki/Utopia

Meditation

This is the "Midas card"—now is the time to realize the fruition of your hard work and the manifestation of your careful plans.

KING OF EARTH

CREATE

Tarot of Creativity

The path represented by this suit is possibly the most difficult of all the paths because matter is the hardest of the four classical elements to manipulate. This is why the King of Earth may think that hard work was necessary in order to achieve his desires. It is far easier to manipulate the raw energy of Fire or Air, or even to swim in Water than to struggle carving out your life from the rocks of the Earth.

If the King of Earth truly reflects on how he got where he is, he knows that the hard work is only a small portion of the equation: the real secret is to enjoy the path, to appreciate whatever part of the path you are on. If that means that you are experiencing difficulty, then the master's way out of the difficulty is to dive in and enjoy the situation to the hilt.

The main theme of the King of Earth is *appreciation*. In the stock market, when a stock appreciates, it gains in value; in the same manner, whatever we appreciate grows. When we assign a great value to something formerly unappreciated, it grows in stature. When we pay attention to something, we make it grow. The King of Earth knows how to use the path of Earth to gain whatever he desires: he knows that whatever he appreciates will grow. The King knows that he must use his attention properly. He isn't obsessed but he knows how to focus his attention in the act of appreciation.

And that is his secret: it has made him a success in every part of his life. He appreciates hard work and so promotes the right people, which makes his business successful. He appreciates his wife and showers her with attention. And finally, he appreciates the garden he has grown: his creative endeavors are flowering and bearing fruit. Like Midas, everything he touches is successful, but unlike Midas, his true wealth is not his gold but his ability to appreciate life itself.

When You get This Card in a Reading

A material master (King of Earth) knows that he has to embody the frequency that matches the frequency of the reality he wants to inhabit. This is the secret to how the King creates: give whatever is in your life your love, appreciate it for what it is, and the world around you transforms into love.

Meditation

Time to birth your ideas into form.

14

KEYWORDS

ignorance/uncon-
scious behavior
lust/uncontrolled desires
control/exploitation
obsession/misuse of power
sexuality/temptation
vice/hedonism
anger/bondage
egoism/self-importance

S = SYMBOLS

CHAINS = materialism, beliefs (misused)
DEVIL = the shadow-self
FEMALE TAIL = sexual power (misused)
INVERTED PENTACLE = power (misused)
MALE TAIL = energy/Spirit (misused)
MAN = self-conscious/ego
TORCH = earthly desire
WOMAN = subconscious/Mother Nature

E = ENERGY

The Devil with bat-like wings dominates the top of this picture, weighing down and suppressing the two figures below.

E = EMOTIONS

Negativity.   Limitation.   Exploitation. Victimhood.

R = NUMBER

THE FIFTEEN is the combination of the One of The Magician with the Five of The Hierophant. This combination shows how a Magician can misuse the power of his intuition and create monsters from the focal point of his attention when the egoic mind of the lower self believes it is in charge of the whole Self.

THE DEVIL

ARCHETYPE

Rider Waite Smith Tarot

THE DEVIL .

The Devil shows how the number of man (the Five) can be corrupted, symbolized in the inverted Pentacle at the top of the card. Reversing this sacred symbol warns us that man can misuse his power and become the inverted man, or the Devil.

The Pentacle is an ancient symbol for man. The five arms of this star symbolize the five senses and the five limbs of man: two legs, two arms, with the fifth arm representing the head. When you turn this symbol upside-down, you reverse the natural order. Note that the "head" of the inverted symbol is placed in the exact center of the Devil's forehead, in the position of the third eye, or pineal gland, indicating that the ego (the head of the inverted star) runs the man.

The Devil dominates both the man and woman below him. The upraised right arm forms a parallel line with the other, downward pointing arm. This carries the eye of the viewer straight to the torch in his hand which seems to be lighting the tail of the male figure. The swooping line of his tail leads your eye to his face, connected by his gaze and by the chains to the female figure. There the movement abruptly stops. The French say, "cherchez la femme." The blame for the problems of the man—the unconscious self-conscious—is projected upon the woman, who represents the subconscious in this card. The subconscious creates according to the projections of the mental self, the mental images that the ego creates. Blaming the subconscious (Nature/God/the Universe/Fate) for what happens is the mark of the unconscious Soul who, without mental and emotional discipline, is eternally condemned to "hell" as a victim of his own unconscious thoughts and emotions: the projections he has forced upon his own nature (the woman/his subconscious Nature).

Evil only exists through our personal will because *we* are the ones who create evil. The idea of evil is only possible in a polarized reality system. It is not necessary or natural—in fact, evil is the opposite of what is natural. The projection of consciousness known as Evil has been achieved at great

15

effort, as it is actually easier to experience goodness. Evil is an experiment in separation—how far can a being that is really only oneness experience otherness? This thought-experiment generated a polarized concept called the *Devil* as a counterpart for the concept of *God*. God represents a principle of wholeness, integrity, and oneness; our original state of innocence in the Garden of Eden—the Garden of Life—while the Devil is an expression of the opposite experience: the pain of separation.

This card shows how a dysfunctional ego can misuse the power of the subconscious. The ego wishes to continue as it is, unchanging and in control, but existence under the domination of fear-based thinking is miserable and terrifying. The trick is to get the stubborn and recalcitrant ego to understand that life will be better if it just surrenders control. It has to understand that losing control isn't a bad thing—change does not equal death. The best way to do this is to give the ego what it really wants: LOVE.

Once the ego realizes that the divine partnership offered by the Higher Self is to its benefit, it relaxes its grip on the mind, and the whole person can flow easily into a new TRINITY of Self; the Higher Self replaces the ego as the CEO of the Self, the ego becomes the personal assistant or executor of the will of the Higher Self, while the body is recognized as the divine material expression of the Self.

Put The Lovers card side by side with The Devil card, and you will see that the images mirror each other. Just as the LIVE is EVIL reversed, so The Devil is the inverse of The Lovers. It is no accident that the number of this card, 15 reduces to 6, the number of The Lovers in the Major Arcana. The Devil is a misguided interpretation of love; The Devil demonstrates what happens when love is interpreted through the core misapprehension of separation and control. The Devil replaces the Angel that hovered over the couple in The Lovers card; in The Devil card, the figures of the male and female are shown chained to the pedestal of the Devil and also to each other. The trees that they stood before in The Lovers card have become tails. The bright day has become night, and the Sun has become an inverted PENTACLE. The only light in this scene comes from the TORCH that the Devil seems to plunge downwards, alighting the tail of the man. In this card, the man looks at the woman not with love, but with an air of lust or exploitation.

With his INVERTED TORCH, symbolizing the Suit of Wands and the element of Fire, The Devil has lit man's (the ego's) desire (TAIL) and he responds by using the woman (the body/subconscious) to help him manifest his desires. The misuse of the subconscious by the ego is what is pictured here. The subconscious, represented by the WOMAN, is at once the physical body of man and the implicate, or the creative force of Spirit, which unfailingly fulfills the wishes or images of the self-conscious. The power of the universal subconscious is here for us to command.

When we are unaware of our own powers, we don't understand that our subconscious automatically executes our commands. The creative process starts with us; we send images from our imagination to our subconscious. The subconscious, as "Mother Nature," then "generates" the "reality" that vibrationally matches the emotional content of the images that we sent it. We miss the connection because we don't understand our role as creators. We don't understand that what we see in the mirror of reality is what we are actually projecting onto it.

The emotionally-charged images from your mind are received by your subconscious as commands. The subconscious responds by manifesting one of the potential realities that has been lying dormant inside the womb of the implicate or *enfolded* reality. The womb of the implicate contains all possibilities; in the Tarot the implicate, or what people may call Source, is symbolized by The High Priestess. Consciousness directs the subconscious to manifest things constantly from the realm of the implicate. Thus, when we create by applying ATTENTION or focus on something, we are directing the forces of creation to express into reality what was simply enfolded as a potential in the implicate up until then. When we are not spiritually aware, as shown in this card, we send negative, unconscious images to the subconscious; the subconscious then automatically creates a reality that matches the vibrational content of whatever we envisioned. The result is that we end up in a hell of unconscious behavior that, paradoxically, we don't realize that we ourselves created. After all, that is the nature of unconscious thinking: irresponsibility.

In The Lovers card, we obtain Heaven on Earth because we have learned respect for the forces of creation; we know that our vibrational awareness is how we create what we see. As aware and awake enlightened beings, we will always choose to LIVE over its opposite, unconscious expression, EVIL. The horror of unconscious behavior represented by the archetype of The Devil can no longer have any power over us because we are now conscious creators. We understand the links and partnerships that exist between our Higher Self, the subconscious/implicate, and the ego/mind/self-conscious.

When You get This Card in a Reading
This may be a chance to look for hidden beliefs that no longer serve you.

Meditation
What chains the ego to the man?

THE DEVIL

THE SHADOW

Tarot of Creativity

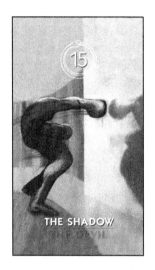

The title in *The Tarot of Creativity* for Key #15 is THE SHADOW. This card shows that karma/duality has taken a turn towards an expression of polarity. This balances the pendulum of karma with an expression of extreme opposites.

In Jungian terms, the Devil is The Shadow: the Shadow represents all the repressed, unmentioned or unmentionable desires that lurk beneath the surface of our acknowledged Selves. The experiment in duality comes to a head as the dark shadow cast by an uncontrolled ego tries to block the light of consciousness itself.

As a light source that is positioned near the ground casts a shadow far larger than the man, so the aggrandized ego sees itself as more than it is; it thinks that it is in control of all that it sees. When the ego is allowed to control the show, it tends to veer towards a polarized view of life. Not knowing or accepting the *Divine Other* as shown in The Lovers/LOVE card, the ego careens out of control in a world defined by loss and separation.

Duality is a binary system; like a computer language, it consists of only ones and zeros. The One is matter, the expression of the individualized consciousness, while the Zero represents Spirit, nothingness, the quantum implicate. The One cannot exist without the Zero, and the Zero cannot express itself without the One. The opposites are bound together by their polarized opposition, like a magnet. The Shadow is necessary in a world of light, if for no other reason than it defines the light by opposing it. In a dualistic reality system, a shadow is necessary in a polarized material-

308

istic expression, but to be all shadow is as impossible as being all light. The shadow of the ego is the shadow cast by the light of the original Self.

Consciousness cannot know itself in duality except by reflection, thus it created an experiment in duality, what we have come to erroneously believe is "reality." Ultimately what Spirit desires with the experiment of duality is not to know itself—which it already does—but to surprise itself with a new, unique reflection of itself, like someone trying to gaze at the reflection of the back of their head by angling two mirrors.

There is another way to look at the Shadow; it is a necessary tool of evolution. Without the tension of opposites, we do not have the necessary energy for creating something new. In a state of oneness, we are at the still point before the Big Bang of creation. In that perfection there is no need to create; in that state of wholeness, there is no desire.

When you walk, you have to engage imbalance momentarily every time you take a step; without the element of imbalance there would be no movement at all. Imbalance is a natural attribute of evolution and time-space. Evolution, like creation, is an illusion of movement. Like the mythological figure of the Ouroborus that turns around to consume its own tail, the goal of change is not evolution but the exploration of consciousness.

15

As long as you are alive, you will have a shadow, you might as well make friends with it. When you accept the shadow, it suddenly reveals itself as a friend. But like a blunt companion, it isn't afraid to point out your erroneous beliefs and energetically wasteful habits. Use it as a wise advisor to keep you on the path with heart.

When You get This Card in a Reading
The proper expression of shadow energy is less extreme, and more balanced. The light of consciousness is defined by its shadow, just as the shadow is defined by light: the Yin/Yang symbol shows this as the dot on each side.

Meditation
Your shadow knows more about you than anyone else; it follows you everywhere. It is the "dark mirror" that reflects the hidden parts of your character.

Related to
The Lovers/LOVE (Key 6)

KEYWORDS
upset/sudden change
disaster/impact
revelation/realization
crisis/disruption
downfall/ruin
dethroning/crash
surrender/fear
divine intervention
divine inspiration

S = SYMBOLS

COUPLE = duality, anima/animus
CROWN = the ego/the intellect
FIRE = spiritual awareness
LIGHTNING = unexpected light/knowledge
TOWER = ego/material values
YOD = spiritual power/feathers of the phoenix

E = ENERGY

The ZIGZAG line of the lightening bolt comes down from right to left, striking the tower and dislodging the yellow crown (the ego). Two figures—a man and a woman—fall and cry out in terror.

E = EMOTIONS

Calamity. Failure. Breakdown. Loss. Inspiration.

R = NUMBER

THE SIXTEEN adds the One of The Magician with the Six of The Lovers; this combination of two principles of consciousness shows how attention when focused with love creates the Seven of spiritual enlightenment.

THE TOWER

ARCHETYPE

Rider Waite Smith Tarot

THE TOWER.

Key #16, The Tower, shows LIGHTNING striking a tower, dislodging a CROWN, and causing the fall of two people. The tower resembles a tree, in this case, the tree is not the Tree of Life or the Tree of Knowledge, but an artificial tree, in the form of a tower, built by man for the glorification of his own ego. A tower is a way to see great distances, which increases understanding and control. The Tower was a way for rulers to dominate both Mother Nature and other men.

The Tarot shows a progression from card to card: after the excesses of the last card, The Devil, the Higher Self intervenes with a karmic lesson. The ego, which built itself up to unnatural heights under the influence of The Devil/THE SHADOW, is now (over)due for a fall. This is the execution of the Law of Karma, which, like the Law of Attraction, is not a moral law but a natural law. The reason why the Law of Karma is invoked is due to duality's need for balance, in fact this law can only exist in a system that doesn't operate as oneness. Oneness is an inert state; it doesn't need to rebalance itself constantly as does the system of duality.

The Higher Self can invoke the Law of Karma to cause the self-conscious or the ego-driven man to look at his life from a more balanced point of view. The falling CROWN represents the head, or ego of man. The LIGHTNING strike comes to topple the ego from the TOWER of greed and control. While this sudden event may be viewed by the ego as catastrophic, the spiritual realization intended by the Higher Self is necessary and right at this point on the path: the BONDAGE to material concerns represented by the last card, The Devil/SHADOW, must be broken. If the Querent does not break the trance of materialism of his own accord, the Higher Self must do it for him. A more awakened individual would not need such a powerful lesson; he would know how to accept the higher meaning of this card: *change/divine inspiration*. In other words, if you are clearly on your path and listening to your intuition, your Higher Self does not need to teach you through polarized events. But if you are not listening, the only way to achieve karmic balance is to live the polar opposite of your current experience.

Thus the pendulum of duality-karma swings. It can swing wildly or it can swing hardly at all. Balance is achieved in stillness as well as in the experience of extreme opposites. Karma is like a pendulum: erratic swings fulfill duality's need for balance, just as well as a pendulum that hardly swings at all. The only choice you really have on this plane is whether you prefer the drama or the stillness. Both are expressions of balance.

There are twenty-two tear-shaped figures, called YOD, that seem to be falling like rain from the sky. The Yod is the root of all Hebrew letters The word, Yod means "open hand." Yod also refers to the candle flame—a symbol of the divine within. These symbols in this image tells us that divine intervention is at hand, for the eventual benefit of all, even if it seems like a disaster from the standpoint of the ego.

When You get This Card in a Reading
If you surrender the ego, then the way forward is full of new changes that are always for the better in the long run.

Meditation
What goes up, must come down.
Pride goeth before a fall.

THE TOWER

THE AWAKENING

Tarot of Creativity

The keyword in *The Tarot of Creativity* for The Tower is THE AWAKENING. The ego must not be in control as it was in the previous card, The Devil/THE SHADOW. Thus a shakeup of the Soul is needed. You can pay attention to the voice of the Higher Self or you can try to hide behind your ego and remain asleep to the storm raging outside your Tower, but the awakening happens regardless.

An awakening often involves what seems to be a disaster for the ego, which is why the figures are falling from the CROWN at the top of the tower in the RWS image. A crown represents the head, the mental body. The tower represents the structure of the false ego, which when struck by the lightning of the Soul's illumination crumbles to the ground.

The hidden lesson of this card is SURRENDER. The ego must surrender to the Higher Self or the Higher Self will break the ego down. The ego is the shell of the Spirit in material form. The shell must be broken by the emerging form, or the bird will die.

The birth of the PHOENIX is a mythological symbol for the spiritual AWAKENING of man. Associated with the Sun, the phoenix obtained new life by arising from the ashes of its predecessor; the old carbon-based man must "burn from within" in order to be born again. The feathers of the phoenix were either red or gold, symbolizing the Sun. There are twenty-two phoenix feathers/Yods falling from the night sky in this picture. Twenty-two is the number of Spirit/THE FOOL. The AWAKENING card refers to the awakening of the pineal gland, sometimes called the "third eye."

> The third eye (also known as the inner eye) is a mystical and esoteric concept referring to a speculative invisible eye which provides perception beyond ordinary sight. In certain dharmic spiritual traditions such as Hinduism, the third eye refers to the ajna, or brow, chakra. In Theosophy it is related to the pineal gland. The third eye refers to the gate that leads

to inner realms and spaces of higher consciousness. In New Age spirituality, the third eye often symbolizes a state of enlightenment or the evocation of mental images having deeply personal spiritual or psychological significance. The third eye is often associated with religious visions, clairvoyance, the ability to observe chakras and auras, precognition, and out-of-body experiences. People who are claimed to have the capacity to utilize their third eyes are sometimes known as seers.

In some traditions such as Hinduism, the third eye is said to be located around the middle of the forehead, slightly above the junction of the eyebrows. In other traditions, as in Theosophy, it is believed to be connected with the pineal gland. According to this theory, humans had in far ancient times an actual third eye in the back of the head with a physical and spiritual function. Over time, as humans evolved, this eye atrophied and sunk into what today is known as the pineal gland. Dr. Rick Strassman has hypothesized that the pineal gland, which maintains light sensitivity, is responsible for the production and release of DMT (dimethyltryptamine), an entheogen which he believes possibly could be excreted in large quantities at the moments of birth and death.[1]

When the pineal gland is broken free of the calcification that surrounds it (the egg shell of the fear-based belief system), it can return to its full, original function: the ability to receive and understand the information streaming from the Higher Self, and from Al That Is.

When You get This Card in a Reading

The ego lives in a dream of its own within the larger dream of the real you. When it wakes, the bubble of the ego's dream bursts and its experiences merge back into flow of your Soul.

Meditation

Hiding your head in the sand won't make things disappear.

Related to

The Chariot/ADVENTURE (Key #7)

1   en.wikipedia.org/wiki/Third_eye

KEYWORDS
meditation/inner silence
listening/intuition
trust/tranquility
hope/serenity
inspiration/faith
harmony/health
renewal/joy

S = SYMBOLS

7 WHITE STARS = 7 chakras
8-POINTED STAR = Higher Self
IBIS = symbol for Thoth/hope
JUGS = containers for Spirit/physical body
LAND = material existence/Earth
NAKED WOMAN =   Spirit/natural Self
POOL = universal subconscious
TREE = Tree of Life
WATER = personal subconscious

E = ENERGY

The gaze of the naked woman directs the eye to the jug in her right hand that she is pouring into the pond.

E = EMOTIONS

Hope. The calm after the storm.

R = NUMBER

THE SEVENTEEN shows what happens when the ONE of The Magician is married with the SEVEN of The Chariot. This combination returns the value of Key #8—Strength/I-MAGE, the union of the lower self (body and mind) with the Higher Self.

THE STAR

ARCHETYPE

Rider Waite Smith Tarot

THE STAR.

Key #17/The Star shows a night filled with eight STARS. A NAKED woman is kneeling on the ground with one foot in a POOL of water. She is pouring one JUG of Water on the GROUND and another JUG into the POOL before her.

The posture of her body with the two jugs in each hand forms the shape of a set of scales, indicating "restored balance." The yellow in her hair matches the huge yellow star in the top center of the image, forming a subliminal correlation in the subconscious mind of the viewer—the star represents her crown chakra, and the sudden illumination of her mind.

After the upset of the last card, The Tower, which served to shake loose the influence of The Devil, this card signifies that hope is returning. The huge 8-POINTED STAR above the head of the woman shines a yellow light upon her, and her YELLOW HAIR is the same color as the STAR. The light of a star at night is only a glimmer compared to the light of the Sun; this is why this card stands for hope—the hope engendered by the return of the light of consciousness.

The stars above the woman in this picture all have eight points, a reference to the 1 + 7 reduction of the card's number, as well as to the wisdom found in the Strength Card (Key #8). Eight stars multiplied by eight points each equals the number 64. Reducing that number returns the number 10, the number of perfection, the number of completion, indicating the beginning of a new cycle. The ruling astrological sign of The Star card is Aquarius; Aquarians are the "people of the future," the new direction of the evolution of mankind. As we leave the Piscean Age of gurus and teachers, we enter a new age of self-direction and personal sovereignty. This means that we have to learn to listen to our higher guidance. When you have achieved the wisdom of the 8-POINTED STAR, you have restored the health of all the lower chakras; you have attained access to the eighth chakra—the Soul or the Higher Self.

The naked woman represents the natural Self, the integrated Self which pours the waters of life upon both the Earth and the POOL of the Universal subconscious. The JUGS represent the vessel of the body holding the water of Spirit—the source underlying all form. The woman pours her personal subconscious or life-force into the POOL of the Universal subconscious or Spirit. She refreshes her awareness as she does so. She nourishes the Self with the water of Spirit, as her personal subconscious nourishes the Higher Self with the experience she has gained on the earthly plane. The water of life nourishes us all.

The motion of the pouring water is like the shape of the Ouroborus, Yin/Yang symbol or lemniscate—always returning to source, always in motion; Spirit coming in and out of material existence. This pouring is analogous to the mystical revelation of the deeper meaning of breathing. The divine breath, or INSPIRATION, is taken through the body to nourish the material plane with SPIRIT. When the body returns the breath in an exhale, the body nourishes the Spirit with the experience of personal existence. Thus, when you breathe out, Spirit breathes in; when you inhale you breathe in Spirit.

When You get This Card in a Reading
The Dark Night of the Soul symbolized in the last card, Key #16 The Tower, is over; hope returns.

Meditation
After the destruction of the old, the stars will come out, lighting the way into a new day.

THE STAR

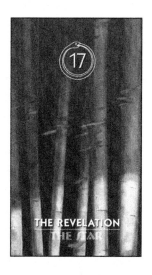

THE REVELATION

Tarot of Creativity

The keyword in *The Tarot of Creativity* for The Star is THE REVELATION. This card represents that moment when a new life suddenly comes in, not in a blaze of glory, but in a sliver of starlight. Light from the stars is reflective of a higher state of consciousness; the state of revelation might be temporary, however, since this card follows the sudden AWAKENING of The Tower card.

The unhealthy, controlling ego represented by the preceding SHADOW card has been dethroned, at least temporarily, so you have in this card a respite, and in that respite, what comes to you is the faint light of Spirit or your Higher Self—your higher consciousness. This light is like a benediction or a blessing, and you bathe yourself in the starlight projected by your Soul.

This card represents how we can choose to recall our natural selves, our innate beings. In doing so, we reach a place of inner silence that results in a state of reverence, not for what is outside the self since there is nothing outside, but for the inner nature of our innate natural selves, in silent communion with the divine trinity of Self—the Higher Self, the Mind, and the Body/subconscious.

When You get This Card in a Reading

Allow the light of your Spirit to fill you, the revelation is in *how* you receive not in *what* you receive.

Meditation

In the eternal silence of the sacred moment, all is revealed; in that moment of clarity, everything loses its name. Nothing will ever be the same.

Related to

Strength/I-MAGE (Key #8)

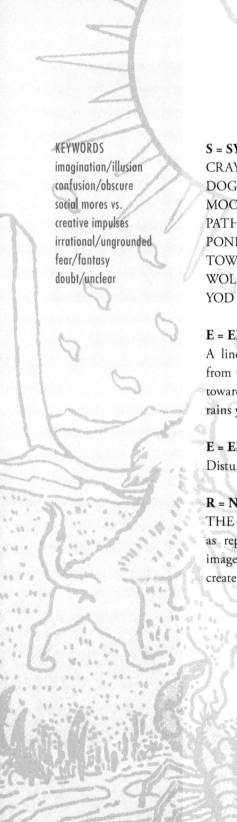

KEYWORDS
imagination/illusion
confusion/obscure
social mores vs.
creative impulses
irrational/ungrounded
fear/fantasy
doubt/unclear

S = SYMBOLS
CRAYFISH = primitive consciousness
DOG = tamed, collective conscious
MOON = reflected light of consciousness
PATH = path of self-knowledge
POND = subconscious, personal and collective
TOWERS = fortress
WOLF = untamed desires
YOD = light or consciousness

E = ENERGY
A line formed by the CRAYFISH emerges from the card title and continues winding up towards the image of the moon, which then rains yods upon the creatures underneath.

E = EMOTIONS
Disturbing. Emotional. Unbalanced. Hidden.

R = NUMBER
THE EIGHTEEN shows how our attention, as represented by The Magician, sends an image to our subconscious as a command to create a dream.

THE MOON

Rider Waite Smith Tarot

THE MOON.

Key #18/THE MOON shows a night scene with two canines howling at the moon. A CRAYFISH crawls to the edge of the POOL at his feet. When the Fool arrives at this card, he is confronted with a scene that makes him uneasy.

The path that he must follow, which is the only path he sees, leads him between two foreboding gray TOWERS, which seem to be battlements that he has to run like a gauntlet. The path is dimly lit, and it seems that it runs directly from the POOL of his own subconscious. He must deal with the dreams and visions that are emerging from his subconscious now. The reflected consciousness of the MOON oversees his journey, while raining down tear-shaped YODS to help light his way.

Evolution is the path of all creatures; even a lowly crayfish is instinctively drawn to the light. The path forward seems to be blocked by two howling canines, a DOG and a WOLF, that represent the choice of two diametrically opposed states of being: social consciousness versus irrationality, intuition or instinct.

Instinct is the intuition of a species, tested over time. For a man, the voice of intuition may seem to be crazy at first. The question is: is the voice the voice of my ego, or the voice of my intuition? The way to tell the difference is this: the ego has needs, so its information is based upon fear; the ideas advanced by the voice of intuition feel expansive and exciting.

The DOG may be tamed, but he is chained to man and therefore cannot go any faster than the slowest man. Clearly, social consciousness symbolized by the dog is not the fastest way to achieve enlightenment. The WOLF, on the other hand, represents the untamed will and desires of the individual; the wolf shows us that if the individual can tame his will to his highest desires, he will achieve success. The wolf indicates that the way to enlightenment is a solitary path beset by the fears and needs of the ego.

The MOON reflects only a pale portion of the light of the Sun; it reflects the fear we often have of our own subconscious, the right brain, or female side of our brain. There are great riches to be discovered in the subconscious if you can walk the path in balance. Everything in this card indicates that the extremes of a polarized existence are to be avoided: being a DOG is no better than being a WOLF, and the prison-like TOWERS are austere reminders that a life lived in the prison of the ego or too-rational mind is a severe and barren existence.

The YODS that seem to pour like drops of light from the MOON are an important symbol, found in many of the cards in traditional Tarot decks. The yod is the smallest letter of the Hebrew alphabet. Literally, it means "hand"—it signifies "creation," and is a symbol for all metaphysical processes; on its own, it is a symbol for Spirit. As the rain of yods fall from the Moon, so the animals in the world beneath look to the light for sustenance, enlightenment, or spiritual evolution.

When You get This Card in a Reading

Think about the things that are in the warehouse of your subconscious. The machine of creation is powered by the energy of the subconscious. The default setting creates what other people want—your family, church, politicians, or school. When you reject the beliefs and emotions that don't support the life you want, you set the machine of creation to a conscious setting.

Meditation

We can choose our thoughts and emotions, step out of the pain of unconsciousness and separation. Thus, the world is at our command.

18—THE MOON

DREAMING

Tarot of Creativity

The title of the The Moon in *The Tarot of Creativity* is DREAMING. The infinite pool of universal subconscious that some may call Source can be accessed through our DREAMS. Our personal subconscious is linked with the universal subconscious through our dreams.

The dream is a marriage of the symbols of the individual—the personal lexicon of the Soul—with universal archetypes. The Moon is an impartial mirror for our emotions and thoughts. It reflects the collective conscious—the ocean of collective dreams—and the personal subconscious equally well.

The river of our individual dreams flows into the ocean of the collective dream. The river feeds the ocean. The rain feeds the streams that feed the river. The rain the water evaporated from the ocean gathers in clouds that fall upon the land, and so it goes. Reality is the dream of the Soul that it has chosen to experience. Karma and the dreams of the incarnated Self in all its myriad forms is the consciousness that is reflected by the MOON. You, as the individual dreamer have access to the collective dream. It cannot be otherwise. The dream you dream unlocks the subconscious like a key.

The MOON reflects the general dream of humanity. The full moon is like the valve on a pressure cooker, it allows the unprocessed emotions of humanity to safely release a bit of the pressure. Once we die, we get to see how we were held down to Earth—kept in physical existence—by the heaviness of our emotions. We see it so clearly when we are no longer affected by it, but the trick is to see it while in the dream of life. This card is linked in thematically to the High Priestess/MEMORY card. The quantum soup of the implicate contains universal and personal symbols known as archetypes. These archetypes are iconic pictures that contain a lot of information in each detail. Dreaming is one way to access the Akashic records. The Akashic records are the etheric records of all that is, all that ever was and all that could ever be. Many times the symbols in a dream are actually archetypes, embedded with huge amounts of non-verbal information. Like a piece of holographic film, an archetype holds a great deal of information; in order to access the information, you have to focus the light of your consciousness at a precise angle—using your power of deliberate focus (The Magician/ATTENTION). Just as language is a collection of symbols that can be strung together in an infinite amount of ways to communicate an infinite amount of thoughts, so the symbols and images in a dream are the language of the subconscious: the language of the right brain.

The Tarot employs the same system of pictures and symbols—meant to by-pass logic and reason—in order to directly communicate with our subconscious. Dreams come from the embedded, unexpressed potentials in the enfolded implicate—the cosmic mind-stuff of universal awareness. In a dream you may act out potential scenarios, interact with the dream-selves of people you know, even live an entirely distinct life with a separate past and different players. By exploring other potential lives in your dreams you don't have to experience these potential realities in your "real" life.

Through your dreams you can communicate with the Souls of other people that you know or don't know; this nightly interaction can certainly smooth things out in your life. Dreams enable us to cram more experience, skills, and experience into our material existence, just like the holographic film that records more information on the surface of the film by angling the light of the recording device. Art and other creative thinking accesses the same pictorial language system that the right brain uses; therefore, DREAMS are very important to creative people. They know how to access their dreams not just at night, but during the day. A daydream is one way for the self-conscious to access the universal and personal Akashic records and thus arrive at new ideas or solutions. Creative people learn to mine their dreams for the richness of personal and universal potential.

All is possible in a DREAM, and those who have accessed the magic of dreaming know that we are alchemists that can transform the pure energy of intent into matter. Under the influence of our focused attention, a wave becomes a particle to exist in time and space, only to collapse back into a wave when we are no longer focused on it. This is the same way a dream works.The ancient Toltec masters said that we are all dreaming one hundred percent of the time. Reality is a dream that issues from us, whether we are consciously directing it or not. We are destined to become what we really are: material masters, alchemists of matter and spirit. We naturally access these skills in our dreams, so we can access the same skills in our "waking" state. If we can dream it, it can be. The Moon/DREAMING card is about the evolution of consciousness from an unaware state to a conscious state; from the person who thinks he is awake but is actually dreaming, to a person who can awake inside the dream in order to dream another dream; one that is more creative, more empowered, more conscious. The goal of the enlightened man is to not stop the dream of material existence, but to wake up to his natural spiritual awareness while inside the dream of the material.

Like a dreamer who suddenly becomes "lucid" inside the dream, the enlightened man realizes that daily awareness is a dream like any other dream. He wakes up to the fact that he is the dreamer dreaming the dreamer who is dreaming that he is real when in fact he is a dream. Material existence then becomes a wonderful game; we see beyond the "smoky mirror" of unconsciousness; we see our role in creating what we then get to experience. Remembering our dreams allows us to narrow the gap between our Higher Selves, our physical bodies, and our self-conscious; we start to merge the three parts of ourselves—the mind-ego, the Higher Self, the body-subconscious—into a new integrated wholeness.

We cannot graduate out of the collective dream until we master the art of dreaming—until we become lucid dreamers, and direct the dream we are dreaming. The conscious dreamer is the one who has woken up to the dream of life while in it; he escapes the gravity of unconscious emotions, and ascends naturally to a frequency outside the laws of physical existence. Spirit in its infinite nature dreamed of the limitation of form and created an independent thought form that incarnated into the physical plane as man. Man can evolve enough to remember his origins, and access his power to recreate himself in a new, chosen dream.

When You get This Card in a Reading

Are you afraid of your dreams? The subconscious has nothing in it to be afraid of: it is merely a messenger with a message to deliver to you. An artist learns to tap into her dreams for creative material. Use your dreams in order to clear your subconscious; then they can help you know your highest desires, the light of the MOON illuminates the path to your dreams.

Meditation

Who is dreaming the dreamer?

Related to

The Hermit/EMERGENCE (Key #9)

KEYWORDS
optimism/expansion
success/positive outcome
vitality/health
confidence/innocence
energy/personal power
happiness/joy
renaissance/rebirth

S = SYMBOLS
BANNER = freed from earthly needs
NUDE CHILD = innocent, new
SUN = Christ consciousness
SUNFLOWERS = turn with the Sun
WHITE HORSE = purity, power
WALL = unconscious beliefs/emotional blocks

E = ENERGY
The image of the Sun dominates this image. The red banner leads the eye from the child that plays on the back of the horse to the Sun shining above.

E = EMOTIONS
Sunshine coming out after weeks of darkness, rain and gloom. Flowers blooming. Innocence. Joy.

R = NUMBER
THE NINETEEN is the combination of the One of the MAGICIAN and the Nine of The Hermit/EMERGENCE. The light of Christ consciousness in the lantern of The Hermit, when used with the razor sharp focus of the ATTENTION of The Magician, creates and recreates the world.

THE SUN

ARCHETYPE

Rider Waite Smith Tarot

THE SUN .

The image on the Sun card pictures a nude CHILD on a WHITE HORSE carrying a RED BANNER under a blazing SUN.

The SUNFLOWER is named after the flower's tendency to follow the Sun as it goes through the sky; the flower always turns to face the Sun. In Key 19, The Sun, the SUNFLOWERS line the top of WALL. The wall represents the barrier of old social systems, personal beliefs, and emotional blocks that the individual had to overcome in order to reach this card. The flowers REFLECT the Sun, but unlike the Moon, they seem to shine with vibrancy and joy. The flowers symbolize success, joy and vitality, but they also show us that LIFE follows the LIGHT of consciousness, just as the SUNFLOWER follows the Sun in its journey around the sky.

The CHILD represents the natural self. For someone on the path of enlightenment, the Earth is not a school where you learn karmic lessons. It is a place of forgetting, a vibrational reality where consciousness is dampened with the density of beliefs, weighed down by the gravity of unconscious emotions, and frozen by the fear of the unknown. The Querent on the Path has only to remember his former existence (vibrational reality) as a being that vibrated with a higher awareness. To become enlightened, or to ascend, is to go back to what is natural for us.

The NUDE CHILD represents that the CHRIST CONSCIOUSNESS has been reborn; the trials of the path of enlightenment are behind him, symbolized by the WALL. The Fool has overcome the old barriers of beliefs, thoughts and emotional blocks in his path; in doing so, he has been restored to his original purity and innocence. He is a child again.

You cannot enter the kingdom of Heaven unless you "become as a child"—innocent to the belief systems and heavy emotional blocks that keep humanity stuck in unconscious, reactive behavior. A CHILD knows nothing of social mores, which is why this child is NUDE. The Fool is finally free of the limitations and beliefs that his fellows regard as reality.

The people that he left behind in his quest for the freedom of enlightenment are behind the WALL in this picture. The others were stopped at the WALL thinking that it represented the end of the world, but the wall was just the symbol of their unprocessed emotions and the delineation of the limits of their beliefs. This same wall defines the perimeter of the Garden of Eden. It represents a frequency barrier—what is behind the wall is the old world of disempowering beliefs and negative emotions. The wall doesn't confine the child on this card; it simply defines the exterior of the perimeter that surrounds the "bubble reality" of the fear-based third dimension.

This card shows this wall from the perspective of the one who has escaped the bubble to play in the greater reality outside. The bubble reality of the old third dimension is like a playpen: it keeps the unevolved individual contained in a limited system so that they can learn certain things and have time to grow.

3D is a petri dish where an experiment is confined in order to play out fully; this is the Matrix of limitation that we think is reality. The bubble reality we live in is a world built upon a single idea, upon a single kernel of programming. The core program behind the "Matrix" bubble reality is the concept of separation (see *Unplug From the Matrix* for more information).

The WALL in this picture is the outside of the bubble that encases and defines the thought experiment of the third dimension. The figure on this card has left the old paradigm, and in doing so, he was reborn into Eden as a CHILD. The number of this card, Nineteen, is a very powerful number: the One represents the individual, while the Nine represents the godhead, or realization of the divinity within. When combined together, a Ten results, which is the symbol that represents the One of the individuated consciousness, paired with the Zero or circle that represents wholeness or spirit. Ten was believed to be the "perfect number" in some esoteric belief systems.

Interestingly enough, the numerology of the word, "Eden" also reduces to 10. Eden = 5+4+5+5 = 19, which is the number of the card, The Sun. The word, "Heaven" also equals a 10. Heaven = 8+5+1+4+5+5 = 28. 2+8 = 10, the "perfect" number of the mystic and sage.

The Sun card represents the ascension of the aspirant to a new frequency, a new base vibration that he has been able to hold consistently. His progress through all the lower cards showed him how to drop all the unconscious beliefs and emotions that held him down in the lower reality. As he rose in consciousness, he dropped the ballast of limiting beliefs and the base emotions. Emotions fix the individual into the evolutionary plane that matches the vibrational frequency of the person's emotional reality. The lower 3rd dimension requires, by default, emotions that keep the individual in karmic situations: "eye for an eye, tooth for a tooth" scenarios and thinking. The core concept of separation underlying the bubble experiment produces thoughts of need and survival. Survival beliefs produce survival emotions: fight or flight, kill or be killed. As long as you are having these thoughts, beliefs, and emotions, you cannot escape the dimensional level that matches these frequencies. When you have learned to take responsibility for your thoughts and emotions, you have attained spiritual maturity. Now you can leave the playpen of karma and escape the confines of 3D.

As a child in the playpen of the lower dimensions represented by the preceding cards, the Fool could not be trusted to create a new world, as he wasn't spiritually mature enough to take responsibility for his creative power. He was living by default: unconsciously reacting to his world, a world he was helping maintain in place with his thoughts and emotions. Like a teenager might learn to be responsible enough to drive the car as he gains spiritual maturity, he knows that he is responsible. Getting through the bubble reality of 3D is a rite of passage and an evolutionary tool. Consciousness is always choice. You can't be conscious or spiritually mature by default, you have to work at it.

The CHILD is NUDE in this picture because he has remembered his natural self, his innocence, the initial being of unlimited power and awareness that he was before he "descended" into material existence. And while he cannot yet do what he could do in a non-dual reality, he has come to appreciate what it means to be his true Self while still in a material form. In other words, he has brought the light of his consciousness into the dense plane of his former existence; he has brought a brighter light of awareness into this plane than ever shone there before. The Sun represents the enlightened man who allows the light of consciousness to shine once again.

When You get This Card in a Reading

The Sun is shining once again. Wake up and be excited by the opportunities that this day will bring you.

Meditation

"Deep in their roots, all flowers keep the light." ~ Theodore Roethke

19—THE SUN

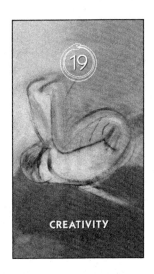

CREATIVITY

Tarot of Creativity

The keyword in *The Tarot of Creativity* for The Sun is CREATIVITY. Creativity is divine play. We play at life—we must not ever forget this and become too serious, too grave.

A child is not serious, he knows that he is always playing; if he can remember this as an adult, he remembers that he has always been playing, if only at being what he thought everyone wanted him to be. "Act your age!" is something that he might have heard growing up. At the time, he may have been fooled into "behaving," but now he knows that he should have paid more attention to the first word in the phrase, "act"—everything in his former life has been just an act. And he can choose to act differently at any time, and go out to play.

A child has no memories to hold him in the prison of unconsciousness, thus he can easily ride the power of his ATTENTION into the light. Remember that the card of ATTENTION is The Magician, and magically, the hidden numerical equivalent of the number Nineteen is One, the number of that card. The CHILD here is not a child without awareness or experience. The discipline of his former life (the preceding 18 cards) has made it possible for him to renew and regenerate his life so he is "as a child" again—reborn, fresh to the world.

Through the magic of CREATIVITY, the Soul is renewed, and the individual becomes like a child again as it remembers its natural Self. While the CHILD of the Soul plays joyously in his new world, he knows that he has created the world in his own image. Everything the individual has endured to get to this point, the tests and lessons in the former cards, is now revealed to be of one piece, and it is good. The Soul is refreshed as it remembers itself.

When You get This Card in a Reading

Your Soul's mission is to play; how will you play today?

Meditation

"Why do you try to understand art? Do you try to understand the song of a bird?" ~ Pablo Picasso

Related to

The Magician/ATTENTION (Key #1)
The Wheel of Fortune/ACCELERATION (Key #10)

19

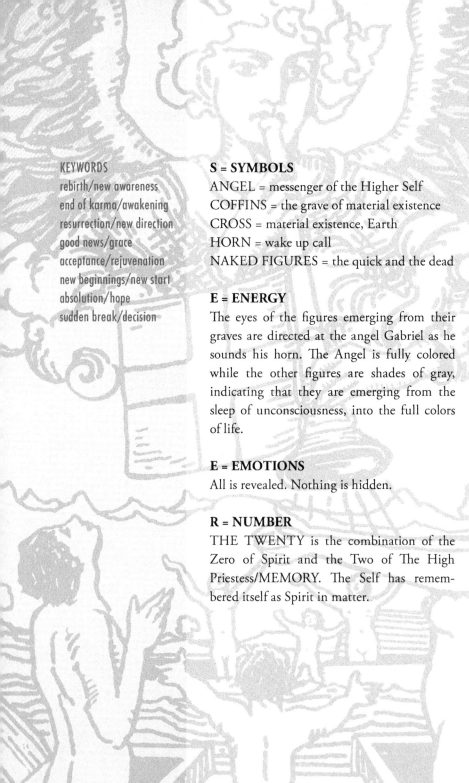

KEYWORDS
rebirth/new awareness
end of karma/awakening
resurrection/new direction
good news/grace
acceptance/rejuvenation
new beginnings/new start
absolution/hope
sudden break/decision

S = SYMBOLS
ANGEL = messenger of the Higher Self
COFFINS = the grave of material existence
CROSS = material existence, Earth
HORN = wake up call
NAKED FIGURES = the quick and the dead

E = ENERGY
The eyes of the figures emerging from their graves are directed at the angel Gabriel as he sounds his horn. The Angel is fully colored while the other figures are shades of gray, indicating that they are emerging from the sleep of unconsciousness, into the full colors of life.

E = EMOTIONS
All is revealed. Nothing is hidden.

R = NUMBER
THE TWENTY is the combination of the Zero of Spirit and the Two of The High Priestess/MEMORY. The Self has remembered itself as Spirit in matter.

JUDGEMENT

ARCHETYPE

Rider Waite Smith Tarot

JUDGEMENT.

JJUDGEMENT shows the ANGEL Gabriel blowing a HORN, and people arising from what appear to be coffins. The FIGURES are gray and nearly colorless, the only color is the gold hair on the woman. The HORN seems to be directed at her. She is the only one—or the first one—in the card who is RISING from the dead, and we know this because her hair is gaining color, the gold of higher consciousness.

The ANGEL Gabriel blows a clarion call to wake up the Self mired in the game of duality. He doesn't just do it at the moment pictured in the card, he does it all the time. No matter when you live, no matter how you live, no matter what your past, no matter how old or young you are, you have the opportunity to awaken from the dream of duality.

Judgment seems to be about being judged at the end of your life by a "higher" being. But the card is not about judgment—in fact, this card means the opposite of what we may think it does. It is about the equality and balance of duality seen from a higher state of consciousness; this is the consciousness that can be obtained by following the path of the FOOL, the map of the Tarot.

The number Twenty brings the Two together with the Zero, and this means that duality is brought together with Spirit; or rather, Spirit now infuses matter at a higher level than previously (when it was just a two, the number of duality).

This is a card that indicates an ending. As a Two it indicates another gateway in the path of spiritual progression. This could be seen as the kind of test that one might encounter at the end of one's life, as in a life review. Everything that one has done or thought comes to the surface. With the energy of the Two brought through the lens of the ZERO, everything is equal and good.

If you believe that there is imbalance, or judge things as being bad or good, then you still are seeing things through the eyes of the limited EGO, and you have to return to the denser plane in order to try to balance things karmically. However, if you can see things without judgment, as Spirit sees them, then you pass the gateway of Judgment.

The card shows the ANGEL blowing a HORN decorated with a FLAG bearing a RED CROSS. The cross with arms of equal length is an ancient symbol that means equilibrium, Earth, the elements, peace, the resolution of opposites, and the marriage of the male and female polarities. It symbolizes material existence in divine balance.

There is an old saying, "The quick and the dead." The word *quick* is an antiquated word that means "alive." The life that this phrase refers to is the life of full consciousness—the awareness of what I call, "the realization of the divinity in the duality:" spiritual enlightenment while inside the illusion of matter. The life that we are taught is real is one filled with egoistic concerns and material distractions. It is "designed" that way as part of the game of awareness that we all came here to play.

To realize the underlying nonjudgmental Spirit behind the illusion of matter is to transcend the game of duality. The "quick" are those who are choosing life over materialism and illusion. They choose to "wake up" to the true reality behind the mirror of duality. In doing so, they see that others behind them are the "dead" that may not wake up, but the realization achieved by their transcendence is that all states of being are OK and equal to any other state of being.

It is in realizing this equality of states that they reach a new form of equilibrium, but this state is not more or better than a less conscious form of existence, it is only different. And the difference is the amazing thing about the experience of separation; difference is how Spirit, represented by the HOLY FOOL, can come to know itself, even if it is under a temporary guise.

When You get This Card in a Reading
What do you judge? What do you accept? Try switching these, as an experiment in the malleability of consciousness. As long as you judge things as lesser or greater, good or bad, you are stuck in the playpen of duality, learning lessons of contrast, choice, and preference.

Meditation
How do you choose among things of equal value?

JUDGEMENT

THE EPIPHANY

Tarot of Creativity

This card is the final step in the Fool's journey, when he "wakes up" to the real life of consciousness through a transcendent moment called an EPIPHANY. The whole path up to this point has been a series of gates that when opened, revealed another passageway to another door.

The title on the card in *The Tarot of Creativity* is THE EPIPHANY: an epiphany is a sudden breakthrough in understanding.

Epiphany: (1) a usually sudden manifestation or perception of the essential nature or meaning of something (2) an intuitive grasp of reality through something (as an event) usually simple and striking (3) an illuminating discovery, realization, or disclosure

The Fool's path is one of self-awareness. There is no other path; there is no bigger game to play. He has journeyed through life and through all the other cards in the Tarot to find out that the thing he has been seeking has been inside himself all along.

He finds out that he can bring this consciousness into the denser plane he exists in by bringing it into himself. The energy is not actually outside him, but he has to deal with the rules of physical existence, otherwise called "The Game;" everyone has told him that what he seeks is outside of him. And that is the rule of the game of material existence: that you begin the game by first forgetting the connection that is YOU.

Then the game is that of RE-MEMBERING the self; of putting back the pieces to the puzzle, one by one. In a way the FOOL is Osiris, who was murdered and dis-membered by his brother SET, who then spread the pieces of his body all over the land. It was only when ISIS (The High Priestess/MEMORY card) reassembled the scattered parts that Osiris was whole again; she did this by RE-MEMBERing him.

And what does The Fool REMEMBER? He remembers himself in his totality. The Self who took the journey of life at the beginning of the game is in truth that infinite totality. The individual transcends the limitations of beliefs, emotions, and physical limitations by REMEMBERING love; remembering the innate goodness of love, the innate goodness of who he is, and becoming whole once again.

But this is not the final truth, and he knows that as he looks around him. He lets go of judgment in exchange for *joy in physical form*. The laboratory of physical existence is merely a bubble reality, one governed by space-time; in order for objects to exist as separate, time had to be created first, which then allowed space to be created. Or was it the other way around?

The FOOL who is now WISE, has the following EPIPHANY: he realizes the meaning of the mirror that duality presents to him no matter which way he turns. The mirror, whether it reflects a vision of darkness or a vision of ethereal beauty has two sides and each are beautiful. As each side becomes aware of itself by the reflection of the Divine Other, it enters a state of non-judgment. All is known to be equal. The mind wants to make meaning, but what if the mind itself is the meaning?

The Mirror is the goddess ISIS. One way to see the wordplay of this name is to see it as two parts that mirror themselves. The name "ISIS" means that each part of the mirror simply IS. But now the two parts, the dark and the light, are *self-aware*. Each side *knows* that it IS, and is also aware of the Other. Each side of the mysterious equation of duality is no longer in judgment because the mind has evolved to a level of understanding that is more holistic in nature. The journey that the FOOL has experienced has brought him to this understanding; the EPIPHANY of wholeness is brought to the level of the ego, transforming it into a force directed by love.

The descent into the darkness of the material plane was a descent into the density of matter. Since the Higher Self could not achieve this descent, it sent a scout ship, the ego/Mind, into this reality. The descent into separation and duality caused amnesia for the FOOL. This amnesia was initially perceived by the ego/Mind as *abandonment*, thus it experienced the primal "wound of incarnation."

The FOOL remembered that something more was to be experienced; he knew deep down that something was "wrong" and incomplete with what he perceived. And so, he went on a search for the something that he had lost. He searched for his MEMORY, for the parts of the dis-membered self in order to rejoin them in wholeness.

The ego, in its blind search, learned to judge. It judged everything it saw as "less than" what it dimly remembered as good. According to the standards imposed on it by the forlorn and abandoned individual mind, nothing could be good enough, bright enough, abundant enough, healthy enough, beautiful enough, wealthy enough, or rich enough. This is because the FOOL, confined by the bounds of the ego, could not see beyond the game. He could not see how beauty, love and abundance followed his every step; he couldn't see the darkness of his ignorance, and couldn't see his own courage in taking the challenge at the beginning of the game—to descend into the darkness and density of matter, into the slow drug of time and space.

Metaphorically, the FOOL took it upon himself to initially incarnate as a rock, the densest form of matter, in which consciousness is very slow. The rock as the densest element of duality evolves very slowly. As the FOOL started to gain wisdom, his vibration raised and the matter-bubble-reality system in which he was embedded started to liquefy and get more fluid. At the point where he has the EPIPHANY represented by this card, he is about to ascend to a higher state of being, let's call it helium, which is lighter than air. Thus he loses the density of unconscious emotions and floats free of the third dimension.

The ability to lighten one's state of being, or more precisely heighten one's vibrational state—is true ALCHEMY, which is nothing less than the enlightenment of the egoic self, the "normal" mind. By changing his own state of being, the aspirant has become a conscious creator emitting a new, higher frequency. As a consequence, The Law of Resonance requires that everything around him has to vibrate at the same frequency. Thus, as he changes, the world changes to align with him. The Fool has REMEMBERED that he is a creator being. The mirror-game of duality has been broken. He has emerged from the cocoon of lower consciousness into a new world.

The physical plane is one of contrast and separation; it is a theatrical play, where consciousness has taken different roles. At Key 20, The FOOL sees beyond the game; he knows the game/bubble was created so that consciousness could see its own reflection, no matter what role it was playing. He came to play in the game with a blindfold over his eyes. As long as he wasn't aware of the game, he could still play it because the object of the game was to awaken to his own self, to see himself in all that is. Once he realizes his true nature is also the nature of his reality—game over.

When You get This Card in a Reading
When you have dropped the masks of the illusion, when you have dropped judgment; the ego has dissolved into the Light of Being, and there is nothing but Consciousness *knowing*, and *seeing* Itself everywhere. Game over.

Meditation
Don't wait for the image in the mirror to smile first.

Related to
The High Priestess/MEMORY (Key #2)
Justice/ILLUMINATION (Key #11)

success/end of cycle
graduation/realization
completion/integration
spiritual awareness
higher consciousness
transcend/ascend
prosperity/contentment
atonement/wholeness

S = SYMBOLS
BULL = Taurus
EAGLE = Scorpio
LION = Leo
HUMAN HEAD = Aquarius
NAKED WOMAN = Higher Self
WANDS = spiritual energy
WREATH = Ouroborus/infinity, life

E = ENERGY
The dominant line in this picture is the circle of the wreath that surrounds the floating woman. The energy circles around and emphasizes the central figure.

E = EMOTIONS
Attainment. Success. Achievement.

R = NUMBER
THE TWENTY-ONE is the combination of the infinite power of the Two with the purified, directed intent of the One.

THE WORLD

ARCHETYPE

Rider Waite Smith Tarot

The number of this card, Twenty-one, symbolizes the marriage of the Divine Feminine (2) with the Divine Masculine (1); the play of the wave and particle; the implicate with the explicate. The product of this marriage is the Divine Child (3).

The World card shows a NAKED WOMAN in the sky surrounded by a WREATH and the symbols of the fixed signs of the Zodiac: Aquarius, Scorpio, Leo, and Taurus. The Lion is Leo, a fire sign; the Bull or calf is Taurus, an earth sign; the Man is Aquarius, an air sign; and the Eagle is Scorpio (the symbol for the evolved Scorpio), a water sign. These signs also represent the classical four elements: fire, earth, air, and water, which are also the elements represented in the four suits of the Minor Arcana in the Tarot.

The NAKED WOMAN holds two WANDS that represent the mastery of spiritual energy, balanced equally in her two hands; these represent a balance of the male and female sides of Nature.

The fixed astrological signs show that she is grounded and works willingly with the principles of Nature. In some decks the WREATH is an Ouroborus. The Ouroborus or Uroboros, from the Greek meaning tail-devouring snake, is an ancient symbol depicting a serpent or dragon eating its own tail.

> The Ouroborus often symbolizes self-reflexivity or cyclicality, especially in the sense of something constantly re-creating itself, the eternal return, and other things such as the phoenix which operate in cycles that begin anew as soon as they end. It can also represent the idea of primordial unity related to something existing in or persisting from the beginning with such force or qualities it cannot be extinguished.[1]

---

1   en.wikipedia.org/wiki/Ouroborus

The four tools/paths of the Tarot were gifts made to the Fool when he set out on the path of individuation; these paths are symbolized by the four fixed signs of the Zodiac at the corners of this image:

WANDS-FIRE—ENERGY/INTENT
SWORDS-AIR—MENTAL
AIR-WATER—EMOTIONAL
PENTACLES-EARTH—MATTER/PHYSICAL

The Master treats each path/gift/tool with respect and learns how to use them together; this creates movement in the time-space continuum. Movement and evolution cannot happen at the level of Oneness; it can only happen when oneness divides into more than one part. The division or opposition of the polarities produces tension, which engenders movement. Movement is the creative evolution that Spirit desires, and the ability to create the evolution of movement *consciously* is the mastery represented by this card.

When we are conscious of the connection between what we think/ feel, and what we experience, we can no longer allow ourselves to project thoughts and emotions that will support and recreate a reality that we no longer choose. We become responsible for what we think and for what we feel. This victimless, responsible state is spiritual adulthood. We go from being unconscious creators to being conscious creators; from being separate from All That Is, to *being* All That Is.

Spiritual adulthood doesn't mean that the achievements and uniqueness of the individual gets lost; the process of Ascension is the appreciation and understanding of the *divinity in duality*; the realization that the distinctiveness of individual expression can be lovingly wrapped in the comprehension of oneness that is the underlying reality.

The World card marks the end of the path of the Seeker; now that she knows how to handle spiritual energy on the material plane, she has graduated. She has achieved a higher level of consciousness; her spiritual apprenticeship is over. The Fool has completed her journey through the Tarot, and through life on the physical plane. She has transcended the world of illusion (the ego) and gained The World of her Higher Self. She has successfully integrated all parts of herself. She has re-membered (see The High Priestess/MEMORY) the totality (divinity) of herself and the divinity of all things, expressed or unexpressed.

When You get This Card in a Reading

The world is your oyster. You are at the center of the universe, where you have always been.

Meditation

"Follow your bliss and the universe will open doors where there were only walls."
~ Joseph Campbell

THE WORLD

TRANSCEND

Tarot of Creativity

The title of The World card in *The Tarot of Creativity* is TRANSCEND.

> [tran-send] verb
> 1. to rise above or go beyond; overpass; exceed: to transcend the limits of thought; kindness transcends courtesy.

> 2. to outdo or exceed in excellence, elevation, extent, degree, etc.; surpass; excel.

> 3. Theology. (of the Deity) to be above and independent of (the universe, time, etc.).

To transcend the world of duality and polarized concepts means to go "above"—to reach a new point of perspective. Visualize the geometric shape of a square: the square exists in the conceptual space of 2D. From the level of this limited perspective you can only see opposites, not unity. Standing at one end of a line, you can see the other point, but not yourself. Some people get to the point where they understand that duality is a "smoky mirror" that reflects yourself as the other, but to really transcend the illusion of duality requires a new perspective.

Imagine a center point to the square that you then project into the space above the surface of the square. Since space cannot exist without time, you are extending the point into the 3rd/4th dimension. Now connect the point in space with all the other points of the square; you have now constructed a pyramid.

The four-sided pyramid symbolizes the evolved Man, the perfected, spiritualized man—the Angel in physical form. The bottom of the pyramid symbolizes the Earth—four points of the square—while the triangular shape of the sides is one of the symbols for God. Combining the Three with the Four returns Seven—the secret number of the manifested world, or 3D. The restoration of the Divine Triad of the evolved Self, places the Higher Self at the top of this pyramid, ruling in complete cooperation and partnership with the Earth, below. This is the "divine marriage" that the alchemists of old sought. Alchemists and ancient mystics sought the transformation of the body into a new form; this lighter vibrational form then "ascends" in consciousness.

The whole point of ascension is not to leave the physical. In fact, as long as we think that the world of matter is lesser or bad, we are still in lower consciousness, in the "playground" of the undeveloped ego-mind. As long as we can't go beyond the lessons of duality, we cannot be let out to play in a larger world. A child cannot be trusted with greater power and freedom until she has learned responsibility for her actions and the rules of the world that lies beyond the playground. In the same way, we cannot achieve our Soul's goal of awakening inside the dream until we have transcended the lower grades of consciousness.

This card marks the Fool's ascension into higher consciousness. In this step, she aligns what she has learned on her journey through life with her original consciousness—that of her Higher Self. In this sense, The Fool relinquishes her life experience in the lower plane of consciousness as a gift to her Higher Self. The Fool has learned how to embody what she has gained from her journey through material existence.

With the knowledge gained from her journey through the Tarot and her sojourn in physical reality, the Fool arrives at a new understanding. Once, she might have called this "wisdom" when she saw it in others, but now she realizes that the truly wise man or woman no longer knows anything, because she has shed all her preconceptions and beliefs. She exists in the Now. She has a natural understanding of all things without needing to resort to words or explanations. She simply knows what she needs to know when she needs to know it, and only acts when she is inspired to do so. Her search through life for the "missing half" of herself resulted in the recognition of the wholeness that was in her all along. Now, she sees everything from the view of her Higher Self, as a divine creative expression. She has become a being of pure potential with the delightful ability to become someone new in every instant and dissolve back into nothing in the next. No longer does she need to search for anything, especially for self-knowledge. She knows less than she has ever known for she understands that "facts" and "absolute truth" belong to the playground of a materialistically-oriented existence that she has left behind. Nor does she desire the "spiritual" over the material, as she knows that any such terms and valuations are only intellectual games that the ego uses to distract and aggrandize itself.

She loves the game of separation and duality because it allowed her Higher Self to gain a rich and unique experience. Those who speak disparagingly of the suffering caused by desire seem now very distant, as she knows that the old value-oriented, wounded ego is what rendered the judgments that cause the perception of suffering. She knows that the point of the human experience is to experience the fullness and variety of material existence, without judging it as good or bad.

The three parts of her Self—the Higher Self, her mind-ego, and her subconscious-body—are now integrated and aligned. As a master of her mental and emotional bodies she no longer wastes energy on useless emotional reactions or thoughts that do not serve her. Her intent is now the same as that of her Higher Self, she has become a Master of awareness. The Master knows that the purpose of her journey through the density of matter wasn't to escape duality, but to transcend the social conditioning of the wounded ego: the beliefs and emotional reactivity that kept her locked in a lower awareness. Emotions connect us to the plane that matches their vibrational resonance. In the old Matrix, "negative emotions" are simply variations on the underlying themes of fear and separation; these are the forces that keep us bound to the Earth.

Negative emotions are like gravity; they keep us connected to a denser version of the Earth; we cannot escape until we shed them. When this emotional baggage is shed, the Master naturally ascends because the gravity of the old paradigm releases her. She transcends the mirror-state of duality, the illusion that she was born into; she sees the primordial nature of Oneness that underlies and supports the experience of duality. As a materialist, she treated everything around her as an objective, separate "thing." Everything was neatly categorized in a collectively agreed-upon system of value. Now that she has ascended in awareness, she sees that everything is equal; it is equally important, precious and unique. The World has opened up like an oyster releasing its pearl. Our journey through the difficult experience of duality and separation is the grain of sand that generated the beautiful pearl.

The Tarot is sometimes called the Journey of the Fool—the journey of Spirit through physical existence. This journey can be traced through the Major Arcana using the Tarot Tableau. Matching the traditional titles of the cards with the modern keyword-titles of *The Tarot of Creativity* provides insight into the progression of the Fool. The twenty-one cards of Major Arcana—excluding the unnumbered Fool—are often arranged in what is called the Tarot Tableau, with three rows of seven cards each.[1]

1. The first row represents the principles and the workings of the universe.
2. The second row represents the faculties of man and the rules of material existence.
3. The third row represents the results of applying rows one and two.

The Journey of the Fool						
1 Magician Attention	2 Priestess Memory	3 Empress Imagination	4 Emperor Insight	5 Hierophant Intuition	6 Lovers Love	7 Chariot Adventure
8 Strength I-Mage	9 Hermit Emergence	10 Fortune Acceleration	11 Justice Illumination	12 Hang Man Reversal	13 Death Metamorphosis	14 Temperance Alchemy
15 Devil Shadow	16 Tower Awakening	17 Star Revelation	18 Moon Dreaming	19 Sun Creativity	20 Judgment Epiphany	21 World Transcend

Coming from the indistinct and undifferentiated heights of oneness and traveling through the valley of duality which allows the experience of separation and individuation, the Fool comes to realize that individual expression and the experience of duality is just another form of Oneness, like a twin yolk inside a single egg. The richness and uniqueness of individual experience is what the Fool sought all along: what she gained in experience has exponential and evolutionary effects in the realm of Spirit.

This card signifies that the Querent has the potential to realize spiritual mastery without the encumbrance of the space-time school of the ego;

---

1   More information on how the cards relate to each other is in the Tarot Tableau section.

former emotional/mental blocks simply lift. The master has transcended the egoic, limited, disconnected self into a completely new plane of existence, governed not by the laws of cause and effect, time-space, or karma, but by the natural laws of the greater universe and the Higher Self.

Mastery is not domination, it is personal sovereignty—self-knowledge. A master rests calm and collected—in at state of perfect balance in the center of the universe—the master is the center point of the circle of individuated consciousness embedded in infinity.

This card represents the enlightenment achieved by the Fool. It shows the perfect partnership of Spirit with Matter, the blueprint for how a conscious individual can exist on a physical plane. The Fool has become a master of awareness; she has awareness of the state of oneness underlying all form while experiencing duality.

As the individual ascends, so does THE WORLD—together they go to a higher level of awareness. Consciousness has remembered itself. It doesn't just recognize the oneness of Spirit behind the mirror of physical existence, but sees the surface of the mirror too—duality as an expression of divinity. In remembering and reconnecting all the pieces of herself, she has reconnected all the pieces of The World as well. And all that she sees is perfect and whole, *as it always has been*.

When You get This Card in a Reading
Recall your natural mastery. Think big. Think of the whole picture. Like a fractal, all the parts of the picture reflect the whole, and the whole is reflected in each part.

Meditation
To see a World in a Grain of Sand
And a Heaven in a Wild Flower,
Hold Infinity in the palm of your hand
And Eternity in an hour.[1]

Related to
The Empress/IMAGINATION (Key #3)
The Hanged Man/REVERSAL (Key #12)

---

1   William Blake

NUMEROLOGY

0. THE ZERO IS SPIRIT

The ancient Greek philosopher and mathematician, Pythagoras, saw the sign of the Zero as the birthplace of all the other numbers, and as the container for all manifested things. It is at once the all and the nothing: the concept of the infinite void and its defining perimeter—the mind that holds the concept in the shape of the symbol. The circle glyph of the Zero represents the empty womb of all possibilities, the void that precedes the act, the moment, if you will, of creation. Ancient cultures all revere the circle as the symbol of spirit, evolution, the definition—or rather the sign—that points to Spirit.

> The Pythagoreans, too, held that void exists, and that it enters the heaven from the unlimited breath—it, so to speak, breathes in void. The void distinguishes the natures of things, since it is the thing that separates and distinguishes the successive terms in a series. This happens in the first case of numbers; for the void distinguishes their nature.[1]

The Zero represents the quantum implicate, where all potential resides; it symbolizes infinity. The circle is timelessness at the center but generates time as it revolves (see Key #10, The Wheel of Fortune). The cycle represented by the outer perimeter of the circle represents the cycle of life as it revolves—the cycle of karma—however, to see the evolution that the circle represents, you have to see the circle from a higher perspective, from a third point outside the two-dimensional symbol; then it reveals that it the circle is really a spiral seen on edge.

> God is an intelligible sphere—a sphere known to mind, not to the senses—whose center is everywhere and whose circumference nowhere.[2]

The spiral is the universal symbol for evolution, echoed in the spiral form of the nautilus and the shape of the galaxy. The Zero births all the other numbers. The Circle of Spirit divides like a cell into two in order to

---

1   en.wikipedia.org/wiki/Pythagoreanism
2   Joseph Campbell, *The Power of Myth*

create duality; it is the mother of the One and Twenty, the male and female principles of duality, which in turn generate all forms. The Zero or circle could be said to represent what we call "God."

THE IMPLICATE/ALL THAT IS

1. THE ONE IS INDEPENDENT

Initiating, pioneering, leadership, , self, aggressor, individuation, the individual, action, new beginnings.

THE MALE PRINCIPLE. INDIVIDUATION ~ The SUN

2. THE TWO SEEKS BALANCE

Cooperation, relationship, tact, diplomacy, balance, union, receptive, changeable, adaptable, consideration of others, partnership, mediating. The number of polarity and balance: think of a pendulum that has to swing equally on each side, equal columns supporting a roof (Justice, High Priestess), justice, fairness, kindness, tact, meditation, planning, discernment, nurturing, and support.

THE FEMALE PRINCIPLE. DUALITY ~ The MOON

3. THE THREE EXPRESSES

Expression, verbalization, socialization, the arts, creativity, magic, innovation, versatility, flexibility, interaction, communication, the joy of living—the Three is the base number of the Master number 33, which signifies Christ Consciousness—enlightenment through love (see number 6).

THE CHILD ~ JUPITER

4. THE FOUR IS STABLE

Foundation, order, system, rational, diligent, endurance, constancy, grounded, limitation, boundaries, production, steady growth, stability, dependability, discipline, dedication, over-cautious, stubborn, protective—the four nurtures, protects, and shelters the growing child.

NUMBER OF EARTH~ URANUS

5. THE FIVE LOVES FREEDOM

Expansion, change, chaos, instability, freedom, visionary, travel, adventure, pioneering, restlessness, innovation, unpredictable, rebellion, opportunistic.

NUMBER OF MAN ~ MERCURY

6. THE SIX EXPLORES LOVE

Balance, harmony, truth, justice, responsibility, protection, nurturing, empathy, healing, marriage, forgiveness, compassion, sympathy, family.
LOVE. ~ VENUS

7. THE SEVEN SEEKS THE UNSEEN

Wisdom, esoteric, spirituality, thought/consciousness, mental, intellectual, spirit, observer, solitary, secretive, analysis, understanding, knowledge, awareness, studious, meditating, hidden. The Seven is the number that combines the divine creativity of the Three with the number of the Earth, which means that divinity is brought into the physical plane. Considered to be the first spiritual number, the Seven shows us how to use the mind as a tool of consciousness and as a path to enlightenment.
SPIRITUALITY ~ NEPTUNE

8. THE EIGHT BUILDS POWER

Union, integration, the balancing of polarity, money, finance, prosperity, success-oriented, materialistic, authority, ambition, organization, practicality, success, abundance, self-reliance, independence, status oriented, power-seeking, karma, self-reliance, inner strength, self-knowledge, giving and receiving, flow, dependability. The Eight is the number of cycles, repetition, success through hard work, determination, and attention to detail. Think of the Eight as a spiral: the spiral goes in a circle that progresses slowly ever higher. So you might build success by counting on the repetition of the cycle to fulfill and manifest. It is the number of karma, the balance of cause and effect. "As you sow, so shall you reap."
MANIFESTATION ~ SATURN

9. THE NINE SUCCEEDS/SERVES

Attainment, fulfillment, completion, success, creative expression; the highest level of personal attainment. If you get this number, it may mean individual attainment or spiritual mastery, depending on your focus. The Nine is the second spiritual number, indicating the attainment of wisdom connected with the energy of the Higher Self. In its spiritual expression, the Nine uses individual mastery for the good of all: humanitarian, giving, wisdom, compassion, patience, universality, tolerance, completion, selflessness, service to others.
INDIVIDUAL ATTAINMENT ~ MARS

10. THE TEN IS UNIVERSAL

The Ten is the number Nine taken up a notch to the level of social awareness. The Zero of Spirit combined with the number 1, indicates another turn on the evolutionary spiral as Spirit comes into matter again at a higher level. Completion, community, bringing Spirit into matter: materialization.
UNITY CONSCIOUSNESS~ The UNIVERSE

MASTER NUMBERS

11. ILLUMINATION

As the first Master number, the Eleven can be seen as a gateway to another level of consciousness, symbolizing a spiritual awakening or initiation. This is the number of the idealist, social activist, iconoclast, inspirational speaker, motivational leader, mystic, and creative dreamer. The Eleven is the number of enlightenment, creativity, expression, and ideals. This number calls us to live our life mission without question or hesitation. The Eleven is the visionary who is inspired to break down old systems in order to establish the new. The eleven means "illumination," or spiritual "enlightenment." The Iconoclast is the demolition expert that removes old structures to pave the way for new structures.
—JUSTICE/ILLUMINATION

22. THE MASTER BUILDER

Building upon the number Two, and taking the concept of the foundation symbolized by the Four to a higher level, this person is only interested in building in a big way; new ideas, new systems, new societies. This number as a double of the number Two emphasizes the feminine inclusive nature of that number. The Master Builder is the contractor that brings practical concrete skills in order to build new paradigms.
—THE FOOL

33. CHRIST CONSCIOUSNESS

With the number Three as its base, the creative, and fresh qualities of the divine Child combined with the Love of the number Six inspires anyone with this number to naturally gravitate towards anything that is socially beneficial for all. As the number for CHRIST CONSCIOUSNESS, the Thirty-three symbolizes the underlying reality of the oneness of all things,

with LOVE as its natural expression. The number of the Master Architect who designs the plans for a new paradigm based upon love.
—THE LOVERS/LOVE

Personal Numbers

There are several personal numbers that you can derive from anyone's name and birthdate. The process involves adding the numbers together until you arrive at a double digit and its single digit reduction, like so: 11/2. If the number you arrive at reduces to a master number (multiple of 11), or a multiple of 10, the meaning is especially powerful.

Life Lesson Number

The "Life Lesson Number" is derived from your birthdate. It indicates the lessons you are to learn in this lifetime, and it can be a great factor in choosing a career that matches your personality. To arrive at this number, you simply add the digits in your birthday. For example, say your birthdate is November 12, 1970:

$$11 + 12 + 1970$$
$$11 + 12 + 17 \ (1 + 9 + 7 + 0)$$
$$11 + 12 + 17 = 40/4$$

The single digit "4" is reduced by adding the first digit to the second. You would then look up the meaning of the number Four, and use this meaning to determine your "Life Lesson" or suggest a career path for you. The Zero doesn't have a value, however, a double-digit Life Lesson Number with a zero tends to accentuate the power of the other digit, in this case the Four. The number Four is the number the Earth; in the Major Arcana of the Tarot, it is the number of The Emperor, called INSIGHT in *The Tarot of Creativity*. The number Four is a conservative, solid number; the number of the diligent, dependable, and practical worker. You should choose a career that allows you to fulfill the life lessons indicated by the number Four.

Letters as Numbers

To deepen your knowledge of numerology, you can use the chart on this page to help you understand how the letters of the alphabet correspond to the nine numbers. Many people use numerology when they evaluate a name or word.

1	2	3	4	5	6	7	8	9
A	B	C	D	E	F	G	H	I
J	K	L	M	N	O	P	Q	R
S	T	U	V	W	X	Y	Z	

Path of Destiny Number

This number is derived from the letters in your name. You can use the numerology section in this book to understand your personal numbers or those of your friends. This number shows what you must do in this life; what you came to manifest. Using a famous name as an example:

$$\begin{array}{cc} \text{EDGAR} & \text{CAYCE} \\ 5 + 4 + 7 + 1 + 9 = 26 & 3 + 1 + 7 + 3 + 5 = 19 \end{array}$$

Add the unreduced numbers of the first name to the last name: 26 + 19 = 36/9 Next, look up the meaning of the single number to arrive at the Path of Destiny meaning. Here is the definition of the number Nine:

9. THE NINE SUCCEEDS/SERVES

Attainment, fulfillment, completion, success, creative expression; the highest level of personal attainment. If you get this number, it may mean individual attainment or spiritual mastery, depending on your focus. The nine is the second spiritual number, indicating the attainment of wisdom connected with the energy of the Higher Self. In its spiritual expression, the Nine uses individual mastery for the good of all: humanitarian, giving, wisdom, compassion, patience, universality, tolerance, completion, selflessness, service to others.

THE TAROT TABLEAU

The Journey of the Fool						
1 Magician Attention	2 Priestess Memory	3 Empress Imagination	4 Emperor Insight	5 Hierophant Intuition	6 Lovers Love	7 Chariot Adventure
8 Strength I-Mage	9 Hermit Emergence	10 Fortune Acceleration	11 Justice Illumination	12 Hang Man Reversal	13 Death Metamorphosis	14 Temperance Alchemy
15 Devil Shadow	16 Tower Awakening	17 Star Revelation	18 Moon Dreaming	19 Sun Creativity	20 Judgment Epiphany	21 World Transcend

The Tarot is sometimes called the Journey of the Fool—the journey of Spirit through physical existence. Matching the traditional titles of the cards with the modern keyword-titles of *The Tarot of Creativity* provides insight into the progression of the Fool. The twenty-one cards of Major Arcana—excluding the unnumbered Fool—are often arranged in what is called the Tarot Tableau, with three rows of seven cards each. Read each column to see how the cards work with each other.

1. The first row represents the principles and the workings of the universe.
2. The second row represents the faculties of man and the rules of existence.
3. The third row represents the results of applying rows one and two.

COLUMN 1—1 Magician + 8 Strength + 15 The Devil

The first column starts with the Magician who represents intent or ATTENTION in the TOC. When combined with the card below, Strength/I-MAGE, which represents the power of imagery, your creative input starts to create form: in this case, the Devil card or THE SHADOW in the TOC. This is a misuse of creative energy; it is a miscreation that stems from the unconscious imagery projected by the will or intent of the self-conscious onto the subconscious. If the individual is conscious of what he is projecting to the subconscious he creates consciously, and the 15 reduces to its higher form, the 6 of Lovers/LOVE:

1 + 5 = 6. If you add the numbers of the cards in the column, and then reduce the number you end up with a six again: 1 + 8 + 15 = 24 = 6.

—The summation of the column: Key #6 The Lovers/LOVE card.

COLUMN 2—2 The High Priestess + 9 The Hermit + 16 The Tower

The second column begins with the principle represented by The High Priestess/MEMORY, the Source or divine implicate. Combined with the evolved consciousness of The Hermit/EMERGENCE, The Tower/THE AWAKENING results: 2 + 9 + 16 = 27 = 9, the number that signifies

—The summation of the column: Key #9 The Hermit/EMERGENCE.

COLUMN 3—3 The Empress + 10 The Wheel of Fortune + 17 The Star

The third column starts with principle represented by The Empress/IMAGINATION, nature or Mother Earth (material existence). When combined with The Wheel of Fortune/ACCELERATION, The Star/THE REVELATION is the result: 3 + 10 + 17 = 30 = 3.

—The summation of the column: Key #3 The Empress/IMAGINATION.

COLUMN 4—4 The Emperor + 11 Justice + 18 The Moon

The fourth column starts with the principle of consciousness represented by The Emperor, the INSIGHT provided by reason. When combined with the natural law of Justice, or the fairness represented by the concept of EQUILIBRIUM, the result is The Moon, which represents the DREAM of life. This dream can be an unconscious creation, or a conscious creation, otherwise called a "lucid dream." It is still a dream but that you can direct through your focus and will. 4 + 11 + 18 = 33. Since 33 is a Master number you can stop there: 33 is the number of Christ Consciousness, but to understand the number you can still add it together: 3 + 3 = 6.

—The summation of the column: Key #6 The Lovers/LOVE.

COLUMN 5—5 Hierophant + 12 The Hanged Man + 19 The Sun

Column five starts with the principle of consciousness represented by The Hierophant, the INTUITION that becomes a natural feature in your life when you are in connection with the greater part of your consciousness, the Higher Self. The next figure in the column is The Hanged Man, who demonstrates how to achieve Self-Knowledge by turning his view upside-down. Incidentally, the light of his consciousness, represented by the halo or nimbus of light that surrounds his head, shows how his act of "sacrifice" enables him to bring a higher consciousness to Earth, or to the material plane, represented by the Tau Cross tree that suspends him. The result of The Hanged Man's selfless act brings general enlightenment, represented by the last figure in the column, The Sun: 5 + 12 + 19 = 36 = 9.

—The summation of the column: Key #9 The Hermit/EMERGENCE.

COLUMN 6—6 The Lovers + 13 Death + 20 Judgment

Column six starts with The Lovers card, which demonstrates the universal principle of LOVE. When you combine the universal principle of LOVE with the natural law of Death/METAMORPHOSIS, or the law of change, the resulting manifestation is Judgment. The Judgment card in the Tarot is not about being judged or valuated, but the inverse. The number of the card gives us a clue: the number 20 is the 2 + 0, the law of the balance of duality of the Two combined with the spiritual knowledge of the Zero. Thus, Judgment is better expressed as the EPIPHANY or spiritual realization of the universal law of EQUALITY or the Oneness of all things, the inverse of the idea of judgment: 6 + 13 + 20 = 39 = 12 = 3.

—The summation of the column: Key #3 The Empress/IMAGINATION.

COLUMN 7—7 The Chariot + 14 Temperance + 21 The World

The seventh column begins with the last card of the first row in the Tarot Tableau, The Chariot, which shows how in this stage of the Soul's evolution, the ego finally submits to the WILL of the Higher Self, becoming finally RECEPTIVE to Spirit. Now starts the grand ADVENTURE of the Soul in material form that the card in the TOC references, meaning the next stage of consciousness, the ego-Mind reunited with the Higher Mind. When combined with the ALCHEMY represented by the Temperance card, the energy produces the Soul's TRANSCENDENCE represented in the card The World: 7 + 14 + 21 = 42 = 6.

—The summation of the column: Key #6 The Lovers/LOVE.

The sums of the columns repeat in a 6-3-9 pattern, which gives us the meaning for the entire tableau: 6 + 9 + 3 = 18 = 9

LOVE + WISDOM + IMAGINATION/NATURE = EMERGENCE

ASTROLOGICAL CORRESPONDENCES

ARIES (March 21 - April 19)
The First House: Identity/Self-Image/Personality
The Emperor/INSIGHT (Key #4)
rational, dependable/boring, overbearing

TAURUS (April 20 - May 20)
The Second House: Value/Security
The Hierophant/INTUITION (Key #5)
teaching, teacher/dogmatic

GEMINI (May 21 - June 20)
The Third House: Communication/Relationships
The Lovers/LOVE (Key #6)
duality/indecision, discrimination

CANCER (June 21 - July 22)
The Fourth House: Home/Possessions/Family
The Chariot/ADVENTURE (Key #7)
resists change/movement within

LEO (July 23 - August 22)
The Fifth House: Self-Expression/Creativity
Strength/I-MAGE (Key #8)
treating the ego with love

VIRGO (Aug. 23 - Sept. 22)
The Sixth House: Health/Service to Others
The Hermit/EMERGENCE (Key #9)
wisdom, learning/separate

LIBRA (Sept. 23 - Oct. 22)
The Seventh House: Partnership/Marriage/Commitment
Justice/ILLUMINATION (Key #11)
balanced/judgmental

SCORPIO (Oct. 23 - Nov. 21)
The Eighth House: Rebirth/Regeneration
Death/METAMORPHOSIS (Key #13)
transformation/mutable

SAGITTARIUS (Nov. 22 - Dec. 21)
The Ninth House: Philosophy/Knowledge/Travel
Temperance/ALCHEMY (Key #14)
understanding/synthesis

CAPRICORN (Dec. 22 - Jan. 19)
The Tenth House: Ambition/Career/Status
The Devil/THE SHADOW (Key #15)
the shadow as a teacher

AQUARIUS(Jan. 20 - Feb. 18)
The Eleventh House: Friendships/Community/Humanitarian
The Star/THE REVELATION (Key #17)
optimistic/spirituality applied to the social level

PISCES (Feb. 19 - March 20)
The Twelfth House: Psychic/Intuitive/Dreams
The Moon/DREAMING (Key #18)
unconscious/emotional/dreams

GLOSSARY OF SYMBOLS

This glossary is offered as a convenient aid for the Tarot scholar. Symbols in the Tarot range from ancient archetypes to images that trigger highly individualized interpretations. As you work with the Tarot, you will find more and more hidden images in the cards, which will help you develop your personal lexicon and deepen your understanding of each card. This list of symbols is very comprehensive, but it is meant to be only a starting point: it can never replace your personal interpretations or intuitive guidance.

SYMBOLS & TERMS

ADAM & EVE = duality, marriage of opposites, the anima and animus
—The Lovers, The Devil

ANGEL = messenger of Spirit, the Higher Self, healing, godhead, perfected man
—The Lovers, Wheel of Fortune, Temperance, Judgment, Queen Swords

ANIMA, ANIMUS = "The anima and animus, in Carl Jung's school of analytical psychology, are the two primary anthropomorphic archetypes of the unconscious mind, as opposed to both the theriomorphic [having an animal form] and inferior function of the shadow archetypes, as well as the abstract symbol sets that formulate the archetype of the Self.

"The anima and animus are described by Jung as elements of his theory of the collective unconscious, a domain of the unconscious that transcends the personal psyche. In the unconscious of the male, this archetype finds expression as a feminine inner personality: anima; equivalently, in the unconscious of the female it is expressed as a masculine inner personality: animus. The anima and animus can be identified as the totality of the unconscious feminine psychological qualities that a male possesses or the masculine ones possessed by the female, respectively. It is an archetype of the collective unconscious and not an aggregate of father or mother, brothers, sisters, aunts, uncles or teachers, though these aspects of the personal unconscious can influence the person for good or ill."[1] (see COUPLE)
—The Lovers, The Devil, Two Cups

---

1   en.wikipedia.org/wiki/Anima_and_animus

ANKH = immortality, Egyptian symbol for "life" graphic of sun rising over horizon; Sanskrit for "eye" meaning clear vision
—The Emperor

ANUBIS = "The Egyptian god Anubis was in charge of ushering souls into the afterlife. One of the roles of Anubis was as the "Guardian of the Scales." The Book of the Dead shows Anubis weighing the heart of the deceased against Ma'at (or "truth"), who was often represented as a feather, Anubis dictated the fate of souls. Souls heavier than a feather would be devoured by Ammit; souls lighter than a feather would ascend to a heavenly existence."[1]
—Wheel of Fortune

ARCH = passage of initiation, passage through difficulty, attainment
—The Lovers, 3 Pentacles, 10 Pentacles, 4 Wands

ARMOR = inner war, might equals right, protection, strength, fortitude, power
—The Emperor, Chariot, Death, Knight Swords, Knight Pentacles, Knight Cups, Knight Wands, 4 Swords

B & J = "B" stands for "Boaz:" "Intellect," "J" stands for "Jakin:" "Spirit"
—The High Priestess

BAT WINGS = darkness, abuse of body, bondage
—The Devil

BEARD = wisdom, rigid, dogmatic, age, wisdom gained through time
—The Emperor, The Hermit

BINDINGS = bondage, slavery. constrictions of old beliefs
—8 Swords

BIRD = spiritual, freedom
—Wheel of Fortune, The Star, (see IBIS), The World

BLINDFOLD = can't see the future, honest, non-judgmental, detached
—2 Swords, 8 Swords

---

1 en.wikipedia.org/wiki/Anubis

BOOK = universal law, esoteric knowledge, Akashic records (see SCROLL)
—The High Priestess

BRICK WALL = barrier to lower consciousness, built to last, brick-by-brick
—The Sun

BRIDGE = emotional connection
—5 Cups

BULL = masculine fertility, power, fixed Zodiacal sign of Taurus, stubborn, intransigent, solid, unmoving, slow.
—Wheel of Fortune, The World, King Pentacles

BUTTERFLY = transformation, metamorphosis
—Queen Swords, King Swords

CADUCEUS = health, healing, balance of opposites, healthy duality, Kundalini, chakra system, pineal gland activation
—Two Cups

CASTLE = defensive, ego, achievement, success, shelter, protection, goals, societal conditioning, beliefs. the past (behind), the future (ahead)
—The Chariot, Ace Wands, 4 Wands, 9 Pentacles, 8 Swords, 5-7 Cups

CAT = psychic power, attention, focus, awareness, energy, flexible
—Queen Wands

CATHEDRAL = sacred building, social structure
—3 Pentacles

CHAIN = bondage, slavery. constrictions of old beliefs
—The Devil

CHARIOT = the "merkaba:" the body as a vehicle for Spirit
—The Chariot

CHILD, CHILDREN = innocence, hope, new beginning, the future
—The Sun, 6 Cups, 10 Cups, 6 Swords, 10 Pentacles

CITY = civilization, group effort, harmony, approved and accepted by others, home, shelter (see VILLAGE)
—4 Pentacles, 6 Pentacles, 8 Pentacle, 10 Pentacles, King Pentacles, 7 Swords, 6 Cups

CIRCLE = the infinite, Spirit, All-That-Is, the Sun (see OUROBORUS)
—The Chariot, The World

CLIFF = danger of falling, descent
—The Fool, 3 Wands

CLOUDS = spiritual, divine inspiration, message, confusion, illusion
—The Lovers, Wheel of Fortune, The Tower, Judgment, The World, Ace Swords, Ace Cups, Ace Wands, Ace Pentacles, 3 Swords, 4 Cups, 5 Swords, 7 Cups, Page Swords, King Swords

COFFIN = what needs to be buried, unconsciousness, death of the old (see TOMB)
—4 Swords, Judgment

COUPLE = duality, balance, opposites, anima and animus, self-conscious, subconscious (see ANIMA/ANIMUS)
—The Lovers, The Devil, The Tower, 10 Cups

CRAFTSMAN = expertise, craftsmanship, skills, creativity, creative genius
—3 Pentacles, 8 Pentacles

CRAYFISH, LOBSTER = rebirth, emerging from lower consciousness
—The Moon

CROSS = (equilateral cross/Maltese cross) ancient symbol of the Earth, representing harmony, dominion, balance of spiritual/material and male/female polarities
—The High Priestess, Judgment, Ace Cups

CROWN = success, victory, crown chakra, intelligence, sovereignty
—The High Priestess, The Hierophant, The Tower, Ace Swords, 4 Pentacles

CUP = emotions, subconscious, vessel for awareness, abundance, offering
—Cups Suit

DANCING = happiness, celebration, partnership
—3 Cups

DEVIL = the shadow-self
—The Devil

DOG = socialized consciousness , loyalty, faith, truth
—The Fool, The Moon, 10 Pentacles

DOOR = passageway, initiation, the future, choice
—Ace Pentacles

DOVE = hope, ascension, Christ consciousness
—Ace Cups

EAGLE = fixed Zodiacal sign of Scorpio, Cups Suit, element of Water
—Wheel of Fortune, The World

FALCON = clear vision; (hooded) Falcon = tamed, domesticated, not-seeing
—9 Pentacles

FEATHER in cap = spiritual information (angels)
—The Fool, Page Wands

FIELD OF GRAIN = fertility, creativity
—The Empress

FIRE = element of energy, creative, destructive
—The Devil, The Tower

FISH = the subconscious, emotions, a gift, life-force, the imagination
—Page Cups, Knight Cups, Queen Cups, King Cups

FLAG= announcement of change
—Death, Sun, Judgment

FLOWER = flowering, happiness, Garden of Eden
—The Fool, The Magician, The Empress, 6 Cups, 4 Wands, Page Cups

FOREST = Mother Earth, nature, untamed, undomesticated
—The Empress

FRUIT = harvest, fall, bounty, abundance
—The High Priestess, 3 Cups

GARDEN = Garden of Eden, life, bounty, abundance, natural, the Earth, harvest
—The Empress, 3 Cups, 9 Pentacles

GARLANDS = celebration
—4 Wands

GLOBE = success, achievement, ruler, mastery, goals (see WORLD)
—The Emperor, 2 Wands, King Pentacles

GRAPES, GRAPEVINE = fertility, abundance
—3 Cups, 4 Wands, 7 Pentacles, 9 Pentacles, 10 Pentacles, King Pentacles

HAMMER = "hammering out the details," hard work, perseverance, consistency
—3 Pentacles, 8 Pentacles

HAND IN CLOUDS = divine force, inspiration
—Ace Wands, Ace Swords, Ace Cups, Ace Pentacles, 4 Cups

HEAD = fixed astrological sign Aquarius
—Swords Suit, element of Air

HEART = love, fertility, abundance
—The Empress, 3 Swords

HERMIT = denial of earthly needs, pilgrim, master, teacher
—The Hermit

HOE = work, harvest, growth, taking care of the land
—7 Pentacles

HORN = announcement as in Gabriel's horn at Jericho
—Judgment

HORSE = power, virility, vitality, motion, masculine power
—Death, The Sun, 6 Wands, Knights Wands, Swords, Cups, Pentacles

HOUSE = home, comfort, family, lineage
—2 Wands/2 Cups, 6 Cups, 8 Wands, 10 Wands, 10 Cups

IBIS = symbol for Thoth, hope
—The Star

JUG = vessel of consciousness, the body
—The Star

JUGGLER = seeking balance in motion, juggling potentials, resources
—2 Pentacles

KEYS = esoteric knowledge, arcane wisdom, unlocks knowledge/wisdom
—The Hierophant

LAND, LANDSCAPE = material existence, Earth
—The Star, 8 Wands, Page Pentacles

LANTERN = container for light of Christ Consciousness, the purified body, mind
—The Hermit

LAURELS = recognition, success
—Ace Swords, 6 Wands

LEMNISCATE = the reciprocal nature of life, infinity, presence of Higher Self, energy to matter to energy conversion, wholeness and completion. The lemniscate is a mathematical symbol representing the concept of infinity
—The Magician, Strength, The World, 2 Pentacles, 9 Cups

LIGHTNING = divine message delivered with force and suddenness, creative inspiration, sudden change
—The Tower

LILY = purified desire, spiritual desire, innocence
—The Magician, Temperance, Ace Pentacles, 2 Wands

LION = the ego, astrological sign Leo, courage, Wands Suit, element of Fire
—Strength, Wheel of Fortune, The World, 2 Cups, Queen Wands, King Wands

LOBSTER = rebirth, emerging from lower consciousness
—The Moon

MONKS = social approval, dogma, patron of the arts
—The Hierophant, 3 Pentacles

MOON = subconscious, reflection, psychic power, dreams, collective unconscious, emotions, emotional awareness
—The High Priestess, The Chariot, The Moon, Page Swords, 8 Cups, 2 Swords

MOUNTAIN (HILL) = contemplation, spiritual, attainment, success, lofty goals, wisdom, high, difficult, unassailable
—The Fool, The Emperor, The Lovers, Strength, The Hermit, Judgment, Ace Wands, 2 Wands, 3 Wands, 7 Wands, 8 Swords, 8 Cups, 8 Swords, 10 Swords, Page Wands, Page Pentacles, Knight Wands, Knight Cups, Queen Pentacles

NAKED FIGURES = natural human, reborn
—The Star, The Sun, Judgment

NIGHT = leaving the past, ignorance, unconscious, confusion, contemplation, rest
—The Hermit, The Devil, The Tower, The Star, The Moon, 8 Cups

OUROBORUS = eternity, cyclical, infinity, the human psyche The Ouroborus or Uroboros, from the Greek meaning tail-devouring snake, is an ancient symbol depicting a serpent or dragon eating its own tail.

"The Ouroborus or Uroboros, from the Greek meaning tail-devouring snake, is an ancient symbol depicting a serpent or dragon eating its own tail. The Ouroborus often symbolizes self-reflexivity or cyclicality, especially in the sense of something constantly re-creating itself, the eternal return, and other things such as the phoenix which operate in cycles that begin anew as soon as they end. It can also represent the idea of primordial unity related to something existing in or persisting from the beginning with such force or qualities it cannot be extinguished.

"First emerging in Ancient Egypt, the Ouroboros has been important in religious and mythological symbolism, but has also been frequently used in alchemical illustrations, where it symbolizes the circular nature of the alchemist's opus. It is also often associated with Gnosticism, and Hermeticism. Carl Jung interpreted the Ouroboros as having an archetypal significance to the human psyche. The Jungian psychologist Erich Neumann writes of it as a representation of the pre-ego "dawn state," depicting the undifferentiated infancy experience of both mankind and the individual child."[1] (see CIRCLE, SUN, SNAKE).
—The Magician (belt), King Wands

PALISADE = barrier, difficulties overcome, rite of passage, initiation
—8 Swords, 9 Wands

PATH = your path, the future, issues, journey
—Temperance, The Moon, Ace Pentacles

PENTACLE = a 5-pointed star inside a circle : talent, wealth, health, physical wellbeing, skills, craftsmanship, magic. "A pentacle is an amulet used in magical evocation, generally made of parchment, paper or metal (although it can be of other materials), on which the symbol of a spirit or energy being evoked is drawn. It is often worn around the neck, or placed within the triangle of evocation. Protective symbols may also be included (sometimes on the reverse), a common one being the five-point form of the Seal of Solomon, called a pentacle of Solomon or pentangle of Solomon.

---

1   en.wikipedia.org/wiki/Ouroboros

"The words *pentacle* and *pentagram* (a five-point unicursal star) are essentially synonymous, according to the Online Oxford English Dictionary (2007 revision), which traces the etymology through both French and Italian back to Latin, but notes that in Middle French the word "pentacle" was used to refer to any talisman. In an extended use, many magical authors treat them as distinct. In many tarot decks pentacles often prominently incorporate a pentagram in their design. The pentacle is representative of the Earth in occult usage. In the Golden Dawn magical system, the Earth Pentacle is one of four elemental tools of an Adept. These weapons are "symbolical representations of the forces employed for the manifestation of the inner self, the elements required for the incarnation of the divine."[1]

If you take the two glyphs that make the symbol of the Pentacle, you can understand the message: the 5-pointed star represents man, and this star is inside the circle, which symbolizes spirit. The star represents the nature of the senses, the nature of manifested matter—man inside the circle of spirit. The pentacle is a symbol that, like the magical and spiritual numbers Zero and Eight, can be traced infinitely. It symbolizes the perfected man the perfected man, Angel, or godhood in material form. Surrounded by the symbol for Spirit or perfection, the Zero or circle, which blesses and supports the symbol for the perfected man who resides in its center.
—Pentacles Suit

PENTAGRAM = the five senses, symbol of man, white magic (upright) evil (reversed). "Heinrich Cornelius Agrippa and others perpetuated the popularity of the pentagram as a magic symbol, attributing the five neoplatonic elements to the five points, in typical Renaissance fashion. With a single point upwards it depicted spirit presiding over the four elements of matter, and was essentially "good." Eliphas Levi called it evil whenever the symbol appeared the other way up. The golden ratio plays an important role in regular pentagons and pentagrams. Each intersection of edges sections the edges in the golden ratio. The pentagram includes ten isosceles triangles: five acute and five obtuse isosceles triangles."[2]
—The Devil (reversed)

PILLARS = tests, duality, balance, passageway, initiation, equilibrium
—The High Priestess, The Hierophant, Justice, The Moon, 3 Pentacles

---

1   en.wikipedia.org/wiki/Pentacle
2   en.wikipedia.org/wiki/Pentagram

POMEGRANATE = fertility, luxury, abundance
—The High Priestess, The Empress

RABBIT = fertility, abundance, the Earth, Mother Nature
—Queen Pentacles

RAGS = poverty consciousness, disease, lack
—5 Pentacles, 6 Pentacles

RAIN = tears, fertility, cleansing, storm
—2 Wands, 3 Swords

RAINBOW = joy, happiness, good omen
—10 Cups

RAM = symbol of Aries, power, dominant, harsh
—The Emperor

ROSE = physical desire, material desire, beauty, love
—The Fool, The Magician, Strength, Death, 2 Wands

SALAMANDER = the salamander was believed to be able to survive in a fire, symbol for the Wands suit and FIRE element
—Page Wands, Knight Wands, King Wands

SCALES = balance, fairness, justice, measuring, investment, karma, cause & effect
—Justice, 6 Pentacles

SCROLL = universal law, esoteric knowledge, Akashic records (see BOOK)
—The High Priestess

SHIELD = defense, sign
—The Empress

SHIP = subconscious thoughts, freedom, voyage, enterprise, resources
—Death, 2 Pentacles, King Cups, 2 Pentacles, 3 Wands, 6 Swords

SNAIL = slow but steady, home-loving
—9 Pentacles

SNAKE = kundalini, rebirth, renewal, evolution, DNA (see OUROBORUS)
—The Magician, The Lovers, Wheel of Fortune, 7 Cups

SNOW = outside society, unsheltered, homeless, cold, difficulties
—The Fool, The Hermit, 5 Pentacles

SPHINX = mysterious, guard of arcane mysteries, the riddle of life
—The Chariot, Wheel of Fortune

SQUARE = number 4, the Earth, material plane, existence, manifestation
—The Chariot

STAFF = authority, rule, mastery, magic, support, intent, energy
—The Fool, The Magician, The Empress, The Emperor, The Chariot, The Hermit, 6 Swords, 8 Cups

STAINED GLASS = vision, sacred window, light of consciousness
—4 Swords, 5 Pentacles

STAR = universal principles, archetypes, guidance, zodiac, 12 states of consciousness
—The Empress, The Chariot, The Star

SUN = happiness, life, Source, element of Fire (see CIRCLE, LEMNISCATE)
—The Fool, The Lovers, Death, Temperance, The Sun

SUNFLOWER = happiness, in French, Tournesol which means "turns with the Sun" or "follows the light"
—The Fool, The Sun, Queen Wands

SWORD = thought, clarity, precision, judgment, beliefs
—Justice, Swords Suit

TABLE = field of attention, the Earth
—The Magician

TOMB = what needs to be buried, unconsciousness, death of the old (see COFFIN)
—4 Swords, Judgment

TOOLS = paths to self-awareness
—The Magician

TORAH book = universal law, principles of consciousness
—The High Priestess

TORCH = illumination (see WAND)
—The Magician, The Devil

TOWER = battlement, challenges, the ego
—The Tower, The Moon

TREE = Tree of Life, Tree of Knowledge
—The Lovers, The Star

TRIANGLE = signifying the number 3; creativity, the child
—Temperance

VILLAGE (CITY)= civilization, group effort, harmony
—4 Pentacles, 6 Pentacles, 10 Wands, 10 Pentacles, King Pentacles, 7 Swords, 6 Cups

WALL = barrier, enclosure, separation, ignorance, protection, shelter
—The Sun, 2 Wands, King Pentacles

WALLET = container for the tools of consciousness (the suits), possessions, the physical body, incarnation
—The Fool

WAND = intent, pure energy, magic, transmits energy from higher consciousness
—The Fool, The World, Wands Suit

WATER, OCEAN, SEA, POND, POOL, LAKE, STREAM = collective conscious, subconscious, emotions, Cosmic mind-stuff, the quantum implicate, Source
—The Star, 2 Wands, 2 Swords, 2 Pentacles, 3 Wands, 5 Swords, 6 Swords, 8 Swords, 8 Cups, 10 Swords, Page Cups, Cups Suit

WATERFALL = flow, emotions, freed subconscious
—High Priestess, Empress, Queen Swords

WATER LILIES = good fortune
—Ace Cups

WAVES = emotional turbulence
—2 Pentacles, 6 Swords

WHEEL = symbol of the goddess Fortuna
—Wheel of Fortune

WINGS = (feathered wings) freedom, spiritual, light
—The Chariot, Wheel of Fortune, Judgment, 2 Cups

WORLD = success, achievement, goals (see GLOBE)
—The Emperor, 2 Wands

WOLF = primal, untamed consciousness
—The Moon, Wheel of Fortune

WORKBENCH = hard work, labor
—8 Pentacles

WREATH = victory, protection, peace, accomplishment (see OUROBORUS)
—The Fool, The World, 6 Wands, 7 Cups

YOD = 10th letter of Hebrew alphabet, meaning "open hand," first letter of "Yahweh," signifies Divine presence, element of Fire. The yod is said to be the basic element in all the letters of the Hebrew language
—Wheel of Fortune, The Tower, Ace Wands, Ace Swords, Ace Cups

ZODIAC = principles, laws of consciousness
—The Empress, The Star, 9 Swords

COLORS

BLACK—negativity rigid, stark, night, conventional, stable, unconsciousness; deep healing, transformational

BLUE—throat chakra, communication, clarity, hearing, inspiration, truth, sincerity, peace: self-expression

BROWN—the Earth, physicality, nature

GRAY—hazy, uncertain, balance of duality/polarity (black and white), indecisive; inner knowledge, wisdom, non-judgmental

GREEN/TURQUOISE—compassion, healing, love, heart chakra, love/unconditional love, seat of the soul, harmony, nature, growth, youth, compassion, summertime; health and well-being, self-acceptance

INDIGO—third eye chakra, pineal gland, mental clarity, vision, truth, intuition

LAVENDER—peace, harmony; inner-strength, wisdom

ORANGE—sacral chakra, emotions, creativity, sexuality, physical desire, vitality, dynamism, courage; a time or situation that requires courage and action

PINK—happiness, harmony, love, forgiveness
RED—root chakra, needs, physical body, connection to Mother Earth

VIOLET—crown chakra, pituitary chakra, connection to Higher Self, intellect, wisdom; spiritual perception and communication

WHITE—contains all the colors in the light spectrum, pure, spiritual, peaceful, new beginnings; universal harmony

YELLOW—solar plexus chakra, self-conscious, will, identity, personal power, control, domination, mental power, life-force, the Sun; self-confidence and positivity

ALSO BY ALIYAH MARR

The Tarot of Creativity
The Oracle of Creative Transformation

The Avatars of Eden
Bringing Heaven to Earth

Unplug From the Matrix
Truth is Sometimes Stranger Than Fiction

Celestial Navigation
The Journey of the Conscious Creative

The Creative Life in 365 Degrees
Daily Inspiration, Wisdom, Motivation,
& Comfort for the Creative Soul

Parallel Mind, The Art of Creativity
The (missing) Manual for Your Right Brain

Do it Yourself Tarot
The Instant, Easy Way to Learn How to Read
the Tarot for Yourself and Others

❧

www.parallelmindzz.com

Did you like this book?

I would appreciate it if you would
post a review via the page below:

http://amzn.to/2e11ngN

Thank you!

Aliyah Marr

CPSIA information can be obtained
at www.ICGtesting.com
Printed in the USA
LVOW13s1456110417
530417LV00012B/934/P